# HENRY JAMES AND MODERN MORAL

In *Henry James and Modern Moral Life,* Professor Robert Pippin argues that Henry James, in his novels and tales, is engaged in a sophisticated, original exploration of moral understanding and moral motivation. Pippin argues that James takes his bearings from what he understood to be the complex and unprecedented historical situation of modernity and that he was able to do full justice to the ambiguities and confusions unavoidable in such a social world, while avoiding skepticism or a narrow aestheticism.

Professor Pippin presents important new interpretations of *The American Scene, The Wings of the Dove, Portrait of a Lady, The Ambassadors, The Golden Bowl,* and several of James's short stories, including *The Beast in the Jungle* and *The Turn of the Screw,* in support of his claim that there is a distinct and philosophically rich Jamesean account of modern moral meaning.

*Henry James and Modern Moral Life* is written by one of the preeminent interpreters of the modern European philosophical tradition and will interest both philosophers and literary critics and theorists. Because Pippin presents his argument without reliance on a particular philosophical or theoretical vocabulary, the book will also engage students and interested readers of Henry James.

Robert B. Pippin is Raymond W. and Martha Hilpert Gruner Distinguished Service Professor in the Committee on Social Thought, the Department of Philosophy, and the College at the University of Chicago. He is the author of several books on the modern philosophical tradition and the nature of European modernity.

# HENRY JAMES AND MODERN MORAL LIFE

ROBERT B. PIPPIN

*University of Chicago*

CAMBRIDGE
UNIVERSITY PRESS

PUBLISHED BY THE PRESS SYNDICATE OF THE UNIVERSITY OF CAMBRIDGE
The Pitt Building, Trumpington Street, Cambridge, United Kingdom

CAMBRIDGE UNIVERSITY PRESS
The Edinburgh Building, Cambridge CB2 2RU, UK
40 West 20th Street, New York, NY 10011-4211, USA
10 Stamford Road, Oakleigh, Melbourne 3166, Australia
Ruiz de Alarcón 13, 28014 Madrid, Spain
Dock House, The Waterfront, Cape Town 8001, South Africa

http://www.cambridge.org

First published 2000
First paperback edition 2001

Printed in the United States of America

*Typeface* Adobe Garamond 11/14 pt.    *System* MagnaType™ [AG]

*A catalog record for this book is available from the British Library*

*Library of Congress Cataloging in Publication data is available*

ISBN 0 521 65230 8 hardback
ISBN 0 521 65547 1 paperback

*In memory of François Furet*

And there appeared, with its windows glowing, small,
In the distance, in the frozen reaches, a cabin;
And we stood before it, amazed at its being there,
And would have gone forward and opened the door,
And stepped into the glow and warmed ourselves there,
But that it was ours by not being ours,
And should remain empty. That was the idea.

– from "The Idea," by Mark Strand

# CONTENTS

# ACKNOWLEDGMENTS

Work on this book began several years ago as a result of a stimulating graduate seminar in the Committee on Social Thought at the University of Chicago. My co-teacher in the seminar was the writer Bette Howland. I am very much indebted to Bette for that seminar, for our many conversations about James, and especially for her encouragement about a book on the themes that I returned to again and again in our discussions.

In the years that followed, I presented versions of Chapters 2 and 3 as public lectures or as colloquia throughout the United States and abroad. I discovered that from Canberra to Colorado to Iowa to Hartford, there were always in the audience, as well as specialists in literature departments, many very dedicated enthusiasts who had, like me, simply been reading and re-reading and thinking about James for years, out of love for the work, and from an intense, almost personal interest in the characters and their fates, and who responded with great generosity and enthusiasm to my somewhat systematic and abstract treatment. Accordingly, I found that discussions after the paper were among the most animated, thoughtful, personal, and, certainly for me, the most helpful of any I have ever experienced. I owe a great debt to those audiences for the questions, criticisms, and comments that I received. This certainly goes as well for the literary critics, many of whom were kind enough not to treat me as an interloper or poacher, and who were often extremely helpful with suggestions and criticisms. It goes just as well for the many interlocutors who had the patience to hear me out, to read drafts of chapters, and to respond and criticize. My thanks especially to John Coetzee, Lorraine Daston, Lisabeth During, Mark Jenkins, Charles Larmore, Glenn Most, Ross Poole, Richard Posner, and Nathan Tarcov.

# Acknowledgments

In the course of writing these chapters, I received for the second time in my career a generous grant from the Alexander von Humboldt Foundation. This *Stipendium,* together with equally generous sabbatical and leave from the University of Chicago and some additional assistance from the Earhart Foundation, allowed me to take up residence with my wife and children for a year's stay in Tübingen, Germany. The grant was given primarily to enable me to continue work on a large project about Hegel's theory of freedom, something I had been working on, on and off, for more than ten years, and that I was able to bring close to completion in Germany. The Jamesean prospect, however, of being an American living in Europe and being able to steal some time away from German philosophy to complete a draft of a book on literature, was too tempting a situation and too romantic an image to resist. Since this would also give me an excuse to re-read *The Ambassadors* during stays in Paris, *The Wings of the Dove* in Venice, *The Golden Bowl* in London, and so forth, I seized the opportunity, and completed the penultimate draft of the manuscript during our first few months in the lovely university town of Tübingen and on several sojourns in Europe. I am grateful to the Humboldt Foundation, to the University of Chicago, to the Dean of its Social Sciences Division, Richard Saller, and to the Earhart Foundation, and grateful for the extraordinary hospitality of my Tübingen hosts for their support and generosity. Manfred Frank and Veronique Zanetti, Toni and Uta Koch, Otfried and Evelyn Höffe, and Axel and Gerlinde Markert were all especially kind and helpful to me and my family, and we shall always remain thankful for their *Gastfreundlichkeit.*

I also owe special debts to the friends who were generous enough to read the completed manuscript and offer detailed comments and extensive criticism and questions. I profited immensely from correspondence and conversation with Fred Olafson, Jay Bernstein, Stanley Rosen, and Dan Brudney, and am much in their debt. I doubt that I have answered their criticisms, but their comments were deeply appreciated, and they certainly prompted many an alteration and attempts at revision. I am just as indebted to the referees for Cambridge University Press, two of whom, Richard Eldridge and David Bromwich, later made their identities known to me. It was extraordinarily kind of all the referees, and especially these latter two, to write such full, detailed, and thoughtful remarks. I hope that in the final draft I managed to do some justice to their concerns. My thanks also to Terry Moore of Cambridge University Press for his support of this project and for his wise counsel about this and many other matters, and to the manuscript editor, Ronald Cohen, for a most judicious and helpful job.

I thank my colleague Mark Strand for permission to reprint from his poem "The Idea" and Donald Justice for permission to reprint "Henry James at the Pacific." A somewhat different version of sections from Chapters 2 and 3 was recently published by the University of Chicago Press in a Festschrift for my colleague David Grene, and I thank the Press and Todd Breyfogle for their cooperation.

Finally, this book is dedicated to the memory of François Furet. François was the co-chair of the Committee on Social Thought when I moved to Chicago in 1992, so I came to owe him all sorts of special personal debts for his thoughtfulness, persuasiveness, and patience during a difficult period of transition. I also quickly realized what extraordinary good fortune it was for me to be able to get to know and learn from one of the twentieth century's greatest historians and wisest interlocutors. James's International Theme was often François's theme, as were both James's worries about modernity – concerns most visible in the land of modernity's future, America – as well as James's hopes and qualified optimism. Completing this book in memory of him was one small way for me to continue imagining how all those conversations about such themes might have continued.

# I

## MODERN MORALS

### I

A remarkably intelligent woman of little means is in love with a talented man of equally few means and no prospects. Both are eager for what a life of wealth will make possible for them. (Great wealth will of course make possible what it always has: a certain kind of freedom – power. But in the modern, secular, competitive society that they inhabit, the prospects for an interesting or even minimally free life without means are rapidly dwindling.) They meet a dying, very young American heiress, herself already infatuated with the young man. The woman conceives the idea that her boyfriend should pursue and marry the heiress. When she dies, after he inherits her fortune, they will then be free to marry; they will have their great wealth and their grand life. No one will be hurt.

The plan almost works. But the heiress learns that her new friend and her supposed lover are engaged. In bitter disappointment, she "turns her face to the wall," to life itself, and succumbs to her illness. But before dying, she makes an extraordinary bequest, leaving the young man a fortune, despite everything. The young man, who has never been enthusiastic about the deception, cannot, he says, simply now take the money and execute the plan. Instead, he proposes to his fiancée that they return the fortune and marry "as they were." But both seem to realize, and the fiancée ends the novel by asserting, that they cannot ever be "as they were." Acting as if no great moral complication would shadow their life is apparently unacceptable to Merton Densher; but accepting such a complication and the need to redeem themselves puts the fiancée, Kate Croy, in the wrong, would thereby change everything in their relationship, and would make any marriage of equal respect and mutual authority impossible. The money, it seems, is in some way morally unacceptable to him, and stands between them in a morally significant sense. Returning it is for him an attempt at expiation, the only way they can at least try to set things right.

So it would seem. The question of the meaning of Densher's renunciation of Milly Theale's bequest and its role in our overall judgment of what has happened turn out to be quite complicated. For one thing, the fiancée plausibly disagrees with this interpretation of the act (as an attempt to set them right again; as if it can prove something, retrospectively, about their motives then or their status now). She thinks it is only motivated by love, not morality; it is a way of keeping faith with a memory he has fallen in love with, of proving that his motives had become finally purer, not merely deceptive. (The fiancée has all along been clever at interpretations that avoid the weight of moral judgments, so we immediately suspect the motives behind her criticism. Despite this, this may be the right reading of Densher; it may also be the best defense she could make to his implied charge; it may be both.) A reader might also see the young man's proposal as an attempt to reject a woman he has fallen out of love with, perhaps as an expression of contempt for what she has come to stand for, perhaps a way of asserting a kind of power over her that he had lost in her grand plan. It (not taking the money) is also disconcertingly consistent with his all-too-passive behavior throughout, with his (disastrous, failed) attempts merely to "keep still" and thereby, he seems to have hoped, to avoid the entanglements his very passivity only deepens. This renunciation might be only a last, consistent act of self-deceit in a whole series. In such a context, with so many very plausible possible psychological interpretations of his rejection of the fortune available, a natural question would be whether that act could ever be said to be rightly understood primarily in moral terms (his or anyone's), whether there ever genuinely are such moral motivations, or, if there are, whether the principles acted on or the good sought is real, has some real claim on us (or is only and always a psychologically valuable weapon). Although such moral considerations are often spoken of as idealizations, what we ought to aspire to base conduct on, even if never unqualifiedly a motive force in action, the other possibilities seem so much more real. The moral dimension and a possible moral motive, without a religious foundation or much resonance left in the world they live in, with so many powerful psychological and self-interested forces at work, seem by contrast always suspicious, as if more a convenient afterthought than the center of things. (And Densher is a man who often invites such suspicion.)

Henry James's *The Wings of the Dove* is, of course, a novel, and James is known as a novelist of manners – an analytical, psychological novelist. So, its being wrong to have deceived and manipulated Milly Theale looks at first like something that seems wrong (in whatever sense it does) to Merton Densher (and especially and interestingly, not to Kate Croy), a donnée within his mental and emotional life, of importance in James's brilliant treatment of what such an experience would mean for a man like that, and why, under what psychological conditions, it would take place.[1]

Yet, because the novelist in question is James, it is likely that we are also being presented with a more ambitious treatment, one wherein the possibility and meaning of that evaluation itself (its being wrong) is also being explored, that James wants us to see what other gears in a complex life that particular wheel turns (let us say, provisionally, in this case, one's entitlement to treatment as a free subject, to a life that is one's own) and what goes missing, disengages, and disrupts other gears, if it is missing or broken. This would involve a way of showing what makes the act wrong, would express in a literary way views about the nature of Milly's entitlement not to be so treated.

There is, of course, no particular reason that Henry James need have such larger views, or that they need play some role in the aesthetic dimensions of the novels. There is no particular reason such views, if they exist, should be independently interesting, apart from our aesthetic appreciation and enjoyment. And the notion of "views" is itself very ambiguous; everything is only implied in how characters explain and defend themselves, and in what ways our sympathies and judgments seem to tip and turn in the face of such evidence about motives and purposes. And the novels have all sorts of exemplary aesthetic and formal virtues on their own. But in some sense, James does have such views, and they are quite interesting.

The former is likely, for one thing, because the theme itself – deception (and a host of related faults: lying, promise breaking, egotism) and the nature of our experience of such things as wrong (or the problem of what is in some way lacking when it is not experienced as wrong) – is at the center of interest in his greatest works. The problem of such a judgment – the problem of its possibility and meaning and authority in such a secular, non-religious, self-interested society – simply seems to have fascinated him.

This is already clear in the way Densher's reaction is described. What Densher seems to experience at the end of *The Wings of the Dove* is not just a feeling of deep sympathy with Milly, or a worry about his reputation, or long-term concerns about what treatment of him under such a principle would be like. He does not just realize that "one doesn't do such things," that he hasn't "gone on" as "they do." Milly, he comes to realize, simply as an individual subject with her own life to lead, just *was* entitled to considerations she did not receive, and so was treated wrongly. Likewise, the "deceived heiresses" in *Washington Square, The Portrait of a Lady, The Golden Bowl,* and other works are his paradigmatic characters not just because of the melodramatic, fairy-tale, and mythic possibilities such a type opens up, but because the phenomenon allows him to raise for his readers the question of the moral reaction without which the novels would not work aesthetically in the first place, would not create the allegiances and revulsions necessary for our engagement. (There always being such a question, though, and its being so difficult, the possibility that such judgments are vestigial or sentimental or finally empty is partly why the moral issues do not just ring down some judgmental curtain at the finale, didactically or programmatically. Offstage, James is more scratching his head, let us say, than wagging his finger.[2] As we shall see, that complexity and tenuousness have their own moral dimension.)[3] The same (intense attention and the question of possibility) is true in many other permutations on the issue of deception and lying (for example, the narrator's falseness in *The Aspern Papers*) or the frequent themes of sacrifice, renunciation, forgiveness, and the problem of "goodness" in characters like Christopher Newman, Fleda Veatch, Isabel, Milly, and Strether.

In other words, James is as aware as we are nowadays that moral categories can be ideological, reflections of the requirements and interests of social position and power, or can be understood psychologically, as a reflection of needs and desires and especially anxieties, never a part of but always behind and motivating the great work of interpretive consciousness that is so much his theme. Moral categories are often and just weapons in this sense. But this is certainly not always or exclusively so in James's fiction, and he also has something to show us about the nature of the moral claim itself, the subjects who cannot but make use of it, the social and historical world within which it fits, and its unique indispensability in an unprecedented historical transition.[4]

This last, historical dimension is quite important and, until recently, somewhat neglected in criticism on James.[5] In exploring such a "moral reaction" (like Densher's), in trying to figure out its status, what makes it possible and effective, James wants to frame the problem in a self-consciously historical and social way. His own characterizations of this "epochal" problem make it reasonable, though a bit grand and somewhat too abstract to be Jamesean, to designate it within the complex of issues usually summarized as the problem of Western modernization. That is, as with most novelists, morality is first of all treated by James as a matter of mores, and that means as a matter of essentially social and historically specific practices, institutions, and largely implicit rules and expectations. And the reactions and judgments he is interested in belong in a certain new historical world (and uniquely in that world). What is most distinctive about this emerging new form of life is apparent immediately: While these individuals always represent and evince aspects of their social position, the interrelation and meaning of such social positions, functions, roles, the depth of meaning in convention and tradition, and so on, do not any longer provide these characters, in this increasingly anomic and disunified social world, with much of a basis for interpretation and assessment. Types and kinds and classes and social position and "blood" and family and races and institutions and social forms and even appeals to "human nature" will no longer function in making possible such mutual understanding, and neither will too hasty a reduction of possible motives to some set of the low, the base, the selfish, or the "natural." (In James's mythic landscape, the name for such a collapse of the reliability of traditional form, such uncertainty and new vacancy as well as radical possibility, is simply "America.")

In this context, James presents his characters as having a very difficult time simply trying to understand what they most need to understand in order to make such evaluations – that is, their own and others' intentions or motives, the right description of the action itself: broadly, the meaning of their own and others' acts and interactions. It is extraordinarily difficult for them to do this precisely because so much of what had made possible such interpretation – the conventions and background assumptions, forms of life in general – has lost a great deal of its cultural authority, at least for the characters James examines, leaving only a kind of void or vacancy. (Here, James's views parallel many others' for whom modernization is a kind of trauma and disorienting loss, not mainly a liberation and discovery.) Precisely what makes necessary understanding an individual somewhat abstractly, even theoretically, as an "agent" or "person" – the unreliability of or lack of common authority for fixed, predictable social norms, the lack of authority for any presumed common good or goods sought by anyone – also makes that attempt intensely problematic. There is often very little to rely on, little way to predict, expect, assume, little basis even for a minimum trust, little clarity about what a "person" is or can be expected to do.

Without much reliability and coordination in mutual expectations and commitments, the question of whether a young man's dalliance in Europe with an older married woman is acceptable or not, the question of just how to describe what he is doing, becomes more and more elusive. The same is even true for Kate Croy's clearly manipulative and deceptive plan, since James also invests a great deal of space convincing us that she is likely the most complex, socially capable, and intelligent character in the novel. (She is representative too: "She was just the contemporary London female, highly modern, inevitably battered, honorably free" *WD*, 40.[6]) Whatever anyone in such a context might settle on as a meaning and evaluation of such an adventure or such a character would have to fit in, play some expanded role in a structure or network of commitments and inferences shared by others, would have to be recognizable by others as right because it could then play some consistent, regular role in further expectations, accounts, and assessments. Such understandings and evaluations must play some role in a whole of some sort if they are to be possible at all. If there isn't much of such a commonality, or if what there is is arbitrary, vestigial, narrow-minded, and inadequate to all it must deal with, if the traditional authority of conventional classifications has begun to break down ("he's been seduced by a fortune hunter," "he's sowing his wild oats," "he's neglecting his responsibilities at home," "she is a selfish egoist," "he is a self-deceived weakling"), then everything, at least to characters of insight and awareness, is left unresolved and indefinite. Hence the constant question that is made so explicit in the ghost, secret, and mystery tales: Am I imagining this (this ascribed meaning or intention or possibility or presence) or is it there?

Of course, being able to distinguish dedication to one's work from greed or egoism, or being able to distinguish concern for a friend from nosiness and manipulation, can often be difficult in any context. But things are much more difficult when the various social conventions and assumptions and traditional categories that might have helped one think through and explore such questions are unavailable; when questions like what one owes a parent or a child, or what it is to marry, or what keeping faith with an old friend whose child seems to need saving amounts to, must all, it seems, be confronted in some historical void, as if anew, on the sole basis of one's sensibility, taste, and especially on the basis of the interchanges and conversations with others; when there is no fixed, agreed-on predictability about such things, only confusion about what examples, paradigm cases, further implications, and so on could be called on to explain and think through such questions. In the modern world described by James, being able to settle on some interpretation cannot now be like discovering some hidden fact of the matter, finding some "truth-maker" in the social and psychological world, even when the fact might be something like "what we think (used to think) about such things." (There is no longer such a "we.") What it (some settling of interpretive possibilities and judgment) is like forms my question in the following. Given the way James presents his historical assumptions about modernity, and given the manifest uncertainties and absences in that world, why isn't James a moral skeptic? What does he think still makes what Densher and Croy do wrong?

I I

This resistance to skepticism, I want to show, is an extremely suggestive response on James's part. His response raises questions both about the nature of the problem as he sees it and the degree of his worry.

In the first place, he introduces what look like a number of serious doubts about various central elements of the moral point of view. Many of these have to do with the uncertainties and unavoidable vagueness of the human condition, uncertainties that mean that even with the best of will, we simply cannot often evaluate or reason well about a possible course of action, cannot come to terms with it until well into the future, and then only retrospectively. These are not considerations the moral point of view usually takes much account of, holding people instead to strict account for the maxims and motives they acted on, however limited and finite the conditions of understanding. To have acted well in a moral sense is usually understood to have acted with the proper sort of deliberation (or attempt at deliberation) and proper attempt at justification. (This is particularly true of one form of justification: justifiability to all those affected by one's deeds, or adopting an impartial criterion that does not privilege one's own case.) This means, among many other things, to have taken the proper

7

account of the results of one's conduct on others (whether in the sense of the brute consequences or in terms of the entitlements of others), to have estimated the value and ill effects of those results, and to have evaluated a course of conduct undertaken now with respect to those future effects and implications and with proper regard to whether we can justify our bringing about those results to those whose lives we change. Anything that might occur because of what I did, but not because of what I intended to do, is regarded as exempt from moral blame.

As Bernard Williams especially has shown,[7] this can present a severe and inhumane picture of what we can claim to stand apart from. Moreover, deeper into the problem as Williams sees it, we, as moralists, often tend to exaggerate the extent of the future events we can anticipate, we presume a capacity to justify what we propose to do in the present on the basis of unrealistic assumptions about our control and knowledge of the future, and, especially, we discount unfairly the ways in which chance future events can affect or effectively determine our sense of what was, or would have been, justified.

These sorts of worries about contingencies in how we determine what is justifiable or not – and so therefore about the role of "moral luck" – are frequently raised in James, and are clearly part of his worry about the rigidity and judgmental rigor of the moral point of view. Kate and Merton consider and justify their actions and plans one way on the assumption that Milly will die before any part of Kate's plan is revealed. And James clearly wants us to consider – especially by making Kate's predicament so sympathetic – what everything would have looked like if Milly *had* died before she found out about them, and perhaps even died blissfully happy and content with Merton. (Of course, the fact that the plan had to be kept secret reveals that their susceptibility to such moral luck, and their attempt to avoid or deny this fact, is not the only thing wrong with it.) The same worry arises in Isabel's retrospective analysis of what she could or should have known about Osmond (much of which she could only have known after having married him), or in the open-ended question of Chad in *The Ambassadors*. (We just won't know how valuable his dalliance will be for some time, and acting as if there is no question about that, as if we know with moral certainty that he ought to return home and keep to his obligations, makes clear what the rigorism objection to morality amounts to.)

These issues and the doubts they raise about the putative "unconditionality" of moral evaluation are familiar enough in many novels. (Williams's example is a fine one: Anna Karenina and how much the question of whether she would have been in any way justified is affected by what happens later, events she could not have anticipated when she had to decide.) But in some ways, James's worries go even deeper. Not only does he appreciate how much justification and evaluation has to be post facto (something that, given the great, uncontrollable contingency of future events, decreases our confidence about what we can hold people to and blame them for when they decide ex ante). But there also appears to be considerable skepticism about the terms of the analysis itself, about any determinacy in the meaning of such terms, or in our being able to assure ourselves that we share such terms of evaluation and share some sense of their claim on us. It is one thing to have to wait to see what will happen to Chad before we can know whether what he is putting his family through was worth it (and to have to make a decision about that beforehand, in such uncertainty); it is another to suspect an indeterminacy and unreliability in the issue of what his being better off might amount to at all, how it might ever be able to count for us as being better off. When we ask about, are prompted by disagreements and misconnections with others to raise questions about, the content of the judgment that Strether is trying to form – is Chad better off – or when we ask about "what" Maggie is trying to save in trying to "save her marriage" or what the harm is that would have been done to Milly had she not known, we are asking, among other things, about the "circulability" or "shareability" of normative terms, whether such assessments can be given and accepted as reasons or justifications in a community whose members are committed to the authority of such notions but must sometimes interpret and apply them in altered circumstances.

This would all be clearly possible if we all, with various degrees of insight and distortion, "saw," or came to know something about, the same objective qualities and states of being in the universe, some of them moral qualities, and so could share such assessments in the way we share knowledge (or fail to share them because of distortions and ignorance, along the model of "missed" opportunities to know). But James seems to have more idealist views about the reality of these moral terms (more on this in a moment), seems more inclined to make them depend somehow (for their sense and authority) on the communities that institute such commitments and sustain them, and that finally begin to alter, shift, abandon, and revise these commitments, often not collectively or all at once, but in confusing periods of transition and renegotiation.

We are – I believe that James believes – in one of the most confusing and complex periods of such transition, but, as already indicated, he does not believe that this means we just don't know what we're about, have lost any shareable assessments, and should be moral skeptics. We might be such skeptics if we held that all such moral assessments depended on several fixed assumptions and principles. Williams often raises doubts about "morality" when morality is understood in some such way – as a futile attempt to transcend and master luck, to put myself in a position where I cannot later be blamed because I took care of all that was in my power to take care of, my deliberation and my own intentions, and so tried to act without privileging my point of view, impartially, as any rational agent, counted equally, one among many. This might, Williams often argues, solve the moral luck and indeterminacy problems by fitting all deliberation into a model almost designed to resolve just such anxieties, but it also leaves me wondering what this stance might have to do with me or my agency, or why I should care about or be committed to such a model or how the relationship between moral and non-moral deliberation should (could ever) be understood.[8]

But taking others into account, giving them their due, need not involve adopting, somewhat mysteriously, some impartial and so alienated a point of view. In the cases that James explores and that will be the focus in the following, the worries about contingency and indeterminacy (which James treats as historical phenomena, ever more a part of the modern social world) need not prompt some attempt at methodological purification, a reaction that looks to impartiality and an assessment tied to a strict attention to an agent's own reasons at a time for acting. The nature of others' claims on me might not be linked so to the requirements of justification and reason, some requirement of impartiality and universality just so that it *be* reasoning. As I suggested earlier, this altered situation of indeterminacy and contingency might itself reveal an altered social state, one wherein those claims are experienced differently, mean something new, are more directly necessary for me to lead my own life, to give it sense, to assess, and judge.[9] The key issue in morality might not be the rational justifiability with which I treat others, but the proper acknowledgment of, and enactment of, a dependence on others without which the process of any justification (any invocation of common normative criteria at all) could not begin.

That is, this uncertainty and doubt and profound ambiguity, unresolveability about meaning, while on the one hand a great loss, an experience of "vacancy," as James often says in describing America, on the other hand makes possible and even requires a form of dependency, a dependency even at the level of possible consciousness itself, and some "lived out" acknowledgment of such dependency, that now makes up the new moral experience, the claims and entitlements of each on others, that he is interested in. (We shall see these two attitudes directly linked in Chapter 2.)

III

Now all of these issues about evaluation and judgment are connected with scores of others in James and in themselves, and there is of course some danger that isolating certain issues (like "morality") from others will simplify and distort. But such simplification needs to be risked a bit further in order to be clear initially about the nature of the problems introduced here. So much (so much in what I want to claim) will depend on the nature of the great social change James is interested in, and how that change bears on the problem of meaning and therewith moral assessment, that at least some more initial orientation is necessary and some outline of the philosophical controversies equally required. It can be put this way.

As suggested, I want to show that James believed that a vast historical alteration had been taking place in Western European and American societies for some time, that this involved a change in basic mores and sensibilities, that it was especially visible in the privileged (reflective, intensely self-conscious, freed-from-the-necessity-of-labor) classes, though not limited to them, and that this had now, as it came to a head – even to a sort of historical crisis – greatly complicated our moral assessments of each other, the way we hold each other to some account for what we do. Modern social existence had become, in the first and crudely obvious sense, just more complex (so complex that when James tries to do justice to what he sees as the magnitude of this new intricacy by inventing a whole new sort language for it, he leaves many readers completely baffled and quite irritated). As we shall see, this complexity has to do with the increasing unavailability of what we used to be able to rely on in interpreting and assessing each other, on the new role of money and the social mobility it made possible, the psychological suspicions it engendered, on new, much more extensive and deeper forms of social dependencies, and on very new ways of understanding the fluid, relatively unfixed, quite variously interpretable dimensions of psychological life.

This altered situation can, with respect to the issue of moral claims, then be understood in either a moderate or a much more radical way. More moderately, it all now introduces a great problem in human judgment, in being able to interpret and apply moral criteria. One might believe that there are and always have been objective moral qualities, states of being, kinds of pleasures, aesthetic forms, human capacities (like intelligence or perhaps the capacity to set one's own ends with as little distortion or subjection to the will of others as possible) that are simply objectively good states and that we always ought to bring about. But our growing appreciation for the complex interdependencies, greater appreciation for the complexity of psychological motivation, and the uncertainties and interpretive vagaries and mutability of modern social life all make it much harder than in more socially stable, hierarchical times to know what, in this new world, will count as an instantiation of such qualities and states. This is especially the case if one believes that it is not enough for such states and qualities to be realized, but that the world as a whole is much better if they are brought about with the right intentions, if people strive to realize them because these qualities or actions are in themselves good, and so have some claim on us. This makes everything even more difficult because we might find it even harder to be confident about our description and assessment of individual psychological motives (and about our own motives in offering various interpretations) than we could be in offering the right interpretation and description of some element of modern social life, some putative fact of the matter.

This is all a "moderate" worry after a fashion because it still holds the nature of moral value stable, and notes that our sophistication and growing ability to cast doubt on our judgment and interpretation, and the growing complexity of what we must make judgements about, all raise mostly an application and interpretation problem. Things might be more complicated and fragile now; we might need to be more cautious and sensitive to error and self-deceit, but the basic human condition remains fundamentally the same. Perhaps our growing hesitancies, suspicion of hasty judgments, resistance to dogmatism and crude moralism might even be counted as moral progress of a sort. The awareness of the great range of such interpretive and motivational possibilities, or of the difficulty of applying Victorian or simplistic categories, means we have simply brought about another good thing, or better achieved what was always a good quality (sensitive judgment), and so have progressed.

One could also believe the same thing if one were not a moral realist and cognitivist in just this form, but some sort of constructivist – that is, if one believed that all value is "legislated" or constructed by human beings, not found or seen in the world, but in a way that must always and everywhere conform to the basic condition of any such value-conferring. Most philosophers who believe something like this believe that that condition is reason and that this constraint of justifiability leads to objective principles that must always and unconditionally be respected in such valuation. If it has become more difficult to differentiate the morally salient features of a situation, to apply this principle consistently and coherently, the basic issue of what is good or right to do is still not much affected.

Things look much different – and immediately much more philosophically problematic – if one thinks that human history can so radically transform people and institutions that one might even say that moral reality itself changes, that the very nature of the kinds of claims human beings can create and hold themselves to, changes. (This would be so if one could say that new "goods" now claim our attention, or new conditions for valuation have come to be.) Many philosophers immediately suspect such a position of being indistinguishable from a claim against any "moral reality" altogether, or they suspect such a move of being reductionist in a sociological, naturalistic, or psychological sense (reducing what is good or right to what people feel or are disposed to feel or in general take to be good or right at a time, in a given society). If that is so, then, so goes the argument, there is no way to account for the claim of the good or right on us, to distinguish between "*we believe this or that ought to be done*" and "*this or that ought to be done.*" Morality, so goes this suspicion, is not a matter of reporting what our tribe believes; and if our tribe does believe anything of this sort, it must be because it claims to know something about the good or to have subscribed to the law. (The holy is loved by the gods because it is holy, goes the old argument in Plato's *Euthyphro*; it is not holy because it is loved by the gods.) If that is what our moral experience depends on, then, so goes this intuition, we ought to hold fast to this realistic or objectivist intuition and worry only about making our way through the new distortions and complexities. Moreover, if the moral dimension of human life itself could change so radically, then a certain sort of relativism seems to some philosophers inevitable. And this too can prompt worries that there is a small step from the concession that this moral dimension changes to the claim that there really is no such moral dimension. It sounds like one might be saying that slavery or the seizure of the lands of indigenous peoples "was" right to a community at a time and "became" wrong later, and that seems like one is saying that there really is no right and wrong; there "really" is only what was taken to be so, given certain conditions, at a time.[10]

James, I want to show, is a member of good standing in both the moderate and more radical camps, but is nevertheless, again surprisingly, no moral skeptic or nihilist. He suggests certain idealist claims about social and psychological reality (makes such a reality depend on how they are experienced and described at a time in a community), reveals there to be such complexity and possibility in that experiencing and describing that he introduces a great fluidity and instability and multiple interpretability, and so radicalizes the judgmental and interpretive problem. But, as we shall see, he also extends his idealism – his view of what depends on us to be what it is, and his sense of how much "we" can change – to the nature of moral authority itself. Here is a relatively typical, well-known expression of his general view:

> Experience is never limited, and it is never complete; it is an im-
> mense sensibility, a kind of huge spider-web of the finest silken
> threads suspended in the chamber of consciousness, and catching
> every air-borne particle in its tissue. It is the very atmosphere of the
> mind; and when the mind is imaginative – much more when it
> happens to be that of a man of genius – it takes to itself the faintest
> hints of life, *it converts the very pulses of the air into revelations*.[11]

Or there is the famous letter to H.G. Wells: "It is art that *makes* life, *makes* interest, *makes* importance, for our consideration and application of these things, and I know of no substitute whatever for the force and beauty of its process."[12]

Accordingly, since we have changed, everything has changed, including what we owe each other and what it would be good to bring about now, and why. The problem is not that we are too confused about what we dimly see must be done, or simply too weak to bring about what (we see) must be done. There is a much more fundamental and justified uncertainty about what must be done in itself; this uncertainty has a distinct historical ground, and threatens the very possibility of moral meaning – threatens, but, I want to suggest throughout, does not destroy or finally undermine it. Densher's dilemma concerns not only the great difficulty in deciding who he is, what it is that he really intended and intends, concerns not only judgment and interpretation, but also how to find at all, or better even how to create and hold to and sustain, any moral compass in the world he inhabits. (The "challenge" of Kate Croy, the challenge of her remarkable intelligence and clear-headedness and desperation, is so compellingly presented precisely just to raise this question, for us as well as for Densher.) He may not succeed, but it would be wrong to say his failure simply evinces a general failure.

That is what I want to claim, and I begin in the next chapter with an account of the modernity analysis that all of this (this particular, Jamesean moral sensibility) is supposed to rest on. I then turn to some of the greatest novels and tales to work through the details of this moral analysis. I describe the structure of the argument in the next section, and conclude this introduction with a brief qualification.

IV

The structure is fairly straightforward. There are five further chapters on James's works, and then a concluding discussion. The goal of the first two is to establish the basic premises of the argument about James's contribution to our understanding of modern moral life; the third is about forms of resistance and denial of this new situation; and the fourth and fifth try to answer skeptical questions that naturally arise from this scenario.

Chapter 2 deals mainly with the *The Awkward Age* and *The American Scene,* and the discussion is meant to show the historical dimensions of the International Theme and especially the relationship between emerging, modern forms of sociality and the problem of shared psychological, normative, and moral understanding. We need to know what James thinks has changed, why he thinks that change so important, and why he thinks this alteration has made for such uncertainty, complexity, and misunderstanding. This will raise questions about the social conditions of understanding that are also at the heart of the revolution James effected in the art novel. That is, many of the standard assumptions in realist and romantic novelists – especially about a struggle between an individual character or couple or group, and the demands of some inexorable social necessity, or the way in which society can now function like fate, crushing individuals or making them conform, or rebel, especially materialistic, commercial societies, bound together by material interest and not by tradition or religion or a common history – all begin to have less and less relevance as a frame or form for James's narration.

In a few instances (*The Bostonians, The Tragic Muse, The Princess Cassimassima*), there is no such struggle. There is plenty of struggle, but it is not "with society" or fate, or with some identifiable objective force, but among individuals, or individual families or members of a family, and it often concerns meaning, most often the meaning and implications of a marriage. This does not mean that James has resigned himself to the total, unopposable power of money in the modern world, and has shifted interest to private attempts at experience and understanding somehow outside (by luck usually) the great capitalist machine. He actually has a far more complicated view of the deep "interpenetration" of these social forms and individual, inner life than has been appreciated, a sense of the inseparability of the social novelties of modern civil society and the way individuals come to fix and hold to understandings of their and others' deeds. Oddly, though, it is not so much the necessities, regularities, deadly conformism, and so forth of such society that James treats as so formative and powerful (though he is interested in that too), but what this new social power has destroyed and how little of what we need it has left in its place. This reorients understanding and judgment among individuals – whom the capitalist world has now essentially rendered strangers to, and suspicious of, each other but who nonetheless must find some way of counting on each other, must find some "modern" moral life.

How they might begin to find it is the theme of Chapter 3, which concentrates on James's masterpiece *The Golden Bowl.* The question here directly concerns the results of modern sociality on possible understanding. I try to show how those results make for a very different understanding and treatment of consciousness itself, or a different sense of what any awareness of one's own states and judgment about others' must involve. In this sort of society, given what has been lost, what looks like "an awareness" turns out to be much more provisional and temporally unstable, often as much an uncertain, hesitant anticipation of another's understanding as anything that could be described cognitively, often as much a first draft of an intention, something that comes to clarity, necessarily, only long after the deed. In *The Golden Bowl,* especially, we begin to see why James thinks certain moral consequences follow from this situation, and what sort of immorality results from denying it.

Denial, resistance, self-deceit, and repression form the theme of the fourth chapter as I examine the ghost and mystery and "secret" stories. My claim is that these form a part of the same theme – the moral dimensions of attempted understanding in Jamesean modernity, let us say – this time by way of negation, or a refusal to accept the uncertainties and anxieties that this situation naturally generates. The paradigmatic case here is John Marcher in *The Beast in the Jungle.* Apropos of my claim, there are two signal elements in this fantastic story: The first is the careful, very self-conscious historical setting sketched by James at the beginning (the meaning of "weather's end" as the setting), and the second is the link between the understanding and uncertainty themes and the problems of reciprocity or moral acknowledgment, here as often figured in James by the "problem" of love, or in this case how we are to understand Marcher's rejection of love. I then extend the case I make about Marcher first to what seems to me a companion story, *The Jolly Corner,* and then to *The Aspern Papers* and *The Turn of the Screw.*

The interpretation offered then suggests two problems. The first is whether any real, humanly recognizable form of genuine intersubjective acceptance and affirmation is ever possible in the social world James describes, whether as a moral acknowledgment or in what is treated as a similar but higher form of such selflessness or bracketing of the egoistic self, in love. It doesn't appear all that often in his fiction. Certainly. (Perhaps the most dramatic of these characterizations comes from James's amanuensis, Theodora Bosanquet, who noted that in the Jamesean universe, it sometimes seemed there were only "children of light" or "creatures of prey.") Renunciation is the thematic term given this problem by so many commentators on James, and there is perhaps no instance of it that has so bothered readers as Isabel Archer's decision at the end of *A Portrait of a Lady* to return to her morally wretched husband, Gilbert Osmond. It is reasonable to think that this and many other examples show that James raises the issue of such a possible mutuality only to show how impossible it is, both morally and romantically. The modern intersubjective world has become simply a zero-sum game, and the moral side of things can only be the "children of light" lining up for their submission to the "creatures of prey." I want to dispute this impression and defend what I think is James's continuing admiration for Isabel.

The other problem concerns the question of how, if ever, all this indeterminacy in negotiations about meaning could ever end. Any postmodern fan of ever-deferred and differing meanings and floating signifiers and shifting gender and social identities and so forth ought to find his hero, it would appear, in the later James.[13] This is especially on view in the sublime, gentle, and often simply beautiful consciousness of Lambert Strether. Here, again, I want to defend what I take to be James's somewhat heroic treatment of Strether, right through to the end of what is never a determinate resolution of his judgmental problem (what to make of Chad) and, apparently, right through to Strether's own "renunciation." I want again, that is, to defend what I think James means us to see, the moral reality Strether confronts and accepts, however fraught with what appears to be an endless interpretive and psychological indeterminacy. However, the discussion throughout should be introduced with a qualification.

V

When we first are introduced to Isabel Archer in *The Portrait of a Lady,* she is alone in the gloomiest room of her house. There is a "crude, cold rain" falling "heavily" outside and she is "trudging over the sandy plains of a history of German Thought" (*PL,* 34). It would fit my purposes well (or introduce the possible internal relevance of philosophical categories to an analysis of James) if she had just gotten to the sections on Kant and Hegel and the problem of freedom, and read some out loud.[14] But the image also hints strongly at all the possible objections to any presumed attempt by some reader to carry that book along with her and make use of it to measure and understand what will happen. That way of trying to understand the world is of course what she will now leave behind, along with the loneliness and gloom of such presumably lifeless, narrow formulae, fit for a small room in New York perhaps, but not for the rich palaces of Rome or Florence.

And so it is, one hears, with the application of philosophical categories, especially moral evaluation, to literature. The density and complexity of psychological experiences and meaning, supposedly, and the uniqueness of aesthetic experience itself, the centrality of beauty and form, the contrary reliance of philosophy on argument and proof, and so on, are all already prima facie objections to the very topic announced earlier, all as if we hadn't got the point of the contrast Mrs. Touchett wants to make between this first, philosophical house for Isabel ("This is very bourgeois") and the "palaces" she wants to show her.[15]

Such a general charge is almost unmanageably abstract, though, and I mention it here only to say that I have no general answer to it. I think it can only be answered in small details, and from the side rather than head on. There are very general remarks that are sometimes offered: about what cannot be "said" in philosophy, but needs nonetheless to be "shown" in literature; the value of literature in casuistic questions; the power of literature in challenging the fixity of our moral categories by revealing difficulties in application and helping us to appreciate shadings and ambiguities; literature's role as Evidence for the Anti-Theoretical, Anti-Universalist Approach to Morality in General (its appropriateness as a judgmental guide, given the truth of a kind of "moral particularism") or Literature's Moral Relevance as a Way of Changing the Moral Subject, Away From Principles and Actions, Toward the Texture and Quality and Goodness of Life, or so on,[16] and the like. But these can be as abstract and elusive as the charge itself, and the important point lies elsewhere. That point is simple: Whatever else is going on in James's fiction, something more than the presentation of examples and illustrations, material for reflection, is being offered; a kind of thinking and reflecting on moral life is going on, and there is much to be learned from that reflection.[17]

I suggest here that we simply begin by noting only that James presents important human conflicts in one way rather than other possible ways, that this involves some way of taking positions or expressing commitments on a number of issues, that his decisions reflect views about the historical and broadly social bases relevant to such views, and that we would do well to consider those implied positions and what appear to be the reasons behind them, as far as reflection on those commitments and possible reasons will take us.

NOTES

1. See Anderson (1992) for a representative view (even if, for reasons of his own, he will not call the mature James a "psychological" novelist): "How, and with what modulations, interferences, quickenings, or delays of pace, one took things in: this was the activity James registered, to our delight" (p. 136). Anderson often calls this a "moral" concern, but what he means is something like the very great importance James supposedly attributes to such a possible awareness and its expansion and deepening. Such

awareness, he means, is simply good, and better if more expansive and deeper. (A great advantage in Anderson's treatment is that he recognizes that this aspiration has a historical dimension. He suggests that we will never understand the importance of such striving for a subjective reality and hope for its universal significance, unless we understand it as reactive, a recoil from the acquisitive, conformist modern world, more manifest in America than anywhere else.) As will become clear, I think James presents such themes on a much wider historical and especially social stage than Anderson does, and the moral issues it raises are more conventionally moral (what are the claims of others and why).

2. Cf. Weisbuch (1998) on James's "original strategy" of renewing "the consequences of evil by problematizing its reality" (p. 103).

3. That is, aside from the question of moral ambiguity, there is often a particular sort of ambiguity about whether a moral category does, or could, apply, could render intelligible the state of things, given the complexity of motives and the limitations of characters. *The American* is an early example of the way James raises both issues, especially the latter. Newman "gives up" revenge he could take on an old French family, the Bellegardes, who have done him grievous wrong, have ruined his life and the life of his beloved. And this appears to be motivated by reflection on what the "right thing" to do would be. As usual, the situation is hardly straightforward. Although the novel is mostly melodrama and fairy tale (evil mother-in-law, secret murder in the past, abused princess, death in a duel, retreat into a convent), one of its great achievements is rendering the subtle complexities of the consciousness of a very unself-conscious man, Newman, especially his confused sense of "the right thing," for him, and in general. He has so much trouble deciding what to do with his damning piece of evidence against the Bellegardes, whipsaws back and forth between inconsistent resolutions, because he understands so little of what happens to him, has no adequate notions with which to understand the old world in which it happens, evincing the link between such issues (between intelligent appreciation and moral appropriateness) that emerges so often in James. And by the end of the novel, right after we are without doubt led to admire his "high road" approach, his tossing his piece of paper into the fire and destroying the evidence that would damn the Bellegardes, thereby rising morally above them, the novel takes us through its final, typical, Jamesean twist. Newman's friend explained that of course they would have counted on that, his natural goodness, that such goodness would only mean for them that Newman was a sucker as well as a clod, all meaning that by rising above them, he has played into their hands and has been manipulated, or also sunk beneath them again. Then the question of whether his gesture was above them or just against them, his own way of proving something to himself and them and so a mode of vengeance, not a release from enmity, is raised a final time. His grand gesture of self-confidence and putative moral integrity gets a final shake. "Newman instinctively turned to see if the little paper was in fact consumed; but there was nothing left of it" (*A*, 306). One last, instinctive change of heart and so one last doubt about what Newman's gesture could mean.

4. I also do not mean to suggest that the question of morality and psychology can be left at this rather abstract opposition. See Chapter VII of Wollheim (1984), Williams (1993), and Pippin (1997b.)

5. I mean, as such exemptions, the work by Posnock (1991), Dawidoff (1992), Furth (1979), Holland (1982), Ozouf (1998), Haviland (1997), and Tanner (1995) referred to briefly later.

6. James goes to other, great lengths to qualify any judgment of Kate; and not to excuse her, but to raise questions about how originally we ought to describe what is going on. There is the somewhat mysterious beginning scene with her father, and the depressing scenes with her sister, but there are also several suggestions about a kind of willful self-deceit in Milly's actions, or, as James puts it in the Preface, there is the question of what Milly "should have known." (Milly *knows* that Kate has not mentioned that she knows the interesting Englishman whom Milly met in New York, but, even as Milly learns more, she refuses or avoids any chance to find out more.)

7. Williams (1981a).

8. Williams (1981b).

9. The image used here and frequently hereafter, that of "leading" a life, raises more questions than can be addressed in this context, especially about the relationship between, on the one hand, individual events in a life and their connection with one another, and, on the other, the relationship between "me" and all those events. That issue opens up onto many others. See Wollheim (1984) and Eldridge (1997), *inter alia.*

10. There is likely not much point in trying to fit James too snugly into any of these categories; he seems to have views that could be characterized in all sorts of ways, and his treatments often challenge the conventional categories. (Cf. the appropriate warnings in Diamond (1995b).) For a clear exposition and defense of the realist/cognitivist option, see McGinn (1997) and Larmore (1996). One could at least say that overall, it is not likely that such realist notions would capture James's views. His philosophical principles are quite idealist (he is obviously very interested in the subjective "take" on claims for the good, as if that is where the claim and reason to act lies) and, especially, he seems so much impressed by historical change. A weakness in the realist position lies in accounting for great shifts in moral sensibility. One has to say either that there really aren't such shifts, away, say, from the acceptability of slavery or toward political and social equality for women. It just looks like there are. Or that there are no great shifts in what really counts as the good, just greater resolve, or, in bad times, more weakness, in bringing them about. Or that there is actual discovery and progress in moral knowledge (the unacceptability of slavery was out there in the world, waiting to be discovered), not all that attractive a claim in the late twentieth century. McGinn tries most of these tacks in his defense of realism. And there is the problem of why knowing that some state should be counted as an objectively better state could thereby give me a reason to act to bring it about. Realists have to say that this just is "part of the meaning of 'good' " and that the question can't arise. McGinn tries this too. And there is also the problem of massive ethical disagreement and cultural differences (of the sort that fascinated Herodotus, say) and many others. The realist answers to such doubts do not seem to me very persuasive, and at any rate James seems (again roughly and with many qualifications possible) headed speedily in other, more historically constructivist (but never skeptical) directions.

11. *AF,* 56, my emphasis.

12. Edel and Ray (1958), p. 267. My emphasis.

13. Cf. Bell (1991), p. 4, p. 39, and throughout on the tension in James's fiction between skepticism about meaning and the unavoidable assumptions about sense and coherence that fiction and the act of reading impose. Bell makes a number of helpful remarks throughout about the importance of "re-reading" in James (and so what I am calling retrospective justification), James's problems with ending narratives (especially with respect to traditional endings like deaths and marriages), the role that unrealized

possibilities play in the meaning of events to characters, and the relationship of all these themes to the general problem of meaning.

14. Olive Chancellor in *The Bostonians* also reads German books, and she too has a "beastly pure mind," as if James is thinking about the link between German moral theory and its internal danger: rigorism, even fanaticism.

15. Not to mention the famous image of James's Preface: "the house of fiction has in short not one window, but a million – a number of possible windows not to be reckoned, rather; every one of which has been pierced, or is still pierceable, in its vast front, by the need of the individual vision, and by the pressure of the individual will" (*PL*, 7). (All this by contrast with Isabel's dreary, bourgeois, closed up, narrow, and infrequently windowed philosophical house, and the contrasting illusion of art and aesthetic freedom, Osmond's palazzo, to which she is so understandably attracted.) He has by this point made his oft-repeated point about the "moral task" of literature: to communicate "felt life" (or to find a way to appreciate and acknowledge genuine individuals, as such). Here he also stresses that while the world may admit of a "million" points of view, whatever we take to be going on in the house depends on which window we look into, and the achievement of such an individual point of view, indeed of individuality itself, is just that – an achievement. The windows, in that most unusual phrase, must be actively "pierced"; indeed all of the great show within is ". . . as nothing without the posted presence of the watcher – without, in other words, the consciousness of the artist." He goes on: "Tell me what the artist is, and I will tell you of what he has been conscious. Thereby I shall express to you at once his boundless freedom and his 'moral' reference" (*ibid.*). Such highly unusual claims – that what the artist "is" amounts to what he "had been conscious of" and that the right achievement of such a perspective amounts to a kind of morality – are not, I claim, vague throw-away lines, but part of an elaborate, certainly idealist view about the situation of morality in modernity.

16. I do not of course mean to imply that reflection on the relevance of literature to thinking about morality or philosophy is limited to superficial speculation. Quite the contrary; I mean only to indicate how difficult the issue is to discuss economically. For admirably economical and insightful discussions of the issues involved, see the helpful essays by Cora Diamond (1995a) and (1995b). See *New Literary History* (1983) for a representative discussion. For other examples of richness and value of many such discussions, one could easily cite the work of Bernstein, Cavell, Eldridge, Williams, and many others. The work of Wayne Booth (1988) in establishing the general relevance of ethical issues in the appreciation of literature is also obviously relevant, but my issue here is not the same as the question of "ethical criticism" as he raises it in *The Company We Keep* or the general issue of what role literature might play in any ethical education. I am interested here more in what position on morality is implied in the novels and tales, and although I am obviously presenting that position sympathetically, I am not here trying to evaluate it as a position.

17. I am indebted to David Bromwich for several suggestions about this theme.

# 2

# "A KIND OF MORBID MODERNITY?"
## (AA, 60)

*Henry James at the Pacific*
*— Coronado Beach, California, March 1905*

In a hotel room by the sea, the Master
Sits brooding on the continent he has crossed.
Not that he foresees immediate disaster,
Only a sort of freshness being lost –
Or should he go on calling it Innocence?
The sad-faced monsters of the plains are gone;
Wall Street controls the wilderness. There's an immense
Novel in all this waiting to be done,
But not, not – sadly enough – by him. His talents,
Such as they may be, want an older theme,
One rather more civilized than this, on balance.
For him now always the consoling dream
Is just the mild dear light of Lamb House falling
Beautifully down the pages of his calling.

                                        Donald Justice

I

In the following, I discuss Henry James's treatment of moral life in its
uniquely modern dimensions. For several reasons, that can be a controversial and easily misunderstood topic. For one thing, to many readers, James
seems manifestly hostile to Puritan or New England moralism, suspicious
of the hypocrisy and smugness that characterize his morally judgmental
characters, and thereby uneasy with the category of morality itself.[1] For
others, his commitment to other values, like "life" and the supreme importance of beauty and taste, might seem to place his deepest interests simply

"beyond good and evil." For still others, the topic itself sounds immediately dreary, unworthy of James and his supreme subtlety – another "lessons for life," edifying, choosing up sides, for the good people, against the bad, anachronistic approach to a work of art, and a modernist, experimental work at that. And, finally, while the novel form itself exhibits, and inevitably offers a treatment of, historically specific social arrangements and mores, that characteristic alone need not mean that a novelist is taking his bearings from ambitious views about the distinct features of the modern world. So I want first to explain what I mean by the general notion invoked ("modern moral life") and why I think it is relevant to James's fiction. In this chapter, this will then also involve some consideration of his understanding of the modern situation itself, and the relevance of those concerns to the morality theme.

First, though, that morality theme can itself be an abstract, endlessly controversial topic. Raising it not only suggests the danger of anachronism and a simplification of James, it also proposes a frame that can be more elaborate and more controversial than the enframed issues in the novels (which would be saying something). Among the issues raised by such a point of view, there is a connected series of themes essential in appreciating both the radicality and the importance of James's treatment. These concern (i) the nature of a distinctively moral evaluation, (ii) the dependence of such evaluations on the possibility of determinate psychological meaning in understanding, explanation, and finally assessment, and (iii) the link between such a possibility (or impossibility) of understanding and specific, historical social forms and conventions criterial in any such understanding. James has all such topics in view, I think, but showing that and explaining what it means will take some time. In this chapter, I shall be especially concerned with the plausibility of (iii). Raising that issue will presuppose the following.

A moral phenomenon is usually characterized by some sort of experience of a tension or conflict between one's own advantage or interest and either the advantage or interests of others or the rights and entitlements of others to consideration (most controversially, to equal consideration). The moral question in general is always some version of the question: Why should I ever suspend in some way the pursuit of my own interests, even my own interests construed very broadly and over a long time, and in their necessary connection with others', for the sake of another's interests or claims of entitlement or for the sake of some purported objective good?

(Since moral claims paradigmatically involve the claims of others, and since that is the issue in James that I want to focus on, I shall concentrate on the nature of the claims of other people on our attention and commitment, and not on the purported claim of some objective good – that a state or relation or quality ought to be brought about. James is quite interested in the latter issue, especially insofar as it involves aesthetic qualities and activities, but in the following I will treat that as a separable concern.) Why, indeed, damage, perhaps permanently, such interests in acknowledgment of such supposed entitlements and claims of others?[2]

Moreover, a moral evaluation is supposed to be an evaluation of an individual. If the distinctive moral failure is, roughly, egoism, making oneself an exception, or in some other way ignoring the claims of others for treatment as like free subjects, then this failure is regarded as my failure, as something I, as an individual, am responsible for having done. The moral point of view is distinguished by its assumption of individual agency and individual responsibility and by an assessment of such responsibility by attention to the intentions or motives of the agent. If the question is whether what I am doing is "protecting my daughter from a fortune hunter," or "refusing, out of fear and selfishness, to acknowledge that she is a separate agent, with her own fate," then settling the question requires settling the question of which among many possible and perhaps actual motives really led to my doing what I did, are the motives that best explain why I did what I did. One can and ought to be held to account for what one did, above all for immoral acts that avoid or ignore these claims of others, but one should be held to account only for what one did or deliberately omitted doing (no inherited or collective guilt), and the question of "what it is" that you did requires that among many other things relevant to the issue of the right description of the action, we know something about what you intended.[3]

This means that the very idea of a moral point of view, tied as it is so deeply to these notions of personal accountability and universal entitlement, and to the question of whether your action did take others into account or not, already presupposes some rather complex understanding of the subjects of such claims and obligations, and the nature of their experience of one another – how, especially, they manage to understand themselves and each other in their evaluations and assessments, how they might correct misunderstanding, might come to appreciate some shared meaning in their interactions. As noted, to understand the simplest elements of any moral evaluation – any sense that my actions have affected others and that they thereby have some claim on me to a consideration of some sort – I have to know something about what another intended, what motivated him even in order simply to describe what it is that he is doing, in what way it can be said that my actions involve, affect others, or not, and if so, which others, in what sense. Likewise, to assess what I may rightfully claim from another, I also must settle on some view of what I am doing, what may be rightfully attributed to my agency and so forth. (It could even be said that one important aspect of a distinctly modern morality itself is some sort of entitlement "*to be properly understood*," some claim on others to an appropriate attempt at understanding. The problem of meaning is the problem of moral acknowledgment too, and a skepticism about meaning can be a deep skepticism about such morality. James suggests this sometimes by identifying a "moral sense" with "great intelligence."[4])

Very often, both the interpretive and evaluative aspects of such efforts are based on very general assumptions, widely and very deeply shared in various historical communities, assumptions about human motivation, religion, the nature of social and political conflict, various types and presumed hierarchies among human beings, and so forth. These assumptions amount to a shared form of life or some achieved like-mindedness (for James, a "tradition"). Actions and motives must be instances of types, kinds, generalities if they are to be understood, and there being such types is some sort of function of participants who acknowledge, are committed to, there being such types (commitments that can change).

Of course, this is all already challengeable philosophically. This formulation has, with its claim of an "*achieved* like-mindedness" and its suggestions about mutability, already – and, it might be charged, in a question-begging way – introduced the historicist and more radical dimensions in a theory of understanding that we discussed earlier, dimensions that we ought to be interested in exploring and arguing for, not just assuming. But I think the details of the interpretations to follow will show that these are the elements of James's "theory of understanding" and that these details themselves make his view very plausible and, up to a point, philosophically compelling.

Moral claims are real in James, in other words, and he is interested in exploring the nature of this claim and its content and the possibility of understanding that it presumes. But we should also note his interest in the place of such claims in a whole life. Since Kant, anyone addressing the topic of morality is presumed to have in mind some claim for morality or duty's decisively trumping any other normative claim on our attention and commitment, from happiness to loyalty or love. But, we shall see, such claims do not have this sort of absolute trumping power in James; nor do they generally, I think, contrary to Kant.[5] Further, morality is itself a limited category, not the supreme, normative category, and there are many others. Justice, for example, is a virtue of institutions; virtues are excellences of human character, and raise questions about the conditions for the formation of character in families and societies, and so forth. Moral issues arise distinctly in respect to actions by people, which can affect, especially impede, the actions of others.[6] And so such moral considerations, of the obligatory and the forbidden, are most deeply (and uniquely) relevant where reliance on others and some sort of possible trust is most expected and appropriate – as in James's frequent treatments of modern romance and marriage. However important, though, such issues involve only a slice of the human attempt to live well, or worthily or properly or righteously, and it should not be exaggerated, or applied abstractly where inappropriate to issues of what, all things considered, one ought to do, or as if moral righteousness simply constitutes what makes life worth living.[7] There is no particular reason to think that either in James or in itself such desiderata cohere neatly in some organic or hierarchical whole.

The great, paradigmatic moral phenomenon, then, is the promise and the subsequent keeping of trust; the moral question always: Why keep such trust apart from my own interest or fear of consequences?[8] And while the always relevant interpretive question of what was really promised, and in what sense, is often an invitation to sophistry and excuse-mongering, in many crucial, life-altering situations (like promises involved in marriage), things are not at all that clear. Such a promise in one society, at one time, within a certain community, is one thing; in another, at another time, among other communities, another thing. And here James's views on the historical problem of meaning – its profound historicity, let us say, and on the nature of human sociality essential to the possibility of such meaning – are extreme, brilliant, and underappreciated.

Most notably, in the historical communities that he describes (especially in novels like *The Spoils of Poynton, The Awkward Age,* and *What Maisie Knew,* and most complexly in the great final novels), this (European, Christian, class-oriented, very stable, fixed social-role) like-mindedness – at least for the most self-conscious, reflexive characters, or for those who have somehow implicitly absorbed such a reflexive realization – has very largely collapsed. It has become a kind of pretense, or theatrical shell, not a "form of life." Hence, given the link between the topics we have been discussing, here is where James's appreciation of the distinctiveness and distinct dangers of modernity for morality arises. There are now very few, if any, such shared, stable assumptions left in such societies for such characters, at least very few that can be reliably assumed by the participants. (And again there is the controversial philosophical assumption: that there must be such stable, historically achieved forms of sociality, such shared presuppositions, as a condition of successful understanding, or shared meaning.) There are of course vestiges of older forms of sociality, but they are now deeply unreliable and are often as ossified, as ghost-like as James's famous ghosts themselves. (In fact, James's major preoccupation in his account of the modern world is just this figure of loss, loss of those forms of social hierarchy, predictability, and expectation that made interpretation, meaning, and some psychological stability and determinacy possible.)

He has a fairly hard-headed sense of the causes of such a failure of social form – he refers most often to the new ways in which money, and therefore power, is made and amassed, and the ways in which the conditions for, and the implications of, such a new way of making money are interwoven into the most intimate details and emotions of individual lives. But he also resists a facile psychological modernism himself, as if we could now see the true, permanent, unavoidable role of self-interest, ego, power, and lust in all human deeds, or the final impossibility of any morality, or the triumph of market societies and their now total manipulation of desire. The "age" is much more "awkward" than such a jejune cynicism can account for, and the imputation of these sorts of baser motives just as problematic and unreliable as other sorts of imputations. And James, as we shall see, mostly takes this moment as it comes, does not treat it as revelatory or decadent; he seems always to insist on seeing his characters within their historically distinctive social positions, roles, relation to particular ways of making money, authority, power, and never, say, either as abstract persons or agents or as "natural" subjects. The persistence of the experience of the claims of morality in such a world, somehow, in some real way (claims beyond cooperative satisfaction of interest) is what makes his novels so interesting philosophically and historically.

That is, while there is everywhere in James a great threat arising from such confusion, mobility, and unpredictability, a threat of complete indeterminacy, or even absolute unresolveability about meaning (a feature of his work that drives many readers to complete frustration), nevertheless, attempts at some resolution of the problems of meaning and evaluation must, and largely still do, go on. Their so going on is the heart of the moral matter as he sees it.

It is in such a context, presented by James as a unique historical situation, one wherein the problems of interpretation and the understanding of meaning are also unique, that the moral theme is addressed and moral skepticism somehow avoided.[9] How it is avoided is not easy to make out, but James's interest in such avoidance is hard to miss. In the first place, it is relatively uncontroversial that James is quite interested in what can be very broadly called ethical or normative matters: how one is to live well, better than one had; what makes for a happy or fulfilling life, what costs might be involved in trying to live well, what conflicts, perhaps tragic and irreconcilable ones, necessarily arise among ends and goals in any such aspiration to a higher or better life. The novels are full of characters who begin their lives as quiet passengers on some busy train of life, and "wake up" for one reason or another, insist on a turn at driving, and must then decide where to go (where it is worth going) and how to get there. The values or ends or goals most often at issue in these adventures and pursuits are distinctly modern ones, and can be summarized (a bit too simply, but not too misleadingly) as "a free life" (and this is always shown to involve necessarily an "aware" or properly "felt" life) and that consummation devoutly wished in the classical novel, enduring human love (a desideratum not always in harmony with the first). But for all the indeterminacy problems just mentioned, almost always in such cases our heroes and heroines also experience a great, intensely felt, indisputably real limitation on such an exploration, something like the claims of others to be and to be treated as free, equally independent end-setting, end-seeking subjects. It is not long before these awakened characters collide with someone (or are run into by some reckless or downright evil driver) and must assess what to make of such collisions.

Violating or ignoring such claims might or might not make one's life better or happier (it usually will), but, apart from that, the characters come to experience some unmistakable "call of conscience" in such cases. The right category – of indisputable reality in James despite the immense difficulties of applying it or thinking it through – just seems to be that ignoring such claims would be wrong. I take this (this claim by others to a kind of acknowledgment) to be a distinctly and somewhat narrowly moral consideration, distinct, that is, from the broadly ethical, "how is one to live well" themes so prominent in, say, Lambert Strether or Isabel Archer. It is not – recognizing or accepting such a claim to acknowledgment – some further component or element of what for us just would be a flourishing or happy life. Such a claim, understood as a moral claim, is not conditional in this way on such an end, and especially not on our desire for it. The nature of the claim is not based on that kind of a reason. Since the basis of this moral experience, first described as such by Kant, is this entitlement to treatment as a free subject (or, in a way, concerns what one also owes to oneself as a free subject, what integrity might mean), this will of course also mean an exploration of how James seems to understand the nature of such freedom, in all its relevant senses: independence, absence of constraint (or, in the Jamesean world, having money), autonomy, authenticity, self-determination, and even in a few works, political freedom.

The moral dimension is perhaps most obvious in what appears to be James's confident insistence on the reality of moral evil,[10] motivated often by egoism, enacted often in deceit (the lie, and especially the unsustainability, the unbearability of the lie, being the moral pivot around which so many novels turn) and by his treatment of the problem of self-sacrifice, especially the sacrifice of one's own happiness or good in recognition of some sort of requirement not relevant to one's happiness or good – which sort of requirement and why required being the problem in much of the following discussion.[11]

In fact, two of James's greatest novels seem elaborately designed in parallel to insist on the problem of sacrifice and thereby to raise the problem of the nature of moral reasons in such a modern world. It is almost as if James designed them both as a complementary pair, although I know of no evidence for this. In the conclusion of *The Portrait of a Lady*, a young American woman declines the overwhelmingly justified option of divorcing her deceitful, manipulative husband, declines the chance to return to America and renew a life "for herself" with a young American in a new marriage, and opts to go back to an utterly failed, hopeless marriage with her smug, Europeanized, American expatriate husband. Readers have been pondering the meaning of such an action, and the justification Isabel thinks compellingly requires it (her duty to her stepdaughter and especially, oddly, "to herself") for generations. In *The Ambassadors,* an older American male forgoes the chance to stay in Europe and begin a life with a supremely intelligent, exquisitely sensitive Europeanized American woman who loves him, and opts instead to return to America where he now has few prospects, and indeed is returning to the wreckage of a failed prospect for marriage with an American dowager who appears to be just as insufferably pompous as Isabel's option. Both do not act for their own good, or happiness, or, it would certainly appear, for a fuller and richer life, and we wonder why. (By apparently "designed," I mean that this elaborately parallel woman-man, younger-older, remaining married-no marriage, staying in Europe, going back to America structure seems designed to raise in a deliberately structured, parallel way the problem of such moral claims and the nature of sacrifice.)

This is especially important to raise in this way, I argue, because for so many readers, such issues of sacrifice seem only to raise psychological or ideological issues, even pathological questions about self-deceit, delusion, fantasy, and self-hatred. James is of course also raising such questions, but even these only properly arise in the context of some morally real and unavoidable claim on such subjects. Without the assumption of such reality and unavoidability, I will show in Chapters 5 and 6, the conflicts and dilemmas faced by characters could not be properly understood, or would be misunderstood if all such normative language were viewed as only the reflection of psychological conflict, defensiveness, and projection.

II

The one book in which the historical theme is richly treated, *The American Scene,* would require a separate study, and I shall return to some of its themes in a moment. But a general acknowledgment of James's historical consciousness is also a fixture in some sense of the standard or received picture of James, and we can begin there and with a novel, the very title of which suggests its relevance.

It is obvious enough that James's characterizations, plots, and dilemmas are everywhere suffused with some sort of claim about the specific historical situation faced by these characters. It is somewhat clumsy to do so, but, as suggested in the first chapter, we can call it the situation of "Western modernization" for want of a better term. The famous International Theme, the "Americans" (New Englanders, mostly, not so much his favored New Yorkers) and the "Europeans" (not so much the British, mostly the French, to some extent the Italians), is clearly not only treated typologically and, one might say, anthropologically, but historically. "Great changes" are coming, warns the elder Mr. Touchett, as they all await "the idea of an interesting woman," the American, Isabel Archer, and "not all for the better" (*PL*, 22), a view of things the "progressive" Lord Warburton quite naively thinks he understands and is prepared for. In *The American Scene*, the question is just as explicit, as James surveys modernizing America: "what turn, on the larger, the general stage, was the game going to take? . . . the great adventure of a society reaching out into the apparent void for the amenities, the consummations, after having earnestly gathered in so many of the preparations and necessities?" (*AS*, 13). And this contrast, between the new and the old, not just between one style and another, is not treated cyclically, as if just another turn of the wheel. Everything of significance in the basic manners of civilized life known heretofore, in the role of history, hierarchy, sensibilities, gender relations, social power, is about to change. The Americans are about to take charge of the planet, and there have never been people like Americans. What will they do with it? is the question that animates many of the more reflective Europeans, or Europeanized Americans.

Such a general claim is easy enough to establish. That these views about modernity (largely implicit except, again, for books like *The American Scene*, where Jamesean modernity is on full view: "Modernity . . . with its pockets full of money and its conscience full of virtue, its heart really full of tenderness" *AS*, 117) are worth taking much more seriously than previously conceded, that they ought to shape a whole interpretation, is another matter. For one thing, such a sensibility, while clearly present, does not seem all that pressing, determining, or even all that visible, not when compared, say, with Hawthorne. For another, there have been complex psychological novels before and after James, full of self-deceit, confusion, shaky interpretations, and uncertainty, and none of that seems to have had much to do with any historical sensibility or any great vortex in world history. Laclos seems not have had any large views about the ever dwindling cultural resources of a mass society, and James himself understood better than anyone how all modern novels of manners and analysis could be said to reveal the play of appearances in modern societies, could penetrate beneath such appearances analytically and often only come up with yet more appearances. And at least since Shakespeare's *Hamlet*, modern tragedies of uncertainty, indeterminacy, and self-doubt, all in contrast with classical depictions of very determinate moral dilemmas, could be cited to undercut any such claim, on James's behalf or independently, for such an epochal self-consciousness.[12]

Finally, in American studies and American literary criticism, James is often grouped together with other American intellectuals who, while all horrified at the regimentation, limited opportunities for expression, and cold aggression obvious in the American market society unfolding so nakedly, without benefit of the moderating and qualifying influences, the denseness, richness, and tradition of European societies, were all also supposedly "ahistorical" in their hopes for redemption, individualist at the core, placing their hopes in a special kind of private "experience," "consciousness" (of a quasi-religious or aesthetic sort) or in a trans-historical unity and truth – the likes of Emerson, Thoreau, Whitman, and even finally Dewey (as in Quentin Anderson's provocative argument).[13]

But this, this resistance to reading James as having such a significant historical consciousness, is all also because the major categories of the International Theme are often treated very much as they appear on the surface of James's narrative, and on the surface they can seem very conventional, very much representative of what James himself calls "the good conservative tradition," the one "that walks apart from the extravagant use of money and the unregulated appeal to 'style,'" and which takes as it principle something like,

> . . . it takes an endless amount of history to make even a little tradition, and an endless amount of tradition to make even a little taste, and an endless amount of taste, by the same token, to make even a little tranquility. Tranquility results largely from taste tactfully applied, taste lighted above all by experience and possessed of a clue for its labyrinth (*AS,* 127).

But no thoughtful reader of James can rest content with any view of him as just straightforwardly representative of "the good conservative tradition," the high-minded critic of "the age of trash triumphant."[14] It is everywhere clear that James believes that many aspects of traditional and, in essence, largely pre-modern European customs, manners, and mores were, by the late nineteenth century, finally in some sort of end-game situation, and that they deserved to be.[15] Upper-class and upper middle-class European life – arranged marriages, rigidly defined, predictable social

classes, accepted notions of honor and social esteem, conventional constraints on conduct and speech, some intuitive sense of, feel for, the higher
and the lower – had all largely become more social theater than social
reality, as James depicts it.[16] Where such forms are observed, or whenever a
character speaks forcefully for them, James is also careful, even if clearly
helping the reader to tilt in such nostalgic directions, to conjure up a whiff
of decay and death, perhaps even cruelty and obsession, certainly self-
serving egoism, ritualistic formalism and rigidity, as with, say, the Bellegardes or the Europeanized Gilbert Osmond, that greatest of Jamesean
villains. (As with Osmond, James is well aware what happens when a
tradition becomes, instead of a matter of habit and trust, or a form of life,
rather an idea, a hope, and ultimately an object of desperate will. It is then
invoked or believed in rather than lived; rather than a form of life, it
becomes a mere artificial form and so dead. And when James really wants
us to appreciate the morbidity of traditions when invoked as ideals, he
makes us watch what such ideals do to children when subjected to them,
whenever they are not allowed to grow and live, but forced to ape and to
repeat.)

James suggests a number of reasons for such exhaustion, the chief of
which is again quite unsentimental: money. Europe and the European
system cannot, simply, historically, finance itself any longer, nor can the
sorts of compromises now necessary with the modern manufacturing
classes make socially possible the preservation of this way of life. Certainly
the participants cannot resist the temptation to make great use of the
mountains of money now being created in perhaps the greatest period of
American capital expansion (that period "of the new remorseless monopo-
lies that operate as no madness of ancient personal power thrilling us on
the historic page ever operated" *AS*, 104).[17] Said more simply, in anticipation of the next section, James is not the ahistorical, apolitical novelist of
sensibility he is sometimes made out to be. His setting is as broadly
ambitious as it can be. It concerns the fate of a secular, capitalist, broadly
materialist, wholly new form of civilized life, and the link between such a
new form and our struggle to understand and evaluate each other.

On the other side of this presumed Jamesean historical situation, neither can one rest content with the standard picture of the American
modernity that comes with this new American money: charm, freshness,
energy, and, in a way, innocence; and with all that, inevitably and in an
inevitably contaminating way, American vulgarity, commercialism, and

historical amnesia, naivete, simplistic moralism, Puritanism, and self-righteousness. It is enough just to note that none of these categories even begins to be relevant to any fair assessment of what we are left with in the greatest Americans, almost "heroically" beyond any European, characters like Isabel Archer, Lambert Strether, or Maggie Verver.

So the familiar account of the historical frame for the Jamesean picture would have cynical, amoral, predatory Europeans on the one hand and either romantic fools or ingenues or self-righteous, pompous prigs on the other American hand ("creatures of prey" and "children of light" again). If this were the right way to understand such a frame, there would be little room within the picture for any very sophisticated portrait of modern moral existence, and we should indeed be led instead to the brilliance of James's aesthetic experiments or the sophistication of his supposedly traditional psychological analyses as the marks of his true value.

However, it is the very presence in James's work of a skeptical and pessimistic attitude toward these very categories that helps separate James from the *fin du siècle* mood surrounding him. Although James, like many other late-nineteenth-century writers, understands his historical context as undeniably empty of the large moral frameworks and categories and typologies within which intelligible human engagement and understanding were formerly possible, it is still the case that the way his novels and stories work, come to engage and grip us, would not be explicable were he not to have succeeded in establishing something like the necessity, the practical unavoidability, of the moral categories his narratives call forth.[18] While much of this moral dimension involves the importance of the possibility of one's actions being justifiable to those whom such actions affect (James's frequent word is being "squared"), the criteria of such acceptance or mutual recognition have nothing to do with natural law, the wisdom of tradition, the approval of the community, religious scripture or religious feeling, pure practical reason, the resolution of class conflict, or some benchmark like a *phronimos,* an experienced man of practical wisdom. In effect, all the major characters are walking a high wire with lots of normative turbulence but without any safety net, dependent wholly on each other and their own talk and negotiations and perceptions for balance. There is plenty of "high modernism" here, in other words, replete with absent gods, and so many other absent minor divinities like mankind, progress, and happiness or prosperity.[19] Yet there is also no metaphysical boredom, no nihilism, no high-culture nostalgia (with America simplistically demonized as *kulturlos* modernity), none of the "secularized" Christianity of Dickens or George Eliot, not even Conradean stoicism, no *symboliste* new religions. The young – Milly Theale, Ralph Touchett – die innocently, unjustly, but no one raises any fists to God. Great moral crises are never resolved, yet no hint of despair or even skepticism sounds in any final tone, however autumnal, even elegiac, in the later works of genius, those tones can sound. There is some great sense of stopped time, a historical *nunc stans,* that some, most radically Kojève, think of as the definitive mood in modernity: the absence of the frontier, of adventure, wars that mean anything, quests, Holy Grails, revolutionary aspirations, and so forth. With James we have begun to settle down in the only wilderness left, "inside," but without a sense of teleological, progressive, developmental stages of success or any road map or goal; we have only the endless chatter and irresolution and revisions and re-revision of the later modern urban world. Even so, perhaps just because so, some sort of real tranquility is intimated, some moral tone in the late novels especially, in some way more than resignation, pessimism, or skepticism, is struck.

Understanding how James accomplishes this tone, what such a moral mutuality amounts to, all depends on understanding the historical and social analysis presupposed in the encounters he presents. Like everything else in James, though, that can be a tricky interpretive question as well, since there is no such thing as non-literary prose, straightforward descriptive journalism, or a truly philosophical statement in James. (Even the New York Edition Prefaces are themselves caught up in great Jamesean literary themes: the presumed authority to revise, the denial that there are original texts, his living his life, even as an author, "too late," or even over again, and so on.)

While such considerations are almost omnipresent in James, they are not all limited to the International Theme, and an example may help make the point. In novels like *The Awkward Age,* for example, the rather odd question of the "right way" a young girl should come to understand for the first time what it is to be a young woman, how she manages her awkward age between one stage and another, is also loaded with the weight of the historical questions we have been considering.[20] The question of such a transition becomes a figure for our own awkward historical age, a transition time between an age of secrets, avoidance, repression, and rigid social control toward a time of dangerous knowledge and a freedom as likely to produce selfishness and fatuity as self-reliance and integrity.

The novel takes its bearings from a salon, a group of rather self-satisfied socialites who think of themselves as very advanced, "votaries of the temple of analysis" (*AA*, 205), a would-be Bloomsbury group *avant la lettre,* witty, cynical, not like a circle around a king because without royalty or established hierarchy or any connection to a public world or court responsibilities. They have a leader, though, Mrs. Brookenham, and she inhabits a world that James insists on describing constantly as, most of all, "modern," the new London.

It is a world, for example, where beauty still counts for something, but now a new, modern "beauty":

> But beauty in London – staring, glaring, obvious, knock-down beauty, as plain as a poster on a wall, an advertisement of soap or whiskey, something that speaks to the crowd or crosses the foot-lights, fetches such a price in the market that the absence of it, for a woman with a girl to marry, inspires endless terrors and constitutes for the wretched pair a sort of social bankruptcy. London doesn't love the latent or the lurking, has neither time, nor taste, nor sense for anything less discernable than the red flag in front of the steam-roller. It wants cash over the counter and letters ten feet high (*AA*, 31–2).

It is a world where the generous but confused Mitchy (he who is "rotten with goodness"), son of a prosperous bootmaker, can have a place, a place earned only by his enormous wealth, and one that allows his colleagues to remind themselves occasionally of who he is.

> "To stay with a person" – Nanda took it up as, apparently, out of delicacy, he fairly failed – "whose father used to take the measure, down on his knees on a little mat, as mamma says, of my grand-father's remarkably large foot? Yes, we none of us mind. Do you think we should?" Nanda asked (*AA*, 139).

"The modern," says Mrs. Brook, "has always been my very own note – I've gone in, frankly for my very own Time – who is one after all, that one should pretend to decline to go where it may lead?" (*AA*, 106).

In such a world, the moral question is portrayed as allowing few options. There is the self-serving, fatuous, hypocritical world of the Harolds, Pethertons, and Trishys, who all represent some sort of apotheosis of the vanity and studied inauthenticity of Rameau's nephew. There is, as a kind of defensive reaction, the even greater hypocrisy represented by the duchess, who pretends that the old, now wholly empty social forms can be retained by willfulness alone, that meaning can be secured and duty thereby recognized as if they were some theater piece (of the absurd), all so long as no one asks to look behind the curtains. And there is the genuine, not hypocritical, morality of nostalgia, of truly better times long ago, that vestige of pre-modern stability and privilege and taste, the world that managed to survive so long into the new world of money, power, vulgarity, and instability. (There is a kind of Rip Van Winkle character in the novel, Mr. Longdon, who emerges from a very long absence from society, full of a genteel horror at what he now finds, carrying a huge torch for an old love, Lady Julia, herself an emblem of what nostalgic moralism always extols, the dead, and so safely extolled, permanently in the past. James is well aware of the various figures such a nostalgic hope can take. Lady Julia is even called a "Greek" (*AA*, 132); Burke himself is quoted (*AA*, 187).)

The interesting characters occupy a position much like that of many other characters in many other novels – in between, unable to "go back" with Mr. Longdon, go forward into a complete surrender to venality like Harold and Petherton, close their eyes and sing on like the duchess, or lurch every which way like Mrs. Brook. Nanda, Mrs. Brook's daughter, and Van, Mrs. Brook's Platonic lover, form the center of the drama, and, as so often, the moral question is concentrated on the concrete issue: "What *makes* a marriage," what can one be said really to owe another in such a pledge of intimacy (an issue treated in no way simply as a question of what one wants to give and another is willing to receive), and especially what could such a question mean in such a world. Again, typically, the problem here is the way in which the naked presence and power of money can so complicate such a question, the understanding of what, exactly, is being offered, and the understanding of motives for those who wish to act well. Mr. Longdon, observing how important money is to all these people, tries to help by pledging to settle a large fortune on Nanda if Van will marry her. This does nothing but complicate everything for Van and makes it impossible for him to sort out what he feels, what he owes (given such gratuitous generosity). Nanda is terribly in love with Van, but is also caught up in her own dilemma. She is a "modern girl," has heard the adult (or "modern") conversations, understands the depths this new world can sink to, and knows enough to know that Van is perilously close to the world of Harold,

Petherton, and Trishy, that he can't be said to stand for very much. (This danger is very much the hidden worry in the European worries about girls being "spoiled" by being allowed into the sitting room "too soon." The assumption is that that erotic attraction on both sides depends on the virginal ignorance of the girl, that it could not be stimulated and sustained if the "real truth" about men and older women were known. That is not true of Nanda, but as we shall see, she wishes it were true and tries to pretend that it was, tries to "act out" the pre-modern fable.) In the novel's deepest irony, her own sense of his being able to transcend "all that" involves her conviction that he would be a suitable suitor if he would "mind" that she knows that about him; he would be the most desirable if he *wouldn't* want her!

> "Do you positively like to love in vain?"
> It was a question, the way she turned back to him seemed to say, that deserved a responsible answer. "Yes." (*AA*, 210).

Unrequited love turns out to be the chief image for the moral conclusion that such complexities produce – a figure for the conclusion that any pledge of intimacy, promise of fidelity, or declaration of commitment requires a kind of understanding, some clarity of vision and determinacy of meaning impossible (or at least extremely difficult) in such a world, and yet that the aspiration for such a meaning and so such a promise cannot be abandoned (the love does not die, it just remains permanently unrequited, permanently unsure of the conditions of its realization), even if the self-doubt it produces in characters like Nanda or the nostalgic idealization it produces in Longdon can look faintly comic. The ways in which the failure of love is linked to the moral meaning problem, and the way in which James's sense of the modernity issue sets the context for both, will return several times in what follows. By the end, Nanda has some sense of what has happened.

> But she continued, with the shadow of her scruple, to explain. "We're many of us, we're most of us – as you long ago saw and showed you felt – extraordinary now. We can't help it. It isn't really our fault. There's so much else that's extraordinary that if we are in it all so much *we* must naturally be." It was all obviously clearer to her than it had ever been, and her sense of it found renewed expression;

so that she might have been, as she wound up, a very much older person than her friend. "Everything's different from what it used to be" (*AA*, 310).[21]

Superficially, *The American Scene* reads like a standard travelogue, in this case written by a grouchy expatriate returning home after twenty years for a ten-month, cross-country visit, reliving old, sweet memories, but grumbling constantly about what he appears to consider the "mongrel" society being created in front of him: a greedy, consumerist, ever changing, tradition-less society, with crude displays of wealth, skyscrapers all out of human scale, a place where manners or mores are hard even to find, much less to analyze. The "restless analyst" is obviously irritated, angry, but, most of all, completely bewildered.

Examples of the critical side of his attitude, and so further evidence for reading the International Theme in the traditional way, seem everywhere. The evidence seems persuasive that James is accepting the familiar Tocquevillean image – America as the great laboratory for the fate of all modernity (that America represents Europe's future, not its infancy) – and that he is accepting Tocqueville's assumptions – whether all that was noble and sweet in the *ancien régime* will be able to survive all that is base and commercial in the New World.[22]

All that the narrator can now find at Sunnyside, Washington Irving's beautiful country estate, is but "the last faint echo of a felicity forever gone" (*AS*, 118)[23]; and elsewhere a whole country organized with a grim efficiency and mirthless economy, as if all were some well-run hotel (*AS*, 80–81); beautiful old Trinity Church still there but ludicrously and "quite horribly" now dwarfed by these "vast money making" structures, "looming through the weather with an insolent cliff-like sublimity" (*AS*, 65); the very "sign" of New York's distinct energy is that "it doesn't believe in itself; it fails to succeed, even at a cost of millions, in persuading you that it does (*AS*, 84); it is a land of great freedom, but "the freedom to grow up to be blighted . . . the only freedom in store for the smaller fry of future generations" (*AS*, 104); a country more given over to an "extreme consideration" of "the dental question" than any other (*AS*, 135), understandable perhaps, given the American obsession with confections. All of which prompts the question: "The wage-earners, the toilers of old, notably in other climes, were known by the wealth of their songs; and has it, on these lines, been given to the American people to be known by the number of their 'candies'?" (*AS,* 147).

However, none of these grumblings (many of which echo James' father's great horror of American commerce and consumerism) are simply presented as such, as observations with a straightforward claim to truth or verisimilitude. They are all represented in a doubly qualified and typically Jamesean way. First, they are all presented in a voice, in character, as if they were the reactions of a distinct and still forming figure, unsure of who he is or what he feels, not so much the historical James as some "Ex-Patriate Stranger," as lively and vivid a presence as any of the scenes or reactions themselves. Various names are given to this presence, and the names recur so frequently that they come to be more prominent in our awareness than any standard first-person singular narrator: The "restless analyst" is the most frequent name, but also the "homeless wanderer," the "fond observer," the "incurable eccentric," a "pilgrim," a "filial mind," a "perverted person," the "restored absentee," the "brooding analyst," and "the repentant absentee."[24] Second, all such recorded reactions are treated as themselves objects of interrogation, rather than reports (hence the importance of the constant third-person references). Such reactions are recorded as occasions for often critical self-interrogation and not as straight statements of "criticism." Most often the question they raise is: What is it to feel this way, to be so disturbed? What then would one have from these people at this time in these conditions? Why am I so interested in them, even obsessed by them? Why do I care, or why does "he" care, this alter ego I am and am not? (Both qualifications presuppose the obvious trope for travel writing, that one is learning by such travels about oneself, traveling through an inner country as well; seeing, in one's relationships and reactions to such circumstances, who one really is, especially in James's treatment, as if one could not be that self except in these relations and reactions.) And as the "repentant absentee" first returns, he warns himself directly about the many "inconsistencies" of "headlong critical or fanciful reaction," and promises himself instead, throughout his journey, to try for

> . . . a kind of fluidity of appreciation – a mild, warm wave that broke over the succession of aspects and objects, according to some odd inward rhythm, and often, no doubt, with a violence that there was little in the phenomena themselves flagrantly to justify (*AS,* 6).

And none of these recorded, sometimes "violent," always "fluid," direct impressions is left standing without some further, often quite contrary take on the same phenomena.

So if the railroad in America seems to have everywhere spoiled "the old felicity of proportion" in the views,

> . . . the heavy, dominant American train that so reverses the relation of the parties concerned, suggesting somehow that the country exists for the "cars," which overhang it like a conquering army, and not the cars for the country . . . (*AS*, 24)

it is also the case that the vast extent of the American transportation apparatus, its trains and train-bearing barges, the very fact that so many views have been "conquered," give our analyst for the first time an approach to New York that allows him to see, just because of this new-fangled and omnipresent apparatus, "its boundless, cool assurance" and its "genius so grandly at play" as he approaches it on the East River (*AS*, 58). The old felicity of proportion has been destroyed, but he also can't resist the attractions of the new.

Not being able to resist the attractions of what he sees, even as he is repelled, makes up many of the reactions, even though articulating and understanding these reactions is extremely difficult in this format. For reasons we shall see presented and explored in much of what follows, the solitary travel writer is not a natural Jamesean form; our "analyst" clearly needs an interlocutor, a presence wherein his own first reactions might be reflected, perhaps opposed or interrogated, and even wherein his own understanding of these reactions-reflected might also then be embodied and seen, all in order finally to be formed, to be settled on, in order for that "settled quality" that comes with some sense of "justification" to be arrived at. Since a Jamesean meditation without conversation of some sort is a virtual impossibility, he has always to imagine them here, to imagine himself even conversing with the wind, or with statues in the park, or with whole communities and peoples personified. None of these speculations is adequate, a fact that helps explain the airy, perplexed, wistful, everywhere unsettled ("discontinuous")[25] tone of the book, a tone itself as evocative of James's appreciation of and dissatisfaction with the modern social world and its fate as any other.

So at the beginning of his initially rather hostile reaction to New York, especially to the "hotel culture" of the Waldorf, he is interrupted by the personified "voice of the air." This voice reminds him of how desperately "interested" he is in just what he "criticizes," that he is even a "victim" of his interest. "You can't escape from it" (*AS*, 83), nor can he escape his "special responsibility" as an American, his ability to see both "its genius and its shame." The voice reminds him that he, James, knows full well that New York, especially as the most vibrant and historical representative aspect of the American Scene, is, in one of James's best phrases about America, a "bad, bold beauty,"

> . . . the creature the most blatant of whose pretensions is that she is one of those to whom everything is always forgiven. On what ground 'forgiven'? of course you ask; but note that you ask it while in the very act of forgiving. Oh, yes you are; you've as much as said so yourself. So there it all is; arrange it as you can. Poor dear bad bold beauty; there must indeed be something about her – ! (*AS*, 84).

When it is not the voice of the wind that consoles and reassures him about the restless modernity of America, that occasions such inevitable forgiveness, he either "hears" something in the atmosphere around him, as if the very buildings speak to him, or he divides himself, creates a persona that reassures him, a voice that can see the "benediction of the future," and so grant "permission not to worry any more" (*AS*, 136). As the Analyst walks by Central Park, on a warm summer afternoon, near the empty homes of the wealthy, gone for the season, he is led by these voices around him to a small meditation on history (though, typically, he "blushes" before such a vast topic). He notes that "history is never, in any rich sense, the immediate crudity of 'what happens,' but the much finer complexity of what we read into it and think in connection with it" (*AS*, 136–7).

What this side of our Analyst does "hear" in the possible future is then stated with subtlety and ellipsis, but the remarks are crucial for understanding the larger relation between the International Theme and the moral complexities of the novels. For what strikes our Analyst so much is precisely the stillness, or *emptiness* of the very fine houses on that day.

> It was the vast, costly, empty newness, redeemed by the rare quiet and coloured by the pretty light, and I scarce know, I confess, why it should have anything murmurous or solicitous to say at all, why its eloquence was not over when it had thus defined itself as intensely rich and intensely modern (*AS*, 137).

The answer to that question about what was so murmurous and solic-itous is, he says, "locked up in that word, 'modern.'" For that half-hour, he claims, he was "more intimately than ever before in touch with the sense of that term" (ibid.). This "last revelation of modernity" is precisely this sense of emptiness, of what is missing, but just thereby what suggests constant possibility yet unfilled; possibilities so closed off, ritualized in predictable cycles in traditional, yet more dependable and stable societies. It is Moder-nity itself that now "speaks," as if from out of these empty homes, in this remarkable passage.

> We have everything, don't you see? every capacity and appetite, every advantage of education and every susceptibility of sense; no "tip" in the world, none that our time is capable of giving, has been lost on us; so that all we now desire is what you, Mr. Auctioneer, have to dispose of, the great "going" chance of a time to come (*AS*, 137).

Our Analyst thus has his permission not to worry; there is no such thing as a "fate" for these people. All the qualities that make them rich and reckless and naive and infantile also make them powerful and open, poten-tially liberated from superstition and ritual, eager, curious, willing. Amer-ica's cultural "emptiness" is real throughout *The American Scene,* and disturbing, but it is precisely just that that also makes it an emptiness now "fillable" with possibilities in a way never before possible in the history of the world, makes it, in that word James finds here so fascinating, "mod-ern." " . . . (F)or what were the Venetians, after all" (the Venetians of Veronese and high style) "but the children of a Republic and of trade?" (*AS*, 138).

And, our Analyst finds, it is not just the radicality of the many pos-sibilities apparent in this unformed society that can be reassuring. There is also ample positive evidence of the emergence, perhaps the reemergence out of the chaos of the long American founding, of the human and so humane scale. Our Analyst is greatly comforted by merely walking the "long, cool" corridors of Presbyterian Hospital, even if they are "halls of pain," admiring "the exquisite art with which in such a medium, it had so managed to invest itself with stillness," "where the genius of the terrible city seemed to filter in with its energy sifted and softened, with its huge good-nature refined" (*AS*, 140–1). Although the "immediate expression" of a foreign visitor to New York is of vulgarity and "the expression of violence," if that impression has not "fatally deafened you," you can always also find that "there is something left, something kept back for you." There is thus another image of this modern world, besides the stillness of possibility suggested by those houses (although that historical sense is deliberately evoked again in the second phrase in the following quotation):

> . . . the image of some garden of the finest flowers – or such as might be on the way to become the finest – masked by an enormous bristling hedge of defensive and aggressive vegetation, lacerating, defiant, not to be touched without blood (*AS,* 141).

There is a moment in *The Awkward Age* that strikes such a similar note that it ought to be cited. Mitchy, that immensely rich son of a bootmaker, knows that he is liked by the old swells largely for his fortune. He cannot dress, is maladroit in numerous ways, the very image of the new man, thoroughly modern. On the surface he appears frivolous, too carefree, too indulgent with his society friends, without sufficient integrity or depth. He is so modern and apparently rootless and almost vulgar that he has all the new ideas. He "has his ideas – he thinks nothing matters. He says we've all come to a pass that's the end of everything" (*AA,* 140). But Mitchy, almost alone among the effete circle he runs in, is constantly inhabiting the viewpoint of those he cares about, is not tied to a role-bound identity, is able to see their lives as his, acknowledging in deeds as well as words his dependence on them all in a way that gives him a sort of independence and integrity. He agrees to a marriage he doesn't want as if it is a kind of duty of love (to another woman, Nanda), and clearly occupies a plane of moral self-consciousness and selflessness that only one another, Mr. Longdon, comes close to inhabiting (but, finally, does not). This exchange between the new and the old closes Book IX and makes much the same elliptical and guardedly hopeful point as *The American Scene.*

"Mr. Longdon, on his side turned a trifle pale: he looked rather hard at the floor. 'I see – I see.' Then he raised his eyes. 'But – to an old fellow like me – it's all so strange.'

'It is strange.' Mitchy spoke very kindly. 'But it's all right.'

Mr. Longdon gave a headshake that was both sad and sharp. 'It's all wrong. But you're all right!' he added in a different tone as he walked hastily away" (*AA,* 280).

And, finally, just before a crucial turn in the book, toward the Bowery and the East End of New York, and a journey throughout the East Coast that will never match the "bristling" and exciting quality of New York (except, he intimates, in monstrous Chicago), one final reassuring moment in the Metropolitan Museum. The great American interest in acquisition, in so many respects so showy and greedy and vulgar, is nevertheless also strangely reassuring, some intimation already that there will be no absolute philistinism, that there seems some inevitable attraction of "values mainly for the mind," that "this New York mind will perform its evolution – an evolution traceable, and with sharpness, in advance" (*AS*, 143). The great period of acquisition (a project that our Wanderer does not shrink from describing as rapacious, unjust, exploitative, and violent, as strong a set of terms as he insisted we should have used in depicting General Sherman) will also be the great period of education. The costs of modernity's new "clean slate" will be immense and "ought to have drawn tears from the eyes" (*AS*, 144). (This is especially so, if, as is also feared, most ominously as the book concludes, there are already signs that the these costs and promises finally will not be redeemed, that there is a real chance that the vulgarity and commercialism will not make something possible, that they will be all there is.) And while many readers of James's treatment of say, Adam Verver, think James is silently crying off stage, aghast at such plunder and power, here such plunderers of old Europe also count as "radiant demonstrations" of something reassuring. "The Museum, in short, was going to be great, and in the geniality of the life to come such sacrifices [for the plundered Europeans], though resembling those of the funeral-pile of Sardanapalus, dwindled to nothing" (*AS*,144). And similarly, later, when remarking on the Library of Congress: "Is the case of this remarkable creation, by exception, a case in which the violent waving of the pecuniary wand *has* produced interest? The answer can only be, I feel, a shy assent" (*AS*, 261).[26]

His reaction to Grant's tomb is just as complex. By European standards, its plain, democratic look offends taste.

> And yet one doesn't conclude, strange to say, that the Riverside pavilion fails of its expression a whit more than the Paris dome; one perhaps even feels it triumph by its use of want of reserve as a very last word (*AS*, 110).

And

One must leave the tomb of Grant to its conditions and its future with the simple note for it that if it be not in fact one of the most effective of commemorations it is one of the most missed. On the whole, I distinctly 'liked' it (*AS*, 110).

These are the impressions and ambiguities collected for those important and largely misunderstood chapters in the book, the heart of the narrator's New York adventures, in the Bowery "and thereabouts," with its strange images of Henry James, of all people, bar hopping throughout working-class and ethnic New York, and thoroughly enjoying himself, "reassured" in a different way.[27] He first allows full reign to one of his divided personnae, the prejudiced, fearful, anxious Wasp, even as his own "immigrant" status works then to evoke a great reassuring sense of the vitality and courage and hope such a plurality evinces. By and large, he "likes" them too. The anti-Semitic fears are balanced by a hope for a "New Jerusalem on earth." The possibility of a new form of moral life means that New York can be a "city of redemption" compared with "the dark, foul, stifling ghettoes of other remembered cities" of Europe. He concludes (in a way that already suggests difficulties with the "meaning" of the "modern"),

> The ambiguity is the element in which the whole thing swims for me – so nocturnal, so bacchanal, so hugely hatted and feathered and flounced, yet apparently so innocent, almost so patriarchal again, and matching, in its mixture, with *nothing one had elsewhere known.* It breathed its simple "New York!" New York!' at every impulse of inquiry; so that I can only echo contentedly, with analysis for once *agreeably baffled,* "Remarkable, unspeakable New York!" (*AS*, 155).

This last passage calls to mind James's much earlier essay on Hawthorne (the impression of which on many, including Howells, seems to have had only to do with the "set up" of the passage, not the resounding conclusion); already a very fine hint of what James will try to get at, both with respect to America and to America as figure of the modern.

> The negative side of the spectacle on which Hawthorne looked out, in his contemplative saunterings and reveries, might, indeed, with a little ingenuity, be made almost ludicrous; one might enumerate the items of high civilization, as it exists in other countries, which

are absent from the texture of American life, until it should become a wonder to know what was left. No State, in the European sense of the word, and indeed barely a specific national name. No sovereign, no court, no personal loyalty, no aristocracy, no church, no clergy, no army, no diplomatic service, no country gentlemen, no palaces, no castles, nor manors, nor old country-houses, nor parsonages, nor thatched cottages nor ivied ruins; no cathedrals, nor abbeys, nor little Norman churches; no great universities nor public schools – no Oxford, nor Eton, nor Harrow; no literature, no novels, no museums, no pictures, no political society, no sporting class – no Epsom nor Ascot! Some such list as that might be drawn up of the absent things in American life – the effect of which, upon an English or a French imagination, would probably as a general thing be appalling. The natural remark, in the almost lurid light of such an indictment, would be that if these things are left out, everything is left out. *The American knows that a good deal remains; what it is that remains, – that is his secret, his joke, as one may say* (my emphasis, H, 351–2).[28]

NOTES

1. James himself is largely responsible for such suspicion, critical of "conscious moral purposes" in the writing of fiction, impatient at George Eliot's moral seriousness, insistent on his role in, virtually, inventing the "fine art" novel, with its central attention to form and "architecture," and so forth. Indeed, in "The Author of Beltraffio" he goes to some length to emphasize the rather deadly dimensions of, especially, religious moralism (of the author's wife and sister; see *AB*, 73, 85, 91). (Although, as always, this is complicated by point of view problems. It looks like the wife was willing to let their son die rather than risk exposing him anymore to the husband's "modern," secular, aesthetic humanism, but we have mostly only the sister's word for this version and it appears to be one that for various reasons, our visiting American wants to believe. The true immorality in the sister's medievalism might be more complex and more fantastic than first appears. At any rate, there is not much to be said "within" the story for the moralism of the author's relatives; that much at least is clear.) But none of this entails any sterile aestheticism, none of it is inconsistent with his insistence on the power of truth in the novel, the moral significance of avoiding the false note and understanding another appropriately. More straightforward examples of characters whose excessive search for evil constitutes the evil they do would include Winterbourne in *Daisy Miller* and the governess in *Turn of the Screw*. See Weisbuch (1998) on this "Ethan Brand" theme, p. 105.
2. The general notions of "claims" of others, experienced as unavoidable in my being able to lead my own life, and of what I owe or cannot but acknowledge owing others in such a common life, are admittedly and deliberately vague. Philosophically, one is tempted to transform such notions into clearer and more traditional notions of obligation, and to raise the question of the status of the principle from which obliga-

tions are putatively derived. But the vagueness and imprecision of James's treatment and this characterization of it do not stem from pre-philosophical unclarity; they have themselves a philosophical point: that moral life is itself a matter of mores, of a common historical fate that we share and cannot but acknowledge, that moral claims are not "deduced" from principles "yielding" obligations that can only be trumped by other obligations, that such moral claims are embedded in ethical life as a whole, where they play a role along with other considerations and derive their normative force from that life; do not "govern" that life. These considerations are certainly complex enough to merit a book-length treatment on their own, like the compelling one by Williams (1985). As will be apparent, I think one can and ought to concede many of the objections Williams makes to modern views of morality as an institution, without accepting the neo-Humean claims he makes about desire and individuality. Cf. the remarks in the "Epilogue" to Eldridge (1989).

3. Such formulations already indicate how controversial any statement of the moral point of view must be. It is already apparent that some view is being taken about the possibility of somehow distinguishing an isolatable subject as the subject of such an evaluation, a subject who must somehow be individually responsible for what happens, in some sense of responsibility, in order to be so assessed; capable of not just such causal or even metaphysical independence, but of such relative self-transparency. James himself, as we shall see, has his doubts about both such assumptions. What one takes oneself to be doing is always in some sense some reflection of what others would take or have taken this sort of action to be, and which formulation I am inclined to act upon, or which gets to be my motive, cannot be simply viewed as a result of my choice, given how much of the "me" doing the deciding is also already some internalization of "who I have been taken to be," or what I have been given by others as a self-understanding. But these doubts, however real and complex, do not extend so far, I shall want to show, as to threaten the experience of all such independence, or the practical, experienced unavoidability of assuming the role of such an individual and attempting such transparency.

4. While a necessary condition for any such moral acknowledgment, however, such an intelligence is clearly not sufficient, or there must be some broader question at stake about the depth and extent of the intelligence required. Mrs. Brook, for example, in *The Awkward Age,* is in some respects as intelligent as they get in James, able to sense at a glance all the various possible implications of an action or the avoidance of an action. But she is also in some sense a moral monster, coldly indifferent to her own children, supremely selfish. One might say that there is something she simply doesn't or can't "see," but that is not in itself clearly a matter of intelligence. We encounter in her something discussed in the next chapter here, her resistance to the kinds of dependencies and contingencies and uncertainties that this new society has made necessary, her insistence that some compromise with the old forms, the old language that she mastered so well, is possible. (Dr. Sloper, in *Washington Square,* could serve as another example, though there the description of his intelligence and its insufficiency makes another point; this time a Hawthornean point about the pretensions of scientific objectivity and empirical observation. Nevertheless, factually, Sloper is always dead-on right, and right because of his insight, however irrelevant to the moral situation that kind of "rightness" turns out to be.

5. There are other reasons, too, why Kant, the supreme theorist of the moral point of view, can be a misleading model here. For one thing, James is not interested in the kind

49

of problems of moral agency that Kant thought required for this point of view, or the conception of agent causality so important to Kant. Being an agent for James much more involves the state of my self-understanding and insight, not a matter of causal power. (I am "freer" to the extent that I understand more and better; there is no insistence on could-have-done-otherwise causal autonomy.) The phenomenon of morality and moral duty is much more a matter of only one of Kant's formulations: respect for others as ends-in-themselves, or morality is a matter of the acknowledgment of a kind of social dependence, or a matter of not denying in one's action such dependence. It was, of course, Hegel who pioneered the notion of such dependence or social acknowledgment as the basic category under which to understand the problem of morality, but that is another story. See Chapters Four and Seventeen in Pippin (1997a), and Pippin (forthcoming).

6. It is always possible, but uselessly abstract, to see all of one's actions as potentially affecting everyone, and so to interpret all actions within a moral framework. Kant does something like this, and it is one version of "moralism."

7. James himself does not treat the possibility of such moral claims as unconditional or absolute, and so as treatable in isolation or autonomously. The moral institution lives within a society; moral subjectivity requires a distinct kind of preparation and socialization, and is connected to other kinds of social norms as well. Marriage, for example, is not only the achievement of some sort of presumed moral mutuality, a special sort of promise. It also has certain sorts of social and financial conditions, and a distinct social function, the raising of children, and that presumes a distinct, shared teleology.

8. The relationship between James and his readers, the trust he asks for, what he promises them, the mutuality that this relationship requires (the honesty or lack of irony in what appears to be his non-omniscience assumption, that he as well as the reader must work to determine the meaning of the narrated events) is a good figure for the moral connections among characters raised and explored. Miller in Chapter Six of (1987) has a number of helpful things to say about this ethical dimension.

9. In other terms, what increasingly begins to qualify as moral authority in modernity is inevitably tied to money, and that must bring with it its own fragility and uncertainty: Cf. Furet's summation of the new class now introduced to the world stage: "Classe sans statut, sans tradition fixe, sans contours établis, elle n'a qu'un titre fragile à la domination: la richesse. Fragile, car il peut appartenir à tous: celui qui est riche aurait pu ne pas l'être. Celui que ne l'est pas auraut pu l'être" (1995, p. 20).

10. By "reality" I do not mean that moral predicates refer to metaphysically real moral properties. I mean that within certain historical communities, agents find that they cannot engage with or understand each other without taking various actions or policies to count as disloyal, egoistic, cruel, selfish or unfair, and so on. All such terms may also count as what they are only within such communities, but all of that is, I think, reality enough. Cf. James's epistemic definition of "the real" in the Preface to *The American*: "The real represents to my perception the things we cannot possibly not know, sooner or later, in one way or another . . . " But that is also another, much longer story.

11. Or, one might say, the sacrifice of retribution, even the sweet, all-too-human pleasures of revenge; as in Newsome's decision at the ending to *The American*.

12. Miller (1987), for example, argues for an "ethics" of reading and rereading that especially in the chapter on de Man (pp. 41–59) resonates with many of the Jamesean themes that will be introduced here. ("To live is to read, or rather to commit again and again the failure to read which is the human lot . . . each reading is, strictly speaking,

ethical, in the sense that it *has* to take place, by an implacable necessity, as the response to a categorical demand, and in the sense that the reader *must* take responsibility for it and for its consequences in the personal, social, and political worlds" p. 59.) But he treats the great difficulties and inevitable failure of "reading" much more as a matter of the structure of language itself ("It is impossible to get outside the limits of language by means of language") and so is led to notions of necessity and categorical demands and "the" reader *an sich* that all seem to me very hard to defend philosophically. James's treatment is much more influenced by considerations of what "makes readings go wrong" now, not in general, and in this he is, I think, on the right track.

13. Anderson (1992). The "ahistorical" characterization is one he uses a good deal for these figures; he includes James in Chapter Four, pp. 133–149, and I think that is a mistake.

14. The phrase is from the funniest Jamesean account of his own failures as a popular writer and dramatist, "The Next Time," about James's own inability to write for the new reading public, to make a "sow's ear out of a silk purse." See *TNT*. James-bashing has taken various forms, inspired by attempts to form a nativist American canon, to the post-modern and cultural criticism of the 1980s (Jameson, Mark Selzer, Caroline Porter). See the discussions in Posnock (1991) and Freedman (1998a). For a considerably more idiosyncratic evaluation of the "James's Reputation" issue, see Rahv (1978), p. 93 ff.

15. This is especially clear in treatments of the adults in *The Awkward Age,* and even more so in his stinging, disgusted tone in *What Maisie Knew.* Dawidoff is quite right that James's attitude is not Tocquevillean; he does not regard the democratic future as "unwelcome" but "unavoidable," something we must just make our peace with, or that we must try to preserve as much as possible of the sweetness of the *ancien regime,* or illuminate the present by as much of the past as possible. See (1992) p. 26, p. 75. And compare the lucid discussion in Ozouf (1998), especially Chapters II and V.

16. Largely, but of course not wholly. One should also mention all the attractions on view, the positive aesthetic side of traditional European society, in *The Princess Cassamassima.*

17. One might also cite Gertrude's complaint about the phoniness of the American/ Puritan pretensions to simplicity and naturalness, or the natural grace of the artificial Eugenia in *The Europeans.*

18. I thus disagree with Sallie Spears (1968) when she has it, as the governing framework for her study, that all James's basic results are "negative," a failure and irresolution so great she will not even call them tragic. See, for example, pp. 38–9. It is true that no writer ever pointed more to the complexities of competing and irreconcilable points of view, and no one relied less on pat syntheses or merely resigned acceptance than James. But Spears's approach too narrowly, I think, categorizes the moral in James (essentially as moralism), and does not do justice to the sources from which our sense of admiration for some, and especially our condemnation of others, stem. It is also just unlikely on the face of it that an imaginative talent like James could be so boldly and undialectically categorized as "negative." Reading a James novel is not like watching some psychological or moral train wreck, a great crash of competing points of view. *What Maisie Knew* is certainly not just all about the "ambiguity of human meaning" (p. 28). Maggie's parents are simply awful, and there is no ambiguity about that at all. The same could be said about Osmond, the (ultimate even if qualified) moral position of Kate Croy, or about the narrow-mindedness of Mrs. Newsome. (Spears's negative take, though, does happily free her somewhat from the great attraction which so many readers seem to feel for that "little nun" of the last novel, Maggie Verver.)

19. James does not raise the issue of religion much, and obviously has little sympathy with the Church, but he is just as obviously horrified by what he presents in Daisy Miller as "replacing" it: a culture of hypocrisy, social conformism and gossip. See the St. Peter's scene in *DM*, p. 42.

20. One of the best discussions of the moral issues raised in this novel can be found in Krook (1962).

21. There is a fine discussion in Ozick (1993) of the role played by *AA* in James's development as a novelist, essentially away from nineteenth-century realism toward modernism, which Ozick describes in a way consistent with the treatment here: as a kind of meaning-overload, something first evident in this oddly theatrical novel. She offers many suggestive details too about the relationship between James's late development and his personal life, especially his theatrical disaster, and the deaths of Alice James and the suicide of Constance Fenimore Woolson.

22. Cf. Dawidoff's discussion again (1992) and what Dawidoff calls James's "tender generosity" toward Americans. David Furth also shows that by the time of *TAS,* James has realized that the question of America cannot be the question of the chances of eventually approximating a European, more organic, settled, tradition-bound society. He is constantly tempted to return to the categories of the Hawthorne essay (even though doubts are present even there; see the quotation cited at the end of this chapter), but realizes that there is no such "Europe" any more, and the category is simply inappropriate as a way of understanding America. David L. Furth (1979), especially the apposite remarks on p. 35.

23. Even so, James's nostalgia for provincial, simple, non-commercialized America is relatively new-found, compared with his harsher comments twenty years earlier about America as largely a question of absences. See the discussion in Furth (1979), pp. 10–22. Along with Dawidoff, Furth is one of the few commentators to note and make much of James's manifest uncertainties about the right tone to take about what he sees, his great hesitancy to play the role of a later Tocqueville, his surprise at himself, that he likes so much of what he would expect himself to loathe.

24. This technique of personification is not limited to *AS.* See the list of such "characters" compiled by Tanner (1995), p. 5. Tanner also gets exactly right James's motives in such a technique. See his comment on "the accommodated haunter," pp. 5–6. Holland's point (1982) about these multiple and oddly named narrators is that James views himself as simultaneously both "participant" and "observer" in the American scene, and this because he realizes that the great emptiness and vacancy of the scene before him is as much also possibility as simply absence, that there is no resisting historical modernity (or no standing outside as mere observer), and one has no choice but to "make" that new sense together with these participants, even as one does so hesitantly, and somewhat ironically (p. 419). Holland claims, in a much more Tocquevillean way than Dawidoff or Furth, that a crucial theme in *The American Scene* is "accommodation" and acquiescence rather than conservative resistance. What seems to me also worth stressing is how such a new sense will be made, that James himself, even as an individual, proposes to do so "dialogically," in reaction and retrospection, even with respect to himself. Hence, again, the "personifications, and the assignment of speaking voices even to buildings and whole cities" – in the mode of "hallucinations and fairy tales." (p. 412)

25. Furth's useful word; see especially his closing discussion, (1979), pp. 45–62, op. cit.

26. Cf. Christopher Newman's remarks: "I am not cultivated, I am not even educated; I

know nothing about history or art, or foreign tongues, or any other learned matters. But I am not a fool either, and I shall undertake to know something about Europe by the time I have done with it. I feel something under my ribs here," he added in a moment, "that I can't explain – a sort of a mighty hankering, a desire to stretch out and haul in" (*A*, 27). James counts a great deal, I think, on that "mighty hankering."

27. For a great deal more on James's historical sense in *AS*, and the relationship between that sense and the problem of meaning, see Haviland (1997). Haviland is particularly persuasive in arguments against both the conventional, conservative readings of *AS* (like Howe's) and contemporary post-modernist or Foucauldean readings (like Selzer's, to cite the most unpleasant example). The connections she makes between James's analytical stance and others, especially with Veblen, are especially helpful.

28. The Hawthorne study, written in 1879, reflects James's attempt to justify to himself his decision to leave an American scene he describes constantly as "provincial," and contrasts sharply with both the nostalgia of *The American Scene* (where ante-bellum American is more often described as simple and peaceful than as "thin in culture" and arid) and with his reconciliation with the "bad, bold" beauty, or modern country that it has become. This contrast and much else that is very helpful about the aesthetic and critical qualities of *AS* are described by Furth (1979). See James's letter to Howells, further defending both the need for the "paraphernalia" of history to "set the novelist in motion" and the uniqueness of the American scene, given the absence of such paraphernalia. (*L*, p. 72). In *Washington Square*, this absence is an important internal element of the novel. It makes understandable the American susceptibility to romance (Aunt Penniman) on the one hand, and the motives for Dr. Sloper's hatred of contingency, chance, and human frailty on the other (convinced as he is without such a tradition, believing that only human will and reason can fashion an acceptable life). Without such "paraphernalia," we are left in that book in a kind of Hawthorne situation: the bland and dangerous innocence of Catherine and the "scientific" willfulness of our new Rappuccini, Sloper.

# 3

# "CRUDITIES OF MUTUAL
# RESISTANCE"

"But thought is one thing, the deed is another, and the image of the deed
still another: the wheel of causality does not roll between them."
                                             "On the Pale Criminal"
                                             *Thus Spoke Zarathustra*
                                             Friedrich Nietzsche


I

One approach to the question of the objectivity and authority of moral
categories is to frame the problem itself as a historical and practical one
rather than as a metaphysical issue. On this understanding, only in certain
sorts of societies, in specific sorts of historical situations, given specific
forms of life and historical memory, economies, opportunities, levels of
education, and so on, would it, for example, be practically necessary in
some way that the norms that constrain conduct be experienced as based
on some sort of fundamental entitlement to a free life as an individual and
some mutual acknowledgment of such claims. In such a society, given such
conditions, the undistorted experience of another subject would have to be
the experience of another equally "entitled" subject. It would, on this
assumption, make no sense to be able to ascribe such capacities to myself
(in a society where I had in fact come to understand *myself* as having such
capacities, as being an agent) without acknowledging that I must be one of
many with such capacities.

In any society, of course, we need to be able to count on and to some
extent trust each other beyond the physical possession and defense of
property and the direct enforcement of agreements through violence. We

do so through some appreciation of the authority of claims to trust and faith-keeping. But, so goes such a claim, in some societies, such norms would be experienced as reciprocal obligations among individuals. Individuals in such a society, we might assume, would have to confront a kind of unavoidable, orienting fact that any consistent way of going on as a subject oneself, leading a life, involves the assumption of minimum, unconditional standards of conduct everyone is owed as a free being, and even that my ability to lead my own life might depend on some such reciprocity and mutuality among free subjects . Such norms would then be understood as made, and as actively sustained, but, contrary to the relativing tendency of much historicizing, their making would not thereby be arbitrary or dispensable. In such societies (and only in such societies), one might argue, something essential to anyone's doing anything, to being a doer of deeds at all, presumes the like capacity of all to do so.

This alone might get us closer only to the war of all free subjects against all, not to any obligated acknowledgment of such like freedom central to the institution of morality. But the *historical* view might allow one to show that not only has one come to experience oneself as, above all else, an individual agent (that it is a certain historical experience that makes this unavoidable), but that within such an experience, given its nature, properly understood, one could not exercise that capacity without such an acknowledgment of and respect for the claims of others, and that I must be able to count on such mutuality in leading my own life. The exercise of my freedom might now involve a profound dependence on others, on a community of free agents. It would not be some sort of metaphysical truth that such dependencies exist, but a historical truth at some level of generality and unavoidability.

This would at least be one way of thinking about the status of such claims by others to such respect, and about my own dependence on there being such reciprocity. Such historical beings have unavoidably (to make that vast assumption again) come to think of themselves as free beings, constraining their own conduct by imposing norms on themselves, and that also moral norms, reflecting an acknowledgment of such mutual freedom, and a dependence on others recognized as free, are the only kind appropriate to such beings. In such societies, commitments to such things as honesty or promise-keeping among individuals or treating others as moral equals (equally free and responsible) do not just function as one way among others of keeping order in the society, or don't just turn out to be adaptive behaviors. An experience of oneself as dependent on a kind of reciprocity in relationships with others has become "who we are" at some constitutive level, as if it were "an agreement in a form of life," in some way such that "opting out" is impossible, or incoherent, or prevents my own realization of freedom. Within such a perspective, it might not be possible to argue in some conclusive, a priori way that this, this particular form of dependence, amounts to "who we've become." We might only be able to "show," in various contexts, in the everyday and in the extreme, that there is no way to go on effectively without acknowledging the force and indispensability of such norms "for us" (even when denied or resisted). It might even be in the nature of such a norm that it could only be shown in this way, all such that the novel might be the great modern philosophical form.

Such a possible account raises, of course, scores of questions. Most obviously, if the general question is whence the bindingness of such putative claims on us by others, and the general answer is that this is simply who we've become, or that not to acknowledge such claims and not somehow to live out that acknowledgment is to risk some unsustainable loss, perhaps the loss of the intelligibility of one's very doings – then the account seems naïve. Those who refuse or ignore such acknowledgment carry on in their own way, after all; they do not collapse into some obvious incoherence, and seem to suffer no loss. But, at least in the context of James's fiction, what is important is what we see they have lost, how little of what they think they understand can fit anywhere, turn any other wheel, in the world they inhabit, especially any wheel of intelligibility, of comprehension. They can easily not know what they don't know, and enact a ritual or performance that just cannot mean what they take it to mean, or much of anything else. Moreover, there is no particular reason that such a reason or account of this bindingness has to be the kind of reason we could give an egoistic agent in order to persuade him to change. The novels can show something about such a claim and about such a loss without providing that sort of reason.

As we have seen, James's view of *modern* societies (his own frequent, complexly used adjective, as we have begun to see) is quite sensitive to the historical distinctness of such societies and is quite unsentimental and somewhat bleak about the fragility of such moral entitlements and the capacity of individuals to acknowledge them. The adults in *What Maisie Knew* seem profoundly representative rather than colorful exceptions, the rich and anomic Americans, and the foppish, effete Europeans of *The*

*Reverberators* just as telling. A new way of making and accumulating money, a dizzying new form of social mobility tied to this new economy, a new culture obsessively dedicated to work and financial success, consumerism, a cult of celebrity and fame, a mass culture based on journalism and advertising, a new conception of individuals as untrustworthy centers of self-interest, a new sort of dependence on the views of others for social esteem, and many other factors mean that things have not simply changed, they have changed in an unprecedented way. They all help to confirm Nanda's simple remark: *"Everything's* different from what it used to be." Even cynical, collective assumptions about greed and venality, much in vogue in the early modern philosophical tradition, do not have much effective purchase, however widespread their presence. One would need some sense of one's own advantage and interest, and some reliable way of anticipating the pursuit of such interests in others, even for that sort of collectivity to function. The modern context, understood by James at a first pass as a massive failure in very much of a common normative structure, makes the assignment of or understanding of determinate meaning – psychological insight, honest self-description, genuinely shared social understanding, reliable act and intention descriptions of all kinds – nearly impossible and certainly very difficult. In such a historical context, any moral judgments of the sort we were just talking about also seem very much threatened, invitations instead – exactly as Hegel once predicted – to hypocrisy, a pretense about criteria of judgment no one can or wants to or knows how to meet, and "hard-heartedness," a non-hypocritical but nearly pathological insistence on a selflessness that renders all actual action unworthy because self-interested.

If one were then to ask what is it about such a society that might positively make moral categories of fidelity, trust, honesty, keeping faith, respect, and the acknowledgment of some sort of mutuality (or all the themes around which so much of James's narratives revolve), *the* problems, and what makes these the issues that are so difficult and so unavoidable, then one would have at least asked James's question. On the one hand, there is clearly much in the historical situation described by James that is only characterizable as a kind of pathology, certainly an occasion of much pathology. The confusion and instability, the threat of radical indeterminacy, creates the setting for so many of James's themes. There are those great, painful doubts shared by so many characters that one "has truly lived," rather than that one has only "pretended" to live. There is that theme itself in general, the difference between pretending to be and being (or the frequent theme of theatricality, of sociality itself as only theatricality, as in *The Tragic Muse*). There is the fear of exposure (as if one would be exposed as, really, nothing), or the general theme of exposing (the debutante ritual or the pretense of initiating someone into a "something" that isn't really "there"). There is the anxiety of being out of place (an "American in Europe" especially) and so the constant wariness about shame, the experience of shame, and then the cycle of revenge and ressentiment so occasioned.[1] There are the bizarre attachments and dependencies, the doubles and twins, the Masters and Slaves, dead authors and living researchers, and other such pathologies of social dependence. There is the constant reality or presence of the unspoken, unsaid because unsayable but nonetheless real (as in Isabel's final knowledge, or Strether's), the fascination with secrets and obsessions about hidden, crucial meanings not yet found, the ghosts and the question of their reality, and so on. All these are reflections of this situation, of modernity as the collapse of reliable forms of sense-making, and the beginning of a kind of sociality that reflects precisely this uncertainty and often desperation and paranoia.

And yet, just in so reflecting it, it also begins to reveal what sense can be made in such a situation. As we shall see, that which makes for the modern situation of loss and failure, if understood, also accepted and properly acknowledged, makes for an unavoidable aspiration to a historically different life, a free life, a freedom inevitably and necessarily cooperative and somehow damaged, lacking for the agents, if not properly mutual. (One hint of all this in *The Wings of the Dove:* Kate Croy's immediate sense that for all of Milly's great goodness, there is something missing in Milly Theale, something directly due to her modern power (great wealth, and so enormous independence) and so, ironically a flaw in her very modern virtues. She lacked "the imagination of terror, of thrift, *the imagination of in any degree the habit of a conscious dependence on others,*" and therewith "was not a person to change places, to change even chances with" (*WD*, 125).[2]

I hope that it is at least plausible that James does not draw skeptical conclusions about indeterminacy, and so the lack of purchase for moral categories; nor is he interested only in the psychology of the types of characters who constrain their actions in some acknowledgment of these sorts of norms (as if, for example, the frequent appearance of sacrifice and selflessness is really a matter only of fear, repression, and avoidance). The norms themselves are often the heart of the matter, and their status is always at issue, never dismissed or psychologized (treated as the particular beliefs of individuals). How he makes out this unavoidability or the practical purchase of such a mode of self- and other-understanding is the question I am raising. And again, whatever practical necessity is being asserted, it is a historical necessity, one no character in such a distinct historical world could avoid and still be a character, a person at all.

## II

Several preliminary things can be said about the way James presents the question of the experience of such necessity, and its meaning, in the lives of these historical agents. For one thing, James's interest lies in the relevance of moral considerations within and not as a mere judge of a life; he is not treating the moral point of view as a kind of external constraint on permissible living, a mere occasional call of conscience. Certainly many of the everyday features of morality are recognizable in the situations (however historically self-conscious) that James presents, especially implied claims about the reality of moral conflict (that there can be a conflict between considerations of one's particular interests and well-being, and some moral claim on us) and the presumption that there are, for all subjects, certain universal moral entitlements. But James has quite a distinctive way of portraying the place of such claims and entitlements within a modern life, distinctive both because of his historical and social sensitivity and because of the way he presents the institution of morality itself. He does not, that is, portray morality as some distinct or separable goal one should formulate and pursue, does not portray moral heroes and heroines, striving to be good or striving not to allow their venal self-interest to get in the motivational way of their duty. His characters, even and especially the best of them, are striving simply for a life, trying to live. (If they are Americans and intelligent, trying for a life appropriately responsive to the vast new possibilities made possible by the American founding, attracted to Europe as to a parent, a source and fund of experience, yet mistrustful of such parents and eager for a thing of one's own; if they are European, trying to preserve, protect, to defend the social forms and conventions that make available the long training and discipline that makes any taste possible, but threatening to kill, mummify what they want to preserve.) For the most part they are simply trying to get or stay married, or to endure a marriage, or to avoid marriage, but all in all the best of them seem to be trying to live, as if figuring out how to lead a life or to have one's own life in such a historical world were now a difficult task, not a course one assumed simply by being alive. And it is within arrangements with each other in such a pursuit that the claims of morality are presented as practically unavoidable if one is to "lead" a life, or avoidable only at very great distinctive cost. Put negatively, the question is then: how James can show what is lost, for these sorts of (historically situated) subjects, from their point of view, not just as objects of blame, when such considerations are neglected, or qualified away in self-deceived rationalizations (as with Densher and Kate Croy).

One way he accomplishes this is by stressing one theme especially, in manifold and complex variations, a consideration that, I believe, he regards as distinctive in the new, somewhat anomic, mass societies being formed around him: the depth and kind of the dependence on each other experienced by distinct free subjects, the experience of the need for some equal acknowledgment of the claims of each on the other, given such dependence and a kind of engagement with others on that basis. And this is an issue also prominent in the International Theme, in his treatment of the implications of the deceptive, even disastrous, American aspirations toward a presumed modern ideal of complete individual independence, or "self-reliance," and the equally deceptive, destructive "European" insistence on the centrality of esteem, pride, or social dependence: on *the* benchmark, being "appropriately seen," more than seeing, or even enacting. If characters like Isabel Archer and Strether and Maggie, in other words, do manage a kind of morally significant independence, do manage to "break free" in some sense, it is not a heroic or romantic independence. It also involves some sort of concession to the specific requirements of modern sociality and others (often in the problem of marriage, what it means in this modern world to seek a romantic marriage, what it is to acknowledge such a dependence and to promise this kind of fidelity, and so why it is a figure for this whole dance of recognition and moral trust; sometimes, in Strether's case, enacted in not marrying).[3] It further involves a concession which, while it can appear resignatory or fatalistic, seems rather evocative of a more complex, Jamesean sense of the sort of independence or freedom possible and possibly valuable in modern societies, and his refusal to be tempted by various false alternatives.

Such a dialectic is constantly on view in James, from little details – as we watch Milly Theale begin to change, to think herself interesting and worthy of a certain kind of life, we realize how much of what she comes to believe is a function of how she comes to be seen in London, that "Milly actually began to borrow from the handsome girl [Kate] a sort of view of her state" (*WD*, 125) – to themes common to many novels in the description of the emotional logic of the lover and the beloved, to the broadest treatments, often played out by James with many historical and gender-bending twists and ironic turns, as well as with many Oedipal echoes of the primeval independence-dependence struggle. (And so the International Theme again: with Americans and Europeans enacting the problem of the founding of a new civilization in these Oedipal terms. Mother Europe devoutly loved and just as devoutly hated for fidelity to the oldest father, custom; the opposing question often being, can these always infantilized Americans grow up?[4]) The dual insufficiency of any straightforward ideal of dependence or independence also suggests by contrast a distinct form of moral mutuality, a way of taking another into proper account, now possible for some, and necessary for any who aspire to live a worthy life. A famous exchange in *The Portrait of a Lady* raises the theme directly, and begins to suggest – and I hope to pull together now – the many related dimensions, some involving radical suggestions about the nature of consciousness and self-consciousness, thereby implied.

Isabel had just remarked about someone's supposedly "ugly brick house," "I don't care anything about his house." Madame Merle replies.

> "That's very crude of you. When you've lived as long as I you'll see that every human being has his shell and that you must take the shell into account. By the shell I mean the whole envelope of circumstances. There's no such thing as an isolated man or woman; we're each of us made up of some cluster of appurtenances. What shall we call our 'self'? Where does it begin? where does it end? It overflows into everything that belongs to us – and then it flows back again. I know a large part of myself is in the clothes I choose to wear. I've a great respect for *things*. One's self – for other people – is one's expression of one's self; and one's house, one's furniture, one's garments, the books one reads, the company one keeps – these things are all expressive."

This was very metaphysical; not more so, however, than several observations Madame Merle had already made. Isabel was fond of metaphysics, but was unable to accompany her friend into this bold analysis of human personality. "I don't agree with you. I think just the other way. I don't know whether I succeed in expressing myself but I know that nothing else expresses me; everything's on the contrary a limit, a barrier, and a perfectly arbitrary one. Certainly the clothes which, as you say, I choose to wear don't express me; and heaven forbid they should!"

"You dress very well," Madame Merle lightly interposed.

"Possibly; but I don't care to be judged by that. My clothes may express my dressmaker, but they don't express me. To begin with it's not my choice that I wear them; they're imposed upon me by society."

"Should you prefer to go without them?" Madame Merle enquired in a tone which virtually terminated the discussion (*PL*, 173).[5]

### III

Such passages reveal already how ambitiously James addresses the problems of modern moral life.[6] As the quotation indicates, what he clearly thinks must be understood, if competing and often opposed claims for certain sorts of treatment and entitlements are to be understood, is nothing less than the nature of intersubjective experience itself, the way in which discursive intelligences can come to settle on some view of what is happening to them, and how any, especially differing, moral claims based on such views are to be themselves settled, or again, to use his familiar word, how one could end up "squared." Since moral issues are often understood to involve something like the unavoidable claims on one by any other, to do or forebear from doing, whatever the costs to one's interest, a great deal depends on how we understand the relevant others, who is or is not affected by what we do, and how we come to understand what is happening to us. And, as already suggested, a great deal depends on the nature of the social dependencies within which these negotiations go on. James's own view is not Madame Merle's, but he takes the point she makes very seriously, and raises the issue in his own voice several times, most famously in this often quoted passage from the preface to *Roderick Hudson*.

Really, universally, relations stop nowhere, and the exquisite problem of the artist is eternally but to draw, by a geometry of his own, the circle within which they shall happily *appear* to do so. He is in the perpetual predicament that the continuity of things is the whole matter, for him, of comedy and tragedy; that this continuity is never, by the space of an instant or an inch, broken, and that, to do anything at all, he has at once intensely to consult and intensely to ignore it (*RHP,* 1041).

Many recent readers of James have begun to appreciate his very unusual and even revolutionary treatment of such issues. Sensitized perhaps by modern literary theory and suspicious of the very possibility of "individually owned" intentions and meanings,[7] and so of the traditionally psychological readings of James, some writers have begun to emphasize what is clearly there in him. Somewhat ironically, they have begun to make a virtue out of what other earlier critics found a vice: first, the great elusiveness of psychological meaning, determinate intentions, or even stable identities in his characters, and second, the complex relationship between consciousness itself and power, or the thin line, in human life as he presents it, between interpreting and understanding, on the one hand, and manufacturing and imposing, on the other. Basing their readings on everything from Freudian to feminist to post-structuralist theories, even to Foucauldean "theories of suspicion," such readers have appropriately drawn great attention to central aspects of that problem of meaning in James's characters most at home in, even prophetic of, our supposedly postmodern world: indeterminacy, absence, knowing and not-knowing the same content.[8]

The most obvious dramatic evocation of this characteristic of Jamesean consciousness is simply failure, the constant failure of characters to understand sufficiently or determinately enough what is going on, what the gestures and words of other characters could mean. Sometimes, of course, this is because the characters are simply dense, or, especially, are being deceived, or trying hard not to understand (Densher being the best example of the last). But the former situation is not where the problems arise, and even these latter explanations are rarely a suitable analysis, since just as often the moral meaning of "deceit" is just as much in question (or so the two deceiving principals in *The Wings of the Dove,* for example, or Madame de Vionnet and Chad, at least try to persuade themselves.)

What is even more at issue, and what is of greatest relevance for the moral themes, is what appears to be the general instability or unreliability of possible mental content in general in James's characters. He clearly has a general interest in how one's beliefs could be said to have content, to be fixed in meaning, and he presents that phenomenon in a way that defies many standard options in explaining it. While there is of course no Jamesean position on consciousness or the ascription of beliefs, no account of perception, mental causes, practical rationality, and so on, at least in the domains where he is clearly taking implicit positions on issues of motivation or the understanding of others' actions, and the like, he does not present us with a receptacle or window view of consciousness, as if a mind just grasps thoughts present for it, or uses its words to fix onto meanings, or as if a mind could be said individually, by effort of thinking, to achieve some intention or insight, to seize on a determinate meaning. In contrast to all such images of searching, finding, disambiguating, and grasping, in the struggles depicted by James, what one could be said to think seems to depend in some complex way on the possible reactions, dispositions, hesitations, and activities of others, as if just to be aware is to be engaged with others in some normative ways, attuned to various proprieties and improprieties, or not. (I shall present an example of this in a moment.) This is often elliptically expressed by James by highlighting what he calls the "negotiated" nature of psychological meaning itself, as if it actually exists somewhere "between" and not "in" persons. And this also makes for great uncertainty and unclarity for those characters and for us. Because of this, there does not appear to be any reassuring way, not just for us, but for them, to identify reliably the content of their own thoughts, to know what they think. And, as he shows us in great detail, it is the kind of context described by *The American Scene* and presented in the International Theme that makes such negotiations and dependencies so much more intense, unreliable, and unavoidable: the absence of the conventional social and political and religious frameworks, the new game required by the American success, its money, social mobility, destabilizing, deracinating effects, its skepticism, secularism.

Of course, to say that many James characters do not seem to know what they think does not mean that they are somehow unaware of their own mental states. It is to note that what I am in fact thinking consciously about my own attitudes, or what I think about others, might but need not have much relevance to what opinions and beliefs may rightly be (eventually) attributed to me about such matters. I may never have "actually thought" the opinions I do have, and what I consciously tell myself I believe may not at all be what I believe.[9] This might still seem to suggest that the problem is some sort of epistemological opacity (there *is* such an opinion and I am blocked somehow from acknowledging it), or am in self-denial, or it is unconscious, and so on. I might be said to reveal what I really believe by what I do, not by what I say or consciously think, for example. But as I shall show in the following chapters, James's position seems much more radical than such "opacity" positions. The question of what belief I actually hold, or what my true motivation was, and so on, is simply not the sort of thing that could be said to be "there" at all, however epistemologically refined our insight might become. It is available retrospectively in some sense only because "there," in the future, is the only place it could "be."

Philosophers have had a hard enough time in the twentieth century explaining the possibility of representational content with the simplest cases of propositional attitudes. To try also to understand the issues involved in the possibility of some shareable psychological and evaluative meaning in such a context, or what one should make of, how one should understand (now, in such a world) the meaning of an American heir's "delay in returning home," or an ex-lover's sudden return before her ex's wedding, say, are all questions so difficult as to be almost without much sustained philosophical treatment, at least not in any way that would begin to help with the question: What it is it one could come properly to think about in any such situation, and why?

And with all this in the air in the fiction, it is understandable that James would again attract the attention of our skeptical age, and that the framework of interrogation should have shifted again. Such contemporary emphases on what, in James too, must always "exceed" what a single consciousness could contain, on the discontinuities of consciousness and even identity in James, on the constant, frustrating "deferral" of meaning, on the treatment of consciousness non-individually, but in terms of competing structures, codes, or conventions, and then on the failure of such structures to permit reliable meaning, on the Jamesean fascination with the secret, hidden, and unavailable, the repressed, what one will not allow oneself to see, and so forth, and the theoretical insistence that this all goes well beyond traditional sorts of ambiguity, tension, and conflict, have all produced quite a different Henry James.[10]

But such emphases have also suggested a set of alternatives – modernist, ego-centered, realist, individualist on the one hand, all versus the priority of discourse, the constant return of the repressed, the artificiality (or constructed nature) of personhood, or the simple failure of meaning on the other – that comprise far too strict a set of alternatives. The attack on the conventional, realist reading gets a number of things right about the oddity of James's treatment of character, but it also misses a great deal of the normative dimension of meaning and intelligibility James is holding onto, however transforming.[11] Understanding in James is still linked to the possibility of getting something right and to assessing the rightness of actions, and the inescapable claim on us of such a possibility is treated quite realistically. What we are trying to get right, what it would be to get it right in our dealings with each other, what especially this all requires now, all form the central core of James's great animating question.[12]

I I I

In fact, the situation alluded to before, in Part One of *The Golden Bowl*, makes the earlier point about the oddities and radical implications of James's treatment of thinking, understanding, and possible meaning, with great compression and complexity, and is treated in a way that directly sets up the enormously complex moral issues of that novel, and so is worth, I hope, an extended discussion here.

Of course, *The Golden Bowl* is not an easy novel to "digress into," and it defies any sort of economical discussion. It is the James novel where the least happens dramatically, but where what does happens means the most. James piles on layer after layer of possible meaning and ambiguity and uncertainty, as if just to see how far he could go, when the "ice" would finally break.

The plot is simple enough. A very rich American businessman and widower, Adam Verver, is traveling through Europe with his daughter Maggie, collecting art for a planned grand museum, apparently a whole town financed by Adam, "America City." Through the matchmaking efforts of an American friend, the most obviously named of all James's characters, Fanny Assingham, Maggie meets and marries an Italian prince, now reduced to some sort of genteel poverty and also very aptly named, as we shall see, Amerigo. Prior to his engagement, Amerigo had been the lover of the formidable but poor American, Charlotte Stant, who, it turns out, is both an old friend of Fanny's and a school friend of Maggie's.[13] Neither Amerigo nor Fanny informs Maggie of this prior romantic relationship. After the wedding, Maggie senses that her father might feel like a fifth wheel in their party, and encourages her father to marry. He does; he marries Charlotte Stant. Maggie and her father assume everyone is "squared" and seem then to revert completely to their life before Maggie's marriage, spending almost all their time with each other and Maggie's new baby, thereby throwing Charlotte and the prince more and more together socially. We are given to believe that there is still considerable electricity between these two, veritable smoke rising from each when they see each other. (They had broken off only because neither had money.) At Charlotte's instigation, they finally begin an adulterous affair. Maggie discovers it, and does not expose them. Instead, she works very hard to keep everything under wraps and in control. She succeeds. Charlotte and Adam end up sailing for America City, a fate, we are led to believe, worse than death, and Maggie and the prince begin their new life together.

The real difficulty in any economical discussion comes from the great subtlety of the moral tone created by the way the story is narrated and the characters presented, a subtlety so complex that the novel inspires nothing but controversy in readers. (The key issue has always been one of great relevance here: what to make morally of, how to evaluate, Maggie's efforts to hold her marriage together and to remove the offending Charlotte.) I can only give a few examples here of the way I think James links together his psychological-historical and moral themes to create this complexity, but they will do very little justice to the controversies.[14]

For example, the meaning of Charlotte Stant's return to London just before the wedding of the prince and Maggie is not, we come to see in Fanny's worried speculations, treated in James's narration as just ambiguous, as if it could be taken in one of two ways, and the problem is to figure out which way has more evidence to support it, that the one right sense is there to be found. It, the meaning, isn't, oddly and frustratingly, there at all, even for Charlotte, even if she thinks her intentions are clear and can explain everything. Such a possible meaning seems dependent instead on a constellation of reactions, expectations, and intentions and assumed proprieties that no one character could grasp as a thought. And this is often presented by James as radically as it sounds, so that the issue is not whether a plausible possible interpretation is correct or confirmable. The very sense of such a possibility is originally in some way a function of a particular social constellation that one does not, as an individual mind, grasp, so much as a be a part of, an ongoing, negotiating, active part. Minds are locked into such tight relations of dependence and mutual reflection in James's presentations that such minds themselves seem nothing but the tissue of their relations and mutual reflections, however uncertain and constantly self-forming.[15] (Part of any such understanding on the part of a putative individual would have to be a kind of correct anticipating of another, something that itself depends on this other, himself or herself, rightly reading, or originally anticipating, such an engagement, or possible anticipation, on the part of the first subject.[16])

Since the possible resolution of such a question is not treated as a hidden thing ever to be found, James must suggest what he thinks is going on when the characters try to resolve their perplexities about it, something they must at least tentatively do if they are to act. The novel, as it introduces us to Charlotte's return, opens with nothing but perplexities like this. It begins by introducing us to Prince Amerigo contemplating his marriage to Maggie, and it opens as if in some odd minor key, full of foreboding and foreshadowing of troubles to come in the symphonic play of themes to follow. (It also opens with a historical allusion that will be important: Amerigo is one of those Romans who prefers London as the center of the new, true "empire," more an empire than the old Rome ever was, an empire of commerce and commercial *imperium.* Amerigo is not entirely proud of his ancestors' Machiavellian past. He has some aspiration to a renewal through these Americans and their commercial empire; he wants to believe in their capacity for good, and does not look down at them, as he might. He is thus, like his namesake, Amerigo Vespucci, some new-old world link, or at least some hope that there can be a link, not just an opposition between the past and the future.)

An ironic and playful conversation with his fiancé, about his being merely added to Adam's collection as a *morceau de musée,* is not quite ironic enough, though. It has a distinct, disturbing edge to it, and the prince feels some strange appeal to "do something or other, before it was too late, for himself" (*GB,* 20), as if, oddly, the marriage is not for him, as if soon things might be "too late." In talking with Fanny Assingham, he talks of the marriage as some "monster" approaching him, jokes with Fanny about how "risky" it had been to bring them together, tells her he has only the old slow-on-the-uptake "Italian" moral sense (if any), not the "elevator speed" sense of Adam and the Americans. Something is off, not right. We don't know what, and are suddenly thrust into the scene as characters ourselves, as disoriented as the prince himself (there is very little sense that he or anyone knows what's wrong), and Fanny, who seems to feel responsible for the situation, is vaguely uneasy.

Then Charlotte Stant hits town. We quickly learn the facts about Charlotte and the prince mostly through Fanny's musings, and we tend to trust instinctively, at least at this point, Fanny's assurances to her husband that they had not gone, physically, to put it delicately, very far, beyond the intensity of their emotional love. (The reason she gives for believing this is a little silly: They "had not enough time," although apparently they had months and months.) We then quickly learn a number of other things, none of which has any meaning assigned to it, so much so that it is difficult (without James's talent) to describe "the facts," as if there are such "facts," in the appropriately elusive and indirect way. As noted earlier, Charlotte and Maggie had been school friends and had spent time together even after Maggie had taken up with the prince. But neither Charlotte, no later the prince, had ever mentioned their romance to Maggie, even after the marriage arrangements. Was this, we are immediately prompted to ask, to protect Maggie? (This is what Fanny insists. Maggie, she claims, is so tenderly incapable of the knowledge of "evil," the oddest word to use about what was just a supposedly incomplete and long past romance. And this is a fact that Fanny's husband quickly notes.) Was it just to avoid "fuss"? Was it strategic, just so as not to complicate the marriage "pursuit"? Or did holding back the knowledge somehow keep the romance symbolically alive, as if they were not "betraying" each other?

Fanny believes Charlotte has acted "generously" in coming back before the wedding, but she is clearly very deeply disturbed by the act, something quite inconsistent with this ascription of motives. She thinks Charlotte has just not calculated the "costs." We have no sense yet of what these may be, and we are confused that Fanny is so worried, if the arrival is so innocent, so much a matter just of possible indelicate but innocent effects, and not of deliberate and perhaps selfish design. Fanny's views on the issue are actually a complex of inconsistencies; she thinks that just as Charlotte voluntarily got out of the way, after it was clear she and the prince could not marry, she has acted now just as "sacrificially," coming back with no thought of herself or of painful memories, but to be of "positive" reassuring help to Maggie. But Fanny has already made clear that the best way to do that would have simply been to stay away. Wishful thinking, guilt at her own optimism about Charlotte and the prince, at her own silence about the two of them to Maggie (which she does not mention), all clearly complicate (and make quite wholly unreliable, despite appearances) her point of view, although she continues to seem to be throughout the novel some sort of critic, making sense of the plot. She even goes so far (so far away from her own expressed views of the innocence of it all) as to hope for Charlotte's eventual marriage, but only as "proof" "that she's cured," that she accepts the situation," as if "proof" were needed.

We learn that Charlotte wants the prince to help her pick out a wedding gift. Fanny, in effect, goes so far as to protest, to offer herself as a guide instead. The prince is also hesitant, and, as a clear pretense, protests that Charlotte hasn't the money for a gift. But Charlotte persists, and they meet, in strange secrecy, agreeing, as if to preserve the surprise, not to visit any areas that Maggie frequents. (This is not a problem; Maggie does not slum in antiquarian shops, looking for values.) Then the key scene. Charlotte makes a speech to the prince while they are out, a strange, elusive, allusive speech. She wants, she says, only to "have had" this moment, before (she can't apparently say the word "marriage") what he's "going to do." She wants only not "to have not had it," this moment alone, when she can "give herself away," willing to "do it for nothing."

But of course it is not for nothing. It must be a secret (the prince has promised), and it does change a great deal; it compromises the prince deeply, whatever spin they put on it. (Imagine you are the wife. You find out from someone else that your new husband had met the (secret, thus far undisclosed) love of his prior life right before your wedding day, and he kept it from you. Your inference?) And she precisely does not, by "giving herself away," *give* herself away. She says, finally, nothing determinate, but thereby everything. She has gotten the prince to go with her, under these odd circumstances, and she has said what she wanted to say: that she wanted there to be something said between them.

On the one hand, of course, modern readers suspect everything in this scene. We suspect Charlotte of trying to compromise the prince, to put him in her power in some way (thanks to the secret), to play on his guilt about his love of money, to initiate some renewal between them, to remind him about whom he really loves and always will, to manipulate him. But there is also something courageous and heroic in her act, and she does seem to be saying good-bye: She will not let what passed between them go unremarked on, swept under the rug of private history. There must be some acknowledgment. And we know enough of the prince already to suspect his weakness, and admire her insistence on a gesture that refuses complete forgetfulness.

And his reaction is just as complex. He is relieved that he has been "let off," that she makes no demands, and asks for no explanation. But, of course, just as she has and has not given herself away, he has and most definitely has *not* been let off. That had been the whole point – not to let him off – something he wants not to see, and so does not. Since he has been let off from a direct response, he lets himself off completely and does not respond to or engage her directly at all, a fatal problem in the possibility of what they are doing meaning anything, as we shall see. (The "figure" for this problem is again a gift, a small gift Charlotte wants to give him, and he refuses.) He does not respond, and his "lips remain closed to the successive vaguenesses of rejoinder, of objection, that rose for him within" (*GB*, 102). (The rejoinders, we note, are still vague for him, as if he only feels some "objection." And what would he be objecting to?)

All of this builds to the great scene and lines that define the problem of the book. Charlotte wants to buy a lovely antiquity, the golden bowl, as a gift. The prince sees immediately that it is flawed, not the gold it pretends to be, but crystal, and walks out of the shop. Charlotte cannot see a flaw, but has deduced from the price that there "must" be one. Hence the great question from the shopkeeper: "But if it's something you can't find out, *isn't it as good as if it were nothing?*" (*GB*, 86). Indeed. That summarizes all at once a very typical, prominent Jamesean question. It might be (as good as nothing), but everything then hangs on whether and how and what it would mean to keep it from someone who would want to "find out." Since so much of the novel's action will turn on characters' pretending or wanting badly not to see, and, especially, refusing to help each other see, this question will later assume the role of the novel's central question. (Would what the prince and Charlotte do be "as good as if it were nothing" if Maggie never found out? Are not the terms on which Maggie and the prince resume their marriage at the novel's end like a positive answer to the shopkeeper's question, pretending to be able to go on because now the flaws "can't be seen"?)[17] The prince has (so he believes) seen immediately that the bowl is flawed, and has stalked out. That is his way of dealing (or pretending to deal) with flaws, and so it is for the other four main characters. But Charlotte alone in the novel will take great risks with flaws, and even goes so far as to lie, directly and finally unambiguously, about the price, making it easier to pretend that she can "afford it." (It is fifteen pounds; she tells the prince it is five pounds.) And the novel is off and running.

Much of this could of course be fit into a conventional framework of intelligibility for actions. We understand what others are doing by understanding their motives and reasons, their desires and beliefs, by understanding what they take themselves to be after and why. This all obviously implies that they can somehow identify what they desire and believe, and either disclose it or not, to others or even to themselves. And, however hard to explain philosophically, it is obvious that in some cases, they might keep their own motives not only from others, but from themselves. Fanny, the prince, and Charlotte might all clearly be trying to avoid admitting to themselves why they act or have acted, even though at "some level" they know. (They would of course have to know in order to keep such motives from themselves.) They all certainly seem busily engaged tying large, obscuring bows and ribbons around their own and others' possible motives, keeping the wedding, and their own later deniability, right on track.

Some of this sort of account is doubtless apt. But it fatally misses the pathos and confusion of the scenes, even the desperation of the problem of meaning for each of them, their own confusion about what is happening to them. (Certainly direct motives to deceive others and act in a strategically self-interested way would be a gross exaggeration of the tone of the treatment here, especially and unfairly harsh on Charlotte.) But the idea of self-deceit here presupposes that something of that basic issue – what is happening, what such a gesture or other would mean (what motives are really behind it) – had been somehow resolved, and that they are now keeping secret from themselves some motive in dealing with it or some motive to see it, or to have seen it, in certain lights.

They are, though, much more at sea than this picture would allow, in large measure because of the kind of world they have to inhabit, a world fully appreciated as such by James. The great density of the opening pages of *The Golden Bowl* is a density of nearly unmanageable possibilities, not of hidden meanings or self-deceived motives, "actually" there, waiting to be seen or exposed. And the resolution of such possibilities does not require honesty or deeper insight, but does require a kind of dependence on and engagement with others, personally and individually, a commonly made meaning, one might say, all as if all and any meaning could be only determined "retrospectively," and "cooperatively," as if life cannot be lived as life, but only as material for remembered life, to allude to Proustean affinities. As with Proust, life seems led in perpetual future perfect tenses and subjunctive moods in the Jamesean universe. Not, my motive for X-ing now is M, given my current understanding of situation S. But, I will have meant to X, because of what will have been M, should the situation have turned out S.

"The merely spontaneous description of the case," as James puts it once, would simply be that agent's motives in such intentional contexts are dependent on certain descriptions. If these descriptions are inaccurate, it may then be true to say, given what they wanted to achieve, that they should have had other motives. But James has introduced such a massive instability into any such possible description, inscribed such complete provisionality into any possible self-understanding, made any description so dependent on various possible interpretations of mutual reflections and inferences, and future actions, that this anodyne formulation is of no help. None of these characters know yet what they intend, not because such motives are hidden from them or because they hide them from themselves, but because James has "placed" their motives in some complex, fluid social space among them all, showing us their incapacity to act except in the light of anticipations and expectations massively uncertain. (There is a fine phrase in *The Ambassadors,* typical of this view. Strether is visiting Madame de Vionnet, is dazzled by her apartment once again, and "he was sure in a moment that, *whatever he should find he had come for,* it wouldn't be for an impression that had previously failed him" (*AM,* 317, my emphasis). The italicized phrase suggests that it is only later that "what he had come for" will be settled.)

And this is meant by James, I think, as radically as it sounds: as if a future negotiation among participants could end up determining what could now count as the "real" motive in the past, almost like "backward causation in physics." The idea is not limited to some great epistemological opacity, such that some future insight, some realization dependent on what one later sees that a possible earlier intention would have meant, provides one simply with a best possible view of what such an intention must have been. There just is no such intention we could ever have relied on as causing or occasioning or justifying the act, not one epistemically opaque. There is some way of resolving "what it would have meant to do that," and so some way of working backward toward "what it would have been for me to desire to do it, to be motivated to do it," given what I now know it means, but we are hardly searching for real hidden causes.

This all does seem to be of great philosophical moment in James. It touches on the much-noted "unreliability" of point of view in his fiction. And he takes up the issue and takes it further by treating the problem of resolution or truth-finding as also complexly evaluative (or normative) as well as psychological or factual. When Strether has to assess, and at the same moment, judge – could not understand without judging appropriately – what it is he is to understand in understanding Chad's "attachment" to Madame de Vionnet, there is little question that James himself is fascinated by the question: for just what, exactly, is he is asking himself, and how could he possibly come to answer it? And he treats it just as much as a question of judgment as of any fact of the matter, a judgment secured by no fixed or objective normative standard. Such an assessment must be arrived at, made, in the kind of empty and frighteningly possible world James described as the American legacy in *The American Scene.* (The hope for some fixed standard is what Strether came to Europe with, what Waymarsh and Mrs. Newsome hold on to, and what he soon finds useless.) Or, when Isabel, in James's great midnight fireside scene, finally "understands" that her husband is not what he seemed to her, and we are treated to what looks like a sudden epiphanic "revelation," what are we to make of the fact that the realization, as if in some great lightning flash of truth, still settles absolutely nothing, has no real content, only opens the way to further problems and implications, only complicates rather than resolves the issue of "who" Osmond "really" is (especially since who he is necessarily involves who Isabel is, or was, or now is or will be)? What especially are we to make of the fact that the very idea that there is something to be seen, ferreted out, some secret, some figure in the carpet, some great basic, and consolingly final truth about a life or deep hidden meaning, while an inevitable attraction to scores of Jamesean characters in their frustratingly modern worlds, is just as often treated with the deftest of Jamesean irony (so deft that many readers persist in ascribing to James the quest for such secrets), treated as the great scourge of the characters' lives, a false temptation, the most destructive (*Beast in the Jungle*), sometimes the silliest (*The Sacred Fount*) thing one could believe or hope?

And finally, even in circumstances where unreliability or perplexities are not prominent, and characters seem to have some sense of what they think or intend, James's treatment of the problems of consciousness and sociality is still marked by a number of challenges to individualist and traditional, mentalist frameworks. He portrays how they come to know what they think or what they believe motivates them, in highly complex relations of minds, and not as introspective revelations. Shortly after Part One in *The Golden Bowl,* after the prince and Maggie have been married a while and have had a child, there passes between Adam and his daughter, in the billiard room at Fawn, one of those "mute passages" of meaning for which James is so renowned. Adam "sees" for the first time in Maggie a concern with his own well-being as a distinct individual with a fate now separate from hers, a kind of concern he had not seen before. (After the marriage of his daughter, Adam has lost one of his shields against fortune-hunting women, and he was being pursued by one when Maggie appeared and saw this fact and the future possibilities and the difference it would make in her father's relation to her, all at once. She sees that she sees it, and she sees that he sees her changed perception, again all at once.)

But what is so interesting about this scene is not now so much the issue of uncertainty and unreliability (although these begin to emerge immediately), but the issue of the nature of the dependence of these consciousnesses on each other. At the very moment when this "silent explosion" of revelation occurs, when Adam sees that Maggie sees him now as a newly independent agent in their relation, he suddenly and for the first time realizes this fact and its many possible implications for himself, but again, only through or because of seeing it in her. He became someone, not mildly amused at this silly woman, looking for a room to escape to, but a man with a problem, a new characteristic. "He became aware himself, for that matter, during the minute Maggie stood there before speaking; and with the sense moreover, of what he saw her see, he had the sense of what she saw *him*" (*GB*, 114). Maggie, in other words, also sees that her father sees this in her, realizes that he has seen her view him in this new way, and the implication is that her relation to him will now change because he will see from now on that she has this new concern. She has become someone with a new characteristic, again, all in this mutual flash.

And as if all these gymnastics weren't enough, James doesn't leave it there. For not only do they come to see each other differently through or by means of these perceptions and perceptions of perception, they both come to see how their relation to each other as a couple in the world has altered by seeing that they are both seen in a new way, even though, to risk turning this summary into what might sound like parody, their new relationship consists wholly in what they see of each other's perception and the way in which that is seen, how the way that they understand that altered mutual perception can itself be seen. For Fanny Assingham is there too, and "her (Fanny's) face couldn't keep it from him (Adam); she had seen on top of everything, in her quick way, what they both were seeing" (*GB*, 114).

The most complex example of the way James's apparent presuppositions about consciousness and meaning (what I am suggesting is the social character of intentionality for him) will undergird his account of moral meaning (the unavoidable claim of the other as distinct and free within the living of one's life) occurs at the beginning of Book Second (Chapter XXVII), after the prince and Charlotte have begun their affair and after Maggie has begun to suspect that something is not right in her relations with her husband. Maggie and her father had been planning a private trip together to Spain. Maggie has delayed bringing it up, wanting to keep up her new campaign to win back the prince, appearing to sense that her father would catch the hint. He did, and volunteers that since everyone is getting on so famously, they had better not go. (We don't know if that is what he thinks, if that is what he thinks Maggie thinks and wants to be accommodating, if that is what he thinks that Maggie thinks, but suspects that she is growing concerned about her husband, as if he knows this about what she thinks before she does, or whether he himself suspects the intensity of his wife's and son-in-law's friendship and is moving to protect his wife. All of the above seems the right answer, but, again, there is no way to "check," *even for Adam.*)

In a carriage together on the way home from the party where Adam had declined to go, Maggie and the prince have an amazingly dense, elusive conversation. Something has gone a bit wrong in Maggie's more intense, new dedication to her husband and her social life. Something is a bit too "beatific" (334) in the way Charlotte and the prince refer to a recent time together in the country, and something resists her being a full, adult member of the scene. She begins to sense a hint of pity and condescension in the great "interest" people take in her "as" the wife of Amerigo (as in: how interesting that someone "like her" should be his wife); she even feels "like a dressed doll" passed back and forth.

In the carriage, what we see in Maggie's and the prince's conversation is the beginning of a mutual exploration of where Adam's decision (and Maggie's new involvement) have "left them." Neither of them can be said to "have views" about this. What they both have are views about the possible views of the other, and, however cumbersome to say, views about what the other's views of their own views are. Again, each will have a motive to respond in a certain way, only on some proper anticipation of the other; but each such possible response by the other is just as conditioned by an expectation of the first.

They cannot find a way to break through this uncertainty, to lay down weapons and embrace. Maggie is expecting the prince to express great happiness that he will not be away from her, and propose a vacation himself for the two of them. He does not, and she is puzzled. But the prince can sense this resistance and expectation and doesn't quite know what to make of it. He must be always vigilant not to assume too robustly the role of paid husband, lest he spoil the illusion of mutuality, so he is clearly always cautious about these things. But what Maggie doesn't know of, of course, is that the affair between the prince and Charlotte has begun, and, in the first place, the prince would not be eager to leave Charlotte, or would at least, in his usual way, be uneasy about her possible response. And he is also mindful of Charlotte's subtle advice about successful lying. Don't be too eager to act well and generously lest you look guilty. But, crucially, James lets us see that he hesitates too because he expects Maggie to say something like "Father could see the real reason we shouldn't go. He sees how much in love with you I am, and how much I am enjoying it." She senses that he expects that (and we sense that the prince needs such an expression, though whether in human or strategic terms is never clear) and perversely or defensively, or for some reason, she deliberately withholds any such affirmation, insistently waiting for him to make the first major move. He senses this insistence and doubly hesitates. She senses the hesitation, and so on . . . They thus end up with what are called "crudities of mutual resistance" (*GB*, 342).[18]

These crudities remain throughout the novel, and it ends, I think, in a great moral crash – all precisely because such resistance is never overcome, and the kind of free mutuality necessary to settle such questions of meaning is experienced only by implication and suggestion and absence. This is not a popular view of the ending or of Maggie. Many readers seem to require a heroine out of all this ambiguity, this "milky fog," "white curtain," or "golden mist," as the prince sees it. And Maggie is often therefore read as a Milly Theale with a steel will, someone willing to love and forgive, but not in the transcendent and other-worldly fashion of Milly; rather with a resolve and even a somewhat Machiavellian tolerance of the moral compromises necessary to save in her life what is worth saving. (This elevation of Maggie is also a function of the widespread desire to read the "last" completed novel as functioning like Shakespeare's *Tempest,* some last farewell and final resolution, or at least heroic acceptance of the ambiguities apparently so unresolved and unacceptable in the fate of Isabel, Strether, or Milly. That temptation alone, to some final resolution, in a writer like James, ought to give more pause than it apparently has.)

It is true that Maggie loses a good deal of her innocence, and seems finally to realize that she must choose between an adult life with her husband or a continuation of her infantilized relation to her father. And she chooses. But to think of her "in intention rather like Beatrice in the *Divine Comedy,* the Lady of Theology," who "suffers the pangs of the highest human love,"[19] is quite a stretch, as much as her own rather self-pitying characterization, willing to suffer everything "for love." What love? There is very little substance or passion in this love, at least that we ever see; it is almost always described in terms of the problem of possession and objects, and Maggie's ardor is usually inflamed most when she sees the prince desired by another, ultimately by Charlotte. She is her father's daughter and wants mostly to keep what she has; she wants above all not "to have been" a fool, to assert herself as an equal, especially if it means first tormenting, then destroying, Charlotte. She plays at the role of suffering-for-their-sins Christ even as Adam plays the God the Father role (allusions that ought to alert us to the heavy irony involved). But there is precious little "forgiveness" in her treatment of Charlotte, the apparent satisfaction she takes in it, or the self-serving pity and crocodile-tear guilt with which she congratulates herself and enacts her power. She even goes so far as to encourage the prince and Charlotte, after all they all have been through, to get together one last time, alone, before Charlotte leaves Europe. The insensitivity and *Schadenfreude* in such a gesture is so manifest that it takes a great act of will to admire Maggie for it, to see it as she does, as truly selfless and beneficent. (It is just as hard to see the prince somehow redeemed by this purported forgiveness. Charlotte was his great link to the social world he loved. There is very little evidence that Maggie, however hard and willful she has become, will ever be able to fill that role, being the prim "little nun," "Roman matron," "Madonna," and "doll" she has always been. We can only imagine the prince spending his time as he does when he waits for Charlotte's exile, arranging and rearranging and re-arranging his books.)[20]

And Adam remains as always, a fatuous romantic whose interest in beauty is never shown to have any dimension other than possession. We saw in *The American Scene* that James is willing to note fairly the great benefits, for America, of all this American "plunder," but that need not mean that he admires the current plunderer. America, and the modern moral world it figures, can indeed produce people like Isabel and Milly and Strether, whose willingness to accept the dangers, uncertainties, and pos-sibilities that the new American situation has created is immense and courageous. But it can also produce people like Adam, the aesthetic ana-logue to New England moralists, resistant to such vast changes, looking for consolation in a presumed past (even though, hypocritically, the brutal market economy that underlay such changes made possible his great wealth) or, in the moral analogue, in some religiously inspired moral code, someone who, like Maggie, believes there must be some "real thing" that the Europeans have in their art and culture, beneath all the surfaces and social light and mirror show. Their fatuous confidence that their great wealth allows them simply to "find" it and "buy" it reflects a parallel moralistic view that evil can be discreetly "located," named, and then by force of will and effort, destroyed. (Here, a great American theme; not for nothing is our national epic *Moby Dick*.) Adam's taciturn, reticent ways, his show of generosity but his isolation and aloof bearing, reflect in his almost complete asociality the consequences of such a romantic hope, as does his manipulative, wholly insensitive "wooing" of Charlotte, and in the greatest figure of all for his detachment, his anti-generative, anti-future stance, his unwillingness (or perhaps even incapacity) to have sex with Charlotte.

Said another way, the great final moments of the final great novel are dominated by something always more complex than conversation in a James novel: silence.[21] After Maggie's brief confrontation with the prince when the golden bowl was broken, he tries to see what she might have told Adam, or even what she might actually know (and he is obviously not eager to ask). She tries to see what he might have told Charlotte, or even something of the nature of their affair, what it was, how far it went (and she is not eager to ask); they both wonder what Adam might see. He occupies the same position as throughout the novel, accumulating great power by never really speaking, by being only the silent object of wonder. And hardly anybody says anything to poor Charlotte, who seems the only character in the book capable of generating real human heat.[22]

None of this, though, should suggest that such a judgment about a moral crash is to be taken as James's last word on Maggie's fate. Of course she is a victim, too, has been treated badly by the prince and Charlotte, has been protected to the point of being controlled and manipulated by her father, and if, while she matures, she acquires a certain will and self-consciousness, she remains a defensive, cold, prim little nun, that is certainly not a completely damning moral failing, not simply and absolutely her (moral) fault. Moreover, there is no question that there is also something at stake morally in her rising to a kind of self-assertion, something that would go missing if she were not to react and protest in some way to what has happened to her.[23] As we shall see with Isabel and Strether (and as can easily be seen with characters like Catherine Sloper at the end of *Washington Square,* or Miriam Rooth in *The Tragic Muse,* or in *An International Episode*), James by no means wants to dissolve his characters' identities into the reflecting mirrors of other selves. A kind of integrity or self-possession is also a moral necessity in this moral universe, even in acknowledgment of one's dependence. All of this does, and ought to, affect a reader's judgment.

Moreover, as noted at the outset, the relevance of the moral category, or any claims about moral failure, only get one so far in understanding the end of the novel. It is an indispensable, and real, category; as enacted by the prince and Maggie, their "crudities of mutual resistance," their refusal to acknowledge and enact their dependence is at the heart of a real failure in the story. But all of this also directly introduces different sets of questions not answerable in moral terms. What, for example, is the source of this resistance to mutual engagement, the basis for the silence, even the refusal to love? It is a moral issue of some significance that there is such silence and evasion at the end of the novel. But that phrase of James about mutual resistance clearly invites a psychological question as well. Why the resistance?

Here, too, a moral category might be partly relevant. Such a refusal of another might be explicable in some sense as motivated simply by morally corrupt motives: self-indulgence, vanity, laziness, venal self-promotion. But it is also true that James does not portray his characters in such a morally final way, as if they are only individual examples of moral turpitude. We often know so little about many of them, and see them during such a small slice of time, that it would be hasty to see such moral evaluations as final or definitive. So much of the dramatic framework, too, is so clearly typological, even mythical, rather than stories only about individuals with moral or psychological failures. That "Basic Plot" for so many of the novels from *Washington Square* on (familiar triangle of the heiress, the fortune hunter, and the duplicitous accomplice, all often complicated by the despotic father) is so frequently and confidently invoked that its presence alone implies some ambition toward a repeated or even archetypal pattern of resistance. Some element of the basic Jamesean human drama (especially in its specifically modern framework) makes self-exposure, the risks of love or even moral acknowledgment, difficult, potentially painful, even frightening. (For example, when the tyrannical father is added to the mix (when the triangle is "squared" as in *Washington Square* or *The Golden Bowl*), the suggestion of some original trauma or fear as source of future resistance – that frequent hint of incest or "unspeakable" desire as source of repression – is not negligible.)[24]

The direction suggested by such questions needs to be explored further, if only to place the moral issues in their proper context. But that moral issue is not reduced away by such considerations, and remains easy to identify and summarize one final time: "But if it's something you can't find out, *isn't it as good as if it were nothing?*"

Indeed. I think James rejects the attitude evinced in this question, and that the silence or refusal or mutual resistances that dominate the end of his great novel are meant to show, even so indirectly and elliptically, what is missed by this refusal, always at the same time, a refusal to struggle with others. Given the golden bowl symbol throughout the novel, it is unlikely that we are meant to understand Maggie and the prince as seeing such flaws and accepting them silently and heroically. (In fact the bowl, or the network of social relations uniting their triangle, has long been shattered beyond repair, and what they are deciding to treat "as good as nothing," what they are refusing to acknowledge, is now well beyond what had been a flawed social and family unity.) It is Maggie who has decided to answer the shopkeeper's question with a firm if self-deceived and cowardly "yes." Calling that dimension and that kind of wrong a "moral" one, a refusal to acknowledge a dependence on others without which even an independent life cannot be led, might seem exaggerated, but that is part of what I intend to show in what follows.

More of course must be shown. This is all, admittedly, programmatic and even somewhat formal in its suggested treatment of relations of moral dependence and achieved independence. Resolutions of such conflicts and doubts cannot be postponed forever, and the question of how such resolutions, even collectively achieved and largely retrospective resolutions, could ever occur in such ambiguous contexts must be addressed. And the problem of the relationship between such moral claims, whatever their possible resolution, and the claims, say, of love, or of art, or the temptations of power, also clearly loom large.

For the moment, James's considerations of characters who cannot resist the temptation to think that some fact of the matter, some hidden secret finally revealed, is still the right way to think of such resolution (characters who resist what I have described as modernity itself for James) should be treated next.

NOTES

1. This is the main theme of Mackenzie's book (1976). Although there is a great deal of valuable discussion in this book about the social setting that would produce such anxiety, Mackenzie's framework is mostly psychological. He wants to contrast the experience of shame and the revenge it inspires with the willingness to sacrifice an obsession with "identity," a willingness that can be secured through honor, or with love. His accounts of how characters constantly come to experience that they are not who they thought they were, and what this does to them, are fascinating and very helpful. I am trying to suggest though that James's interest is not in some inevitable failure of honor, mutual respect, or love, but in the contingent and false expectations that instigate such cycles. The kind of intimations of tranquility suggested in the preceding chapter in the discussion of James's modernity theme point to the moral situation and the kind of reconciliation that James wishes to attend to.

2. This is all also doubly, perhaps triply, ironic. First, who knows, even at this early stage, why Kate would want to set up Milly as so divinely independent, what stake she already has in believing that Milly is so free and unaffectable. Second, it is not wholly true. Millie's all too human dependence will soon become obvious. Third, the worry about changing places is all too true, but for a reason Kate does not know and that is wholly, fatally, independent of any power that Milly's money can bring her.

3. Cf. the summary of the views on marriage of Henry James Sr. given by Haviland in Chapter 8 (1997) and her extraordinary animadversions on James Sr. and Lacan.

4. In *The Ambassadors,* Strether feels that being compelled to return to America would be like being "recommitted to Woollett as juvenile offenders are committed to reformatories" (*AM,* 201). Chad also remarks about his compatriots: "They're children; they play at life!" (*AM,* 203). Cf. also, in *The American,* this formulation of the problem: "In America, Newman reflected, lads of twenty-five and thirty have old heads and young hearts, or at least young morals; here they have young heads and very aged hearts, morals the most grizzled and wrinkled" (*A,* 79).

5. Cf. also a similar discussion in *The Awkward Age,* after Mr. Longdon had asked Nanda, "What you suggest is that the things you speak of depend upon other people?" Her response indicates James's awareness of the historical as well as the social character of

such dependence, and of how deep the dependence goes. The "her" in question in the following is Nanda's grandmother, Lady Julia, an almost mythic figure of nostalgia in the novel for the "lost time" of premodern sensibilities. Nanda says, "If we're both partly the result of other people, *her other people were so different*" (*AA*, 141, my emphasis). And in a formulation with a perfect Jamesean grammatical pitch: "Granny wasn't the kind of girl she couldn't be – and so neither am I" (*AA*, p. 141). Perhaps the best figure for the problem James is getting at occurs in *The Ambassadors* in the famous "live all you can speech" in Gloriani's garden, discussed in Chapter Six.

6.  I don't mean to suggest that James simply identifies with Madame Merle's views (they already hint at her self-serving cynicism); just that her remarks introduce the framework within which James understands the problem, and especially the problem of Isabel's contrasting innocence and willfulness.

7.  Interestingly, the position James could be said to be opposing is often expressed in William James's individualism, and his claim that we speak not of that thought but "my thought, every thought being owned." James (1983), p. 221. This, and much else, is pointed out and developed in persuasive detail in one of the best recent books on James, Posnock (1991). A first pass at a statement of disagreement: Posnock, like Cameron in note 12, states James's aesthetic and ethic in terms still too indebted to Adorno, too captivated by the importance of some "negative" moment in James's picture of modern life, as if the irruption of some ineffable, "inevitable deviation," the "illegible," or "unassimilable particularity" shows the eternal impossibility of any "totalized" modern, instrumentalist, commercialized world. I disagree with this picture of Jamesean redemption as, or at least mostly as, some commitment to "nonidentity thinking," or the "mimetic," or as transgression, violation of limits, excess, and so on. (This is true even if one concedes Posnock's point that Mead, Dewey, Adorno, and Henry James can be read as attempts "to socialize the Jamesean (W.)/Bergsonian abandonment of identity logic," p. 136) For all the greater historical and social sensitivity captured by Posnock's picture, and for all his attempts to differentiate himself from approaches like Trilling's (cf. p. 83), such a negative dialectic still shares too much of Trilling's original high modernist celebration of ambiguity as the great ideal of the truly liberal imagination.

8.  Even many of the older criticisms of James have been given new and more interesting life under such influences. For example, on the issue of consciousness and the supposed limitations of James's treatment (an issue as old as Gide's frustration), Bersani (1969), especially in pp. 128–155, "The Jamesian Lie," claims that James is "remarkably resistant to an interest in psychological depth." This forms the basis for his criticisms of the achievements of James's fiction, summarized in the following extreme reading: "The mind of the Jamesean center of consciousness is free in the sense that it invents and satisfies desires which meet only a minimal resistance from either the external world or internal depths. Language would no longer be principally a reflection or sublimation of given desires; it would promote new versions of being (p. 146)." This, he says, "re-enslaves consciousness in James," because "intelligence detached from psychology traces designs that belong to no one . . ." and "the absorption of character into language can also be the dehumanization of desire" (p. 146). This view seems based on a (purported, Jamesean) view of language itself as a kind of "neutral territory," "always 'outside' any particular self" (ibid.). This is most definitely not James's view of language or intelligence, I want to show; he sees it much more as a social practice among selves, rather than a "system" outside selves, and the Jamesean "I" is

most definitely always and everywhere "limited," and radically dependent – on other such selves in a constant enactment of a struggle for mutuality that resonates with moral claims and thereby, most definitely, with a distinctly human desire.

9. For a fine discussion of this and other similar phenomena, see the essay by van Frassen (1988), pp. 123–57, especially pp. 125–7.

10. This represents a sea change in the terms with which attacks and defenses of James often took place. The old criticism was usually that James's interests were so fastidiously formal, epistemological, and hyperreflective (as if James should count as a peculiar sort of ethnic fiction for wealthy Wasps, an altar for the living dead, the neurotic New England pale faces) that nothing human was left over. One of the most well-known examples: F.R. Leavis's discontent with *The Golden Bowl*, as expressed in his (1954), p. 196. Or: "Magnificent pretensions, petty performances! – the fruits of an irresponsible imagination, or a deranged sense of values, of a mind working in a void, uncorrected by any clear consciousness of human causes and effects," in the words of Van Wyck Brooks (1925), an extreme critic, not, apparently at all sympathetic to the Jamesean, or at least "later," Jamesean adventure. Brooks is certainly not alone in such judgments, and the company is, at least in terms of influence, important: Granville Hicks, Charles Beard, V. L. Parrington, Marxist or Marxist-inspired critiques like Terry Eagleton's or Frederick Jameson's, all the way to mindless attacks like Maxwell Geismar's, Habbeger's, and on and on. (Of course, with Pound, Eliot, Fitzgerald, Edmund Wilson, Richard Blackmur, and, later, Dupee, Quentin Anderson, and Lionel Trilling on his side, James did not go undefended. But those defenses locked him into the High Modernist Culture Camp that only perpetuated, this time favorably, many of the James Myths.) There is a fine guide through the thickets of such conventional accounts in Chapter Three of Posnock (1991) (which also makes an excellent case against the "narrow, dualistic and repetitive" form of the old "Jacobite" vs. "anti-Jacobite" battle over James).

11. Thus, consider Wayne Booth's remarks (about the unreliable narrator in *The Aspern Papers*) that "Again and again in the story one is forced to throw up his hands and decide that James has simply provided insufficient clues for the judgments which he still quite clearly expects us to be able to make." Booth (1962), p. 361. But there are no "clues" and there can't be. There is no "figure in the carpet" or "real thing" to be found. This again does not mean there is just moral skepticism everywhere in James. That absence is precisely the moral point, precisely what binds us together in a distinctly normative dependence. Or such is my thesis here.

12. One of the most interesting of such contemporary discussions (and a valuable guide through many others) is Cameron (1989). Cameron is a persuasive critic of the psychologically realist reading of James (even James's own in his Prefaces). She makes interesting use throughout of spatial metaphors in analyzing, mainly, *The American Scene, What Maisie Knew, The Golden Bowl*, and *The Wings of the Dove*, to show that James, despite what he says, does not portray consciousness as "stable, subjective, interior" or as "unitary," p. 77. I think she is quite right to say, and will try also to defend, such things as, "For in the novels consciousness is disengaged from the self. It is reconceived as extrinsic, made to take shape – indeed to become social – as an intersubjective phenomenon" (p. 77). However valuable, though, the spatial framework throughout makes it easier for Cameron to defend claims about where consciousness isn't, about what always "exceeds" any "container" view of awareness and so forth, than they can contribute to James's positive view. We don't get a richer sense of what James is trying to

show us – how that "in between" where real consciousness exists gets established and sustained within the mutual reflections and corrections, and the mutual caring and normative constraints, constitutive of modern social life. Cameron is thus quite right, I think, at p. 175, to criticize phenomenological readings of James like Paul Armstrong's (1983), but also right to suspect that "earlier" forms of a phenomenology, like Hegel's, might provide a model both of a less subject-centered and more morally rich intersubjectivity. That is partly what I am trying to show here. A consequence of this problem: When faced herself with the problem of meaning and its shareability (given all the many things it cannot be in James), Cameron resorts to what is, finally, a familiar formula of untrustworthy speech, impenetrable thought, and "therefore" the "imposition" of meaning (p. 108). This is how, especially, she treats Maggie. In the view I am presenting, by contrast, it is not because "we are unable to sustain the idea of meaning as a question" that we "moralize about the novel, see its thematic as one of morality, which is an ultimate act of codifying the arbitrariness of our interpretation by making a special case for its inevitability" (p. 120). It is rather precisely because of our acknowledgment, in reading the novel, and the characters' realization in living, of the unavailability of individually owned, discoverable, even hidden or secret meaning that morality – a certain sort of acknowledgment of our dependence on others and their entitlements – arises unavoidably in the first place.

13. One curious aspect of this novel is that James doesn't give us much of Charlotte, not compared with that other "contemporary London female, highly modern, inevitably battered, honorably free" Kate Croy in *The Wings of the Dove*, p. 40. But her similarity, both to the modernity, and therewith to the moral complexity, of Kate, is obvious, and functions much the same way: to raise the question of where moral constraints are supposed to come from, how they are supposed to apply to characters like this, why even they should acknowledge them. (With Kate, James lets us see the Condrips, gives us the smell of boiled meat in Marion's little room, the "greasy children," and much more to prepare us for this question.)

14. There are scores of other such passages one could pick for illustration. An especially brilliant treatment is given at the beginning of *The Wings of The Dove*, as Milly begins, playfully at first, to speculate on what it meant, now means, that her fast new intimate friend Kate never mentioned a word about her much-frowned-upon relation to Densher. This quickly becomes entangled in the question of why Densher, when he saw them in America, did not let on that he was so attached, and acted, even if slightly, as if free to "call on" Milly under other assumptions. Both gaps then raise the question of what it would now mean to raise either or both of such issues with Kate, when it would then become, as an event, inevitably shadowed by Kate's realization that Milly would now be raising the issue in the light of her (Kate's) not having done so. Kate's silence, then, is not to be "explained" or understood by reference to a hidden, eventually discovered motive at that time, even a self-deceived one. What it would be "now" to assign such a motive "then" determines, in some way retrospectively and in some joint linkage among them all, several elements of the supposed fact of the matter "then" that commonsensically should settle the matter. (The simplest Jamesean account of all of this is that Kate really did not know why she kept silent, and might be said to be herself "waiting" to find out.)

15. After Charlotte and the prince return to London from a time together in the country, during which their affair has begun, Maggie has begun to sense that something is not quite right in her relationship with the prince. She tells herself that the problem is her

own over-zealous attention to her father, that she has let the prince assume that she expects him to play only a marginal role in her life. She resolves to correct this by attending to the prince much more zealously. What is happening, what her new attention means, could be described in any number of ways: as it appears, some evidence of marital drift, with incomplete evidence for why, with Maggie forming a reasonable but far too innocent a hypothesis. Or self-deceit. Maggie is already intimidated by and somewhat jealous of Charlotte's clothes and worldliness, and must sense the differences in the prince's reactions to Charlotte and to the "little," "prim" "nun like" Maggie, but she keeps from herself a full formulation of what she knows. Or Maggie only now begins to want the prince when she realizes he is desired by her "rival" and in some true sense of the word, stepmother. (God knows how complicated this could be: In pulling the prince away from Charlotte, she is proving that she is more desirable than the woman who sleeps with her father?) The same problems emerge in explaining her motives in asking everyone who was at Matcham (in the country) for all the details. In some sense, while she tells herself that this is part of her new strategy of more intense involvement in the prince's life, she is also clearly checking the stories against one another, but also just as clearly doesn't know that, or won't let herself admit it, and so on. But any of these sorts of explanations would, I think, presume something not yet there, something of Maggie's own sense of who she is, where she fits in, what is at stake in her marriage, what she wants. She doesn't have hidden, or self-deceived, or unconscious views about any of these. She has no possible views, and must enter this intensely sophisticated world of supremely intelligent mirrors and lights and shadows in order to form views. This is particularly manifest in the incredible carriage scene described later.

16. One effect of this sort of ambiguity is that James ends up making far greater and far different sorts of demands on the reader than almost any other novelist. Not only is it "hard" to figure out what is going on, James, in effect, keeps hinting that he doesn't know either, and rather invites us to enter the novel as characters, often giving us figures for The Reader, like Fanny here, or Maria Gostrey, or Henrietta Stackpole, or Susan Shepard Stringham, while showing us through them how easy it is to get things wrong. (This partly explains the unusual tone, or at least I find it unusual, of so much criticism of James, a kind of foot-stomping impatience with all the supposed fussiness and folderol.) And this fact – how much trust James asks for, with so little promised – touches again the question of moral reality in his books. This is the hardest issue to state properly, but by far the most important. That is, again: The fact that there can be no final fact of the matter to settle everything (one of the implications of his historical theme) does not mean that is the whole question of "getting it right" is hopeless, or ends in skepticism. I will say more about this, in bits and pieces, throughout the analysis that follows in the next three chapters.

17. This question can be used just as well to dramatize the issue in *The Wings of the Dove:* It is in effect Kate's question to Merton about Milly. What is wrong, she wants to know, if we are happy and she can't find the flaw, or dies before she can? I don't think there is any question that James is treating such an attitude as a wrong, and the interesting issue is why he thinks that, what else he must be committed to in order to believe it. It has, I am suggesting, something to do with the loss we suffer when others are so treated, the way the absence of such free, opposing other subjects (an absence we often engineer) turns our own aspirations and projects into self-contained fantasies that cannot be satisfying.

18. Although I am making heavy use here of *The Golden Bowl* to make these points about consciousness and motivation, I should also take note of the great interest the book inspires in James's moral or ethical outlook in general. I am thinking especially of Martha Nussbaum's (1990a) and (1990b) and Olafson (1988). Since I find the ending of *The Golden Bowl* a moral as well as a personal disaster for all four of the principals, my disagreements with Nussbaum's reading, and with the ethical ideal she sees finally evinced in Maggie (see p. 134, but see also Nussbaum's later discussion in (1995)), would require much more space than a footnote in order to do the disagreement justice. The same would be true for my disagreements with Brudney's attempt (1990) to defend Maggie's "tact." (Both Nussbaum and Brudney are defending a reading of Maggie long a fixture of pro-realist literary criticism of the 1950s and 1960s. See Sabin (1998), p. 223, and compare Posner's helpful skepticism, Posner (1998), pp. 315–8.)

    I agree with Olafson's claim (1988) that the novel's resolution still rests on a tissue of lies, that this is bad and understood by James to be bad, and that one need not be either soft-hearted about what a successful marriage requires, or a narrow moralist, to see why such a state is unacceptable (pp. 303–312). But in exploring the question of how James shows us just what is wrong in Kate Croy's and Maggie's actions, Olafson relies on Kantian and even Habermasean criteria of publicity and the conditions of communication that do not fit James's use of the International Theme (or rather on transcendental concerns that do not fit with James's historical understanding of modern moral life), nor the more radical conceptions of consciousness and meaning that underlie his moral sense. Or so I am trying to show.

19. Blackmur (1983) , p. 51.

20. For a discussion of the differences in the critical literature, especially with respect to Charlotte, see Sabin (1987), pp. 65–81. Sabin's later discussion of the ending (1998) is also valuable, especially her very effective counter to Edel, Holland, and others who see Maggie's lie as (with Edel) "constructive," the "lies by which civilization can be held together." Sabin is quite right that this sounds like, and sounds as empty as, the lie at the end of Conrad's *Heart of Darkness,* and her general case against such readings is quite effective.

21. I take seriously here Mackenzie's point in Chapter IV of (1976) that there is a kind of knowledge obtained by James's characters that cannot be shared or spoken at all. There is indeed much that is and must be unspoken in Isabel's resolve or Strether's decision, or in *What Maisie Knew,* for that matter. But here James seem so intent on treating this sort of silence not as an acknowledgment of the simply unsayable, as a way of not knowing what one knows, or as a wise way to avoid a scandal and preserve a marriage, but, as noted, as "crudities of mutual resistance," a pretense to hide in plain sight. It is true that this reading breaks the string of heroic Americans like Isabel and Strether and Milly, but I have tried to show how dark are the shadows around Adam's collecting and pretensions and Maggie's egoism, as these are both painted by James.

22. The problem remains, as it was very early, in 1878 with *Daisy Miller,* or in 1880 in *Confidence,* the possibility of trust, confidence, a fundamental acknowledgment and acceptance of the other, all in a way consistent with the ideal of a free life. One sometimes hears that James simply did not believe such trust was possible, that all love was a zero-sum game, someone gaining, someone losing. (Bell (1991) comes close to this often.) What is more interesting, I think, is that James treats the aspiration to such mutuality, however difficult, unlikely or risky, as unavoidable in any attempt at a free or independent life, and that he does not treat the failure of such hopes as due to the

nature of things, as if human love is subject to some cruel cosmic fate. It is essential to note that the questions of equality and mutuality are also treated as reflections of the modern problem of money and power, and that these issues are treated historically and so contingently, not essentially, or as if products of some psychological necessity.

23. The situation is complex enough certainly to justify Dorothea Krook's interesting strategy (1962): one chapter "for Maggie," one "against" her. I see the point, but that goes too far, as argued before. (This split-the-difference or flip-flopping about Maggie is not unusual in the literature and betrays some understandable anxiety about the moral point of view itself. The cases of Nussbaum and Krook have already been mentioned. Perhaps the clearest example is that of Blackmur's two Prefaces, to the Grove edition of 1952 (very pro-Maggie, from which the Beatrice quotation cited earlier is taken) and to the Laurel edition in 1963 (very much the contrary.) (1983, p. 147 ff., and p.221 ff.) The latter also, I think, still fails to get it right, since it is based on a harsh and inaccurate understanding of the place of morality in James's assessment of his characters.

24. In a paper on *Washington Square,* Bette Howland (1996) has shown in detail how important this basic triangle is in the most important of James's novels, and how variations on it work. I am much indebted to this article.

# 4

## BEASTS, SECRETS, AND GHOSTS

"My best McGuffin, and by that I mean the emptiest, the most non-existent, and the most absurd is the one we used in *North by Northwest* . . . the McGuffin has boiled down to its purest expression: nothing at all."

Alfred Hitchcock[1]

"Das Sein – ein McGuffin"

Hans Blumenberg[2]

### I

James gives his characters a setting, and has them confront kinds of problems that suggest his own complex claims about the social world they inhabit and about his views of its historical novelty. A major recurring element in this complex is a certain kind of threat to the possibility of their being able to understand and rely on each other, an indeterminacy or unresolveability about some elements of practical meaning, the elements one needs in order to be able to count on others or commit oneself to anything. In the simplest sense, this is about being able to understand the dimensions and implications of my own and others' intentions well enough to promise, expect, blame, and especially trust, to fulfill the minimum conditions of any social world. As we have seen, sometimes this incomprehension is a result of stupidity or a self-serving refusal to comprehend. As we shall see in this chapter, sometimes it also results from an inability or a refusal to understand the threat itself, an attempt to rely on means of resolution and determination no longer available. (In *The Turn of the Screw*, a kind of rage to understand takes over in the face of this threat, demanding to the point of insanity and death that questions be resolved, no matter what.) But in such cases too, the deeper source of the difficulty itself is not simply the result of individual failure in the normal sense or obstinacy or a disastrous insistence, or at least not exclusively so (the failure to understand is almost always itself a complex of motives and conditions).[3]

This can sound like a far-fetched danger. We seem to be able to get each other right enough of the time to catch planes, coordinate meetings, show up in the same classroom, and so on. But obviously there is understanding someone, and then there is understanding *someone*. And the suspicion that at any significant level of understanding, we fail more than we succeed, or perhaps always fail, is not so far-fetched.[4] What is interesting about James's worry is that rather than invoking the failures of individuals, or the depressing nature of fundamental human limitations, James intimates that this anxiety is a specifically modern one, that it arises because a certain kind of deep agreement in a form of life has failed, the kind of agreement and orientation at play when such expectations, promises, and especially inferences were successfully undertaken. "Europe" has "died," exists only as "the murmur of extinguished life."[5]

This is, of course, a wider and much, much more controversial set of claims than James's mere intimations could ever justify. It goes to the issue of whether and if so how a certain community could be said to suffer something like a loss of meaning, in the way we sometimes speak of that happening to an individual. We usually mean thereby that some teleological structure has lost its authority for the individual and no longer seems, or is experienced as, worthy of allegiance. A hierarchy of ends, whereby this was important for that, and that for some higher goal, and so on, has broken down in some way, or some crucial element in it has failed (can no longer command allegiance) and caused all else to topple over. Accordingly, the desires animated by and animating such a structure have also simply failed. It is not easy to find the words to describe how such a thing could happen (that nothing could now seem "worth wanting"), but it would be foolish to deny it happens. Melancholy of such a sort is not unknown in the fiction, drama, and poetry of the late modern world. And while it is admittedly controversial and quite abstract to begin to use the same language to describe what might happen when some common structure of ends, or teleological complex of ideals, loses its social authority for a whole community, anyone reading literature from, let's say Hölderlin to David Mamet, would have a hard time not making use of some such language. This situation in James is no less grim if so many of his characters ignore it or deny it, no less ominous if his language is not apocalyptic.

In the settings James describes, I have been suggesting that either reliance on some older set of conventions and expectations somehow loses its power to orient, inform, explain (sometimes in ways unnoticed by those still relying on it) or some new form of life is as yet or in itself insufficient to orient or help resolve the problems of interpretation without which reliable relations of trust and dependence cannot be formed. European traditions and American modernity often do duty for these alternatives.

Yet none of this is set out as a prelude either for an extreme reactionary position or for a radical moral skepticism. Here again, though, James of course is a novelist; he provides no theory about either why such mutual dependencies and acknowledgments, or morality itself, is still experienced as practically unavoidable, or how contested questions of meaning and the imputation of intention could ever get resolved in such a setting. He does show, with characters like Madame Merle or Kate Croy, or Charlotte Stant or John Marcher, what is lost, what goes so fundamentally missing that the possibility of leading one's own life at all goes missing, when such claims are ignored or when the new difficulties in understanding are simplified. This is not quite the right way to put it either because it sounds like it is all an attempt to give us (by showing) a reason to behave well (otherwise these unpleasant things are likely, and so on). That would presume a model of subjectivity and reflection, though, a model of reflective subjects who stand apart from possible courses of action that could be "theirs," and decide on the basis of reasons which such courses of action shall be. In some sense, that sort of thing happens all the time, of course, but at the level of generality we are now discussing, it is an extremely artificial and even fantastic way of looking at how a course of life "gets" to be mine ("by my deciding on it"). Nevertheless, there is something to the claim that James can "show" how much is lost, what else can't be done, what simply cannot be understood, if such claims by others are rejected. Since he is not trying to change anybody's mind by offering reasons, how all of this should be understood in relation to a philosophical theory or in relation to the kind of reason that might be able actually to convince someone to constrain his interest in an acceptance of such a claim can be left for another discussion.

In other words, a certain kind of reliability in the claims at issue between characters is the problem, and not just because these characters must always suspect duplicity or deceit. As they engage each other, they must make serious, wide-ranging assumptions about fundamental interpretative possibilities, and they must do so without much of a basis, for reasons we have already discussed. They must often "wait" to see if the reactions and counterinterpretations of others bear out such assumptions. (Said more simply, they must often act without knowing what they are doing or why, not simply in ignorance of their motives.) But this reliability question is always also a question for them. Some avoid it in solipsism and often egoism, a self-certifying but deadly smugness. Some revert to traditional social forms of understanding or narrow moralistic categories. Some aestheticize everything. Others, though, see ghosts, or become obsessed with secrets, and in those stories, the question of reliability, truth, and James's interests in a subjective idealism about meaning come together in a particularly forceful way. Those stories, and the ones about secrets, lost papers, or hidden meanings, all raise again the question of who someone really is, or was, or what an author finally, really meant, or in the most famous (*The Turn of the Screw*), what "really" happened, all in ways that will raise again not just the question of reliability (especially in one's presentation of a self-identity) but possible resolvability, and the link between that issue and the moral question.

II

The lead character in the 1903 tale *Beast in the Jungle,* John Marcher, could not be called James's most ironically or flamboyantly named character, not with competitors like a "Marquise de Cliche" from *The Reverberator* or the unbelievable "Ulick" from "The Pupil" in the running. But the irony is clear, even heavy, enough. The last thing poor John Marcher does is "march" anywhere, not toward any goal, not even just for show. He is part of no parade or army, not even part of a business, a group, a family. (In the story's second sentence, we are told that in his view at least, he is always "lost in the crowd.") He does not even drift or stroll; he simply waits, and the importance and pain, for him, of such waiting assume a kind of biblical proportion. We first meet him as he heads into middle age, and so his name also, together with that of an acquaintance from ten years earlier, "May" Bartram, together with the time when they meet again (October), together with the name of the house where they meet (Weatherend), all call to mind the temporal frame for the story, and eventually suggest that spring season of youth, March/May, has, for him, become only a terribly "stalled" time, all the more obvious and poignant as it now begins to pass him (them) by, as the end of all weather, or turbulence, or the end of life itself, is in sight.

Moreover, the first scene in the story – his meeting again at a "historical" house on display for tourists an acquaintance whom he met very casually ten years before – also gently suggests the larger historical themes (the modernity theme especially) discussed earlier, and so gives a larger significance to the theme of stalled time and the image of waiting. The decisive reencounter is set in a house taken out of time, where the displayed objects give themselves up to "mysterious appreciations and measurements." Something like the latter is apparently more in order than the former, given that the tourists are described as moving about "as with the emphasis of an excited sense of smell" (*Be*, 277) and that Marcher's companions do not so much appreciate the "poetry and history" that press on Marcher (causing him, instructively, to wander alone) but are better compared to "dogs sniffing at cupboards." The house and form of life it represents is not marching forward either; it simply sits, as if waiting, for appreciators it cannot find. If Weatherend is really the setting for the story of Marcher's waiting and opens the question of what that waiting means, then the setting itself figures some sort of deeply stalled history, and thus must count as a bizarre, very harsh opening image: a European scene or context (or at least the one that had poetry and history) now only to be visited, not lived in, visited by would-be appreciators who rather resemble dogs sniffing about. Marcher, for all his pathos and self-deceit and pomposity, at least stands apart at the beginning, by being alone, by having some sense that there is or was here "poetry and history." (This all prefigures both his distinctness and pathos in the main narrative. He senses that the ordinariness of his life would swallow him up were it not possible to hold on to some secret meaning or fate. This redemptive meaning must be temporal, not transcendent or stoic; it must be some real, coming event that can put the past in its right context, as preparation and setting for this moment. But it cannot be sought or worked for. That would require that we know what it is. We don't and cannot know such a thing; hence the unformed, indeterminate wait for some "beast.")

This setting and the somewhat abstract, almost metaphysical treatment of the "waiting" theme introduce anti-romantic, ironic "reverse-quest" images that will recur in later modernist literature, from Eliot's missing *Fisher King*, to Kafka's *The Trial*, to the obvious Beckett play, and will pull together, condense, and reverse a number of conventional Christian themes, especially the idea of a redemptive moment in time, a future coming that will redeem and make whole all past time (the idea of redemption so important for the modern notion of revolution). James's irony about such redemptive hopes is as thick as other modernist treatments, an irony that replays and undermines the very self-image of modernity itself as "what had been waited for," as the putative decisive leap of the historical beast. Marcher stands, of course, on the other side of such a redemptive aspiration. His unique sort of expectation and fear of the future is what robs him of the traditional hero's (or revolutionary's) role and makes him so much a figure for such ironically self-consciousness modernism: he knows that a courageous man ought to know "what he's afraid of – or not afraid of? I don't know that, you see. I don't focus it. I can't name it. I only know I'm exposed" (*Be,* 292). A fine modernist, perhaps even Heideggerean, sentiment.

On a conventional reading, though, James's ironic treatment of this man Marcher is the main thing. It is a case study – James at work portraying a type. In this case, Marcher's hesitancy to live, his feeling that he is destined for something so disruptive he must only wait, that something awful and huge will eventually happen to him and greatly distinguish him, that some beast will finally leap from the jungle, all are often taken to reflect a psychologically explicable resistance to life itself. On such a reading, this may be the most dramatic and extreme treatment of the Strether Problem, the problem of those characters whom some ironic self-consciousness, or illness, or aesthetic distance and awareness, or moral scruple or unconscious self-loathing or just bad luck have removed from the partiality and violence and great flow of life itself and who must sit on the sidelines and either observe or wait; who, like poor Catherine Sloper or perhaps James himself in his moments of self-pity, must return to their "morsel of fancy-work – for life, as it were." In this case, Marcher waits rather than lives, we are told, because such waiting is an expression of a kind of weakness or woundedness, a constitutional inability to live and love. He would simply much rather wait than live, all in the self-deceived expectation that he must be ready, cannot tie himself down or take much pleasure in any present. His reaction to the offer of love clearly made to him by the patient, long-suffering May is simply fear. His own suspicion of his egotism or even narcissism in using the excuse of his great expectation to keep her at arm's length, and yet in making use of her companionship and love (with only an occasional perfunctory regard for what such a wait must mean for her), draws any reader's attention immediately to this palpably real fear, rationalization, self-deceit, and pathos. When it turns out that May has guessed his secret (or seems to believe that she has guessed it) and that she believes that it has already occurred (or so he believes), and when finally he thinks that his great fate was to have been the one man in existence to whom nothing ever happened, any reader going through the story the first time naturally falls into Marcher's point of view, takes his claim (and his bitter self-reproach) about his pathetic fate at face value, and begins to reflect on the psychological causes that might have led to such a destructive fantasy. And, as noted, coupled with the usual doubts about James's celibacy, his treatment of the renunciation or loneliness theme in characters like Catherine Sloper, Isabel, and especially Strether (who does seem some sort of echo of Marcher and the "missed life" or life-too-late theme), we do then seem led back to some "reflection vs. life" issue, or fear of sex and of the messiness and dependence of intimacy, or even, more recently, homosexual panic, all as the psychological source of Marcher's self-suspicions and consequent self-renunciation.

It is certainly true that here, as in so many stories, James's Picasso-like talent for sketching, with the fewest details, a full, real character whom we care about even as we criticize is, with both May and Marcher, on full display. Yet it is also true that we know even less about Marcher and May than we know about other characters sketched so quickly and dropped into some dramatic setting. Relatives, other friends, confidants, money, business affairs, and even most of daily life (apart from a few dinners and opera trips) have been stripped away, giving the story a much more mythic and hardly psychological frame. Marcher's sense that he must wait, that he is being "kept for something rare and strange, possibly prodigious and terrible" (*Be,* 282), is idiosyncratic in the extreme and faintly comic. Of course, it makes us ask what led this particular man to such an absurd fantasy of self-importance, such a destructive asceticism, so like a religious prophet's, except for the one thing without which the prophet's waiting would also be faintly comic: an idea of what he is waiting for.

Yet, as noted, there is very little psychologically to work with, and it would be hasty to leap to a full psychological reading, a Jamesean treatment of that "resistance to life" or a resistance to love that is supposed to function like some universal *explicans* in so many contexts. For the historical frame with which the story begins, and the odd (and as far as I can tell, largely undiscussed) fact that May, for most readers a paragon of patience, understanding, and sanity, believes him, believes this nearly insane scenario (and not ironically, or as if just to wait the poor fellow out), all suggest a different and more general ambition than a psychological typology.

It is that setting and also the problem of memory that suggest different issues. They met first, ten years before, amid ruins as well, though the ruins of an extinct, and (presumably) possibly still active volcano, Pompeii (suggesting, obviously, both the sparks that flew between them then and the depths at which they remained buried). And they must, in an odd dance with each other, struggle to build a common memory of what happened and ultimately what it meant that it happened. (May knows instinctively that what happened between them won't mean what it now could, if Marcher is simply told the facts by her.) Marcher is thirty-five now, and has carried around this fantasy of his future for at least that long, revealing it only one single time in his life, to May, in the casual way travelers often speak with exhilarating frankness to each other. But although she looks vaguely familiar to him, he doesn't remember this unusual, distinct fact. In fact, his difficulties with time and memory (he knows he has met her, but gets all the places and people wrong) again begin to suggest larger problems with historical time and this historical time in particular. The current episode, for example, "affected him as the sequel of something of which he had lost the beginning. He knew it, and for the time quite welcomed it, *as a continuation, but didn't know what it continued*" (*Be*, 278, my emphasis). This formulation has a suggestive air, a faint invitation to a reading with a more archetypal ambition. (The house itself, the present age, the scene, is itself some sort of "continuation," for all the ruptures and revolutions, a continuation we have to be able to put together and live through in order to live at all, however poorly that is being accomplished by all the "sniffers." Marcher's waiting and hesitation might not be so idiosyncratic, as with his tendency to forgetfulness, his inability to remember, to place in any narrative, even the most unusual and meaningful of his past adventures. One might, in such a situation, come to hope that that house's past and one's own might be connected to some future that would make it possible for the past to be properly recollected and "carried forward.") Not for nothing does James connect the slow flood of memories over Marcher, finally reanimating his connection with May, to the spread of evening light over the objects *in the house*, a figure for the possible reanimating of their meaning through the right kind of memory, all in this era when any future depends first on the right kind of recollection.

> It was in the way the autumn day looked into the high windows as it waned; in the way the red light, breaking at the close from under a low, somber sky, reached out in a long shaft and played over old wainscots, old tapestry, old gold, old colour (*Be,* 278).

But May remembers the facts perfectly, although, wisely, she does not pretend simply to possess the meaning of what she remembers. "She had not lost it, but she wouldn't give it back to him, he saw, without some putting forth of his hand for it" (*Be,* 278). This already suggests themes of mutuality and dependence we have seen before, although it would be too soon to say that May understands that she can't just "give" him this past memory, that whatever it is and whatever it means that he spoke so to her depends on them both (is "in between" them and unformed yet) and so also depends on what will happen next.

However, even after the factual enlightenment, Marcher still cannot recall the revelation of his great secret, testimony to the powers of repression in his psyche, and this fact is still puzzling, as puzzling as May's immediate, wholehearted trust. In fact, James's treatment of the recollection and the beginning of the narrative proper in the story is quite striking. It is, first, interesting that Marcher is relieved that what she remembers and he doesn't is not some expression of love or a romantic episode at all (as we shall see, for Marcher, love is not enough to redeem the ordinariness he seems so afraid of, and later he seems to understand any shared fate as a diminution of his own distinctness) and that they both keep getting their personal pronouns confused (they stumble over "who has lived away from who they were," an initial presentiment of their deepest problem: distinguishing what will happen to Marcher from what will happen to her). For the story is just as much about the failure of May's offer of love (and so about something else hard to integrate into a reading of Marcher: that May also waits and in effect wastes her life) as it is about Marcher's expectation that some determinate sense to his life, an answer to the question of who he is and what he is "for" can be found, delivered up to him somehow. It is largely the latter, I suggest, that is responsible for the former, a theme and a link so often at issue in the secret and ghost stories, especially "The Figure in the Carpet," "The Aspern Papers," "The Jolly Corner," and with the greatest complexity and self-consciousness, *The Turn of the Screw.* These are stories, I suggest, that all portray different kinds of resistance to the situation of modernity itself, as James understands it, a failure to appreciate and acknowledge how the "continuities" Marcher only senses must be made out and sustained, or a failure to acknowledge the kind of dependencies and the appropriate forms of mutuality without which life cannot now be led. Because the deepest and most dangerous expressions of such reciprocity – trust and faith-keeping – are romantic ones, the resistance in question has its most disastrous results there.

Put another way, May does trust and believe Marcher and could help build the continuity Marcher seeks in himself and between them, and so she figures also this possibility historically, what is needed for these autumnal shades and light to be "May" again. (Although again, some aspect of her unusual authority in the story seems to be her realization that the only thing to wait for is the realization, the acknowledgment, that there is nothing to wait for, that it has always already happened, and the question is one's reaction, not one's expectation.) Not for nothing is she the official guide to the "meaning" of the objects of the house (although she can leave such a museum and, after the death of her aunt, take up residence in the contemporary world too); not for nothing are their activities together trips to the National Gallery and the South Kensington Museum, or their conversations so much about Italy and its ruins. (This is the backward journey, the attempted recovery that May seems to understand, as she "waits" patiently for Marcher to stop waiting; Marcher can only pretend to himself that it all is a journey, no longer stalled at the headwaters, but pushed off and flowing with the current.)

As just suggested, although the question of what gives May the kind of authority she has in the story, despite her complicity with the fantasy (apart from the inevitably favorable contrast with poor Marcher), is a complex one, there are early and late indications that she believes Marcher's intimations of a Great Coming Event because she believes it has already happened. The secret is, as it so often is, hidden in plain sight. "Isn't what you describe perhaps but the expectation – or at least, at any rate, the sense of danger, familiar to so many people – of falling in love?" (*Be,* 283).

As the story develops, we see that the right formulation here would be: to have been loved devotedly and selflessly, really loved. But if this were the Beast, it wouldn't have the temporal character that Marcher wants or demands; it would only begin something still messy and unfinishable, something still open and indefinite, rather than be an event that would decisively end his waiting. That could not mean what he needs the event to mean, and it wouldn't satisfy the narcissism of his self-image. Everyone falls in love and is loved; that is at once too common-place or bourgeois and too frustrating a fantasy of redemption. (He wants something more; something like a revelation or especially an ending.)

His reaction, though, is interesting, and forms the oddest element of the beginning here. He claims that "till now," he too has taken the Beast to have been just that, a love affair. Until now, he seems to suggest, he had been disappointed that that was all it was, and so the expectation of such an event had largely been forgotten, had been somehow absorbed, taken for granted. It is only with the realization that he had "accidentally" described his life this way once to May Bartram that he "now" realizes that love could not have been "the real truth" about him, and that the "wait" itself must begin anew, in earnest.

> He had with his own hands dug up this little hoard, brought to light the object of value, the hiding-place of which he had, after putting it into the ground himself, so strangely so long forgotten. The exquisite luck of having again just stumbled on the spot made him indifferent to any other question (*Be,* 285).

It is May who has made all the difference in his sense of his mission and his sense of her importance for it. For Marcher appears to have some presentiment of what will later assume a great importance, that any such event, any presumed real truth, would have to seem to him, as he says, "natural." He seems to sense something of the actual truth that happens: that whatever it is, he might actually "miss" it. It might be some great thing, and it will be distinctive, his alone, not what happens to everyone, even though "for him," the distinctiveness will be lost. There can't be some natural marker to the event, no objective sign that will show what truly elevates a life above the ordinary. In the world inhabited by James's characters, all of that natural hierarchy and objective position is gone, lost in a new play of unending, subjective mutual reflection and negotiation. Marcher cannot know what he is waiting for because there is no way to anticipate what sort of a life-event would be in itself distinctive. The distinctive, the extraordinary are social categories, not natural or transcendent. This means that May's reaction, not any quality of the event, will be able to signal the distinctiveness of the thing. What will happen will be an elevation above the ordinary, but the ordinary is what is taken to be or accepted as ordinary. One might privately feel among all this ordinariness that one is exposed to some indeterminate threat, an impending great thing, but, again ironically, it's being a great thing, its having happened at all, is a public matter. It is only within the mutual expectations that make up the ordinary that something can stand out. Therefore, the event can, he realizes, seem strange to her. He will see "in her" what it will be and what it will mean. He will need her, he goes so far as to say, even to know if he was afraid or not! (Marcher, later, so stalled in time, cannot even realize he is old; he has to see it in May finally, to realize it about himself (*Be,* 295).)

Thus begins their unusual, profound relation of dependence, as much based on Marcher's waiting as it on May's watching him wait (or her waiting for him to stop waiting), an appearance of or imitation of a relationship and friendship that will last for the rest of May's life. Or at least so it seems to Marcher, who, if he cannot accept the idea of marriage because it would be unfair to ask May to share it, given the calamity that will befall him, cannot for the same reason accept that they are bound together in the current form of their friendship. They only seem to others like a couple, he believes. That saves Marcher, he also believes, from any suspicion by others that he has some dark secret, that there is some reason he is living his life alone and aloof, or that he is damaged or dangerous in some way. The question of what "saves" May from similar suspicions is left open for a while, although, typically, Marcher decides that what saves her is that he looks like an ordinary man, and that fact somehow covers her.

The ironies here are quite thick. Marcher has asked May to wait with him, has in effect made her the arbiter of what The Real Truth is and what it will mean; he has actually asked her for more than a marriage. The pretense or fantasy is not that they are a couple but that they are not. They seem like an ordinary spinster-bachelor couple because that is what they are. May looks like she is living for him and his secret, because she is. Marcher appears deadly ordinary, because he is. Everything is again hidden in plain sight. ("She looked older because inevitably, after so many years, she *was* old" (*Be,* 295).) Everything about Marcher is what it is only as reflected in May's or the public's mind, and for him this would be intolerable without his secret. However, in another ironic turn, even his great secret had lain hidden and forgotten until it turned out another person understood and believed, until it could live again in this reflection.

And this all sets up and informs the moral problem raised by their relationship. That moral problem clearly begins and ends with Marcher's narcissism, not an uncommon pathology in a world where traditional forms of identity, position, and importance have been lost. (The greater the threat that one is no one, the more uncertain or unreliable the criteria that might mark one off as distinct and distinctly worthy, the greater the anxiety about one's lack of definition, and so the greater the temptation to fantasies of importance, the greater the need to inflate or even manufacture such a worth, even at the expense of others.) Being a minor government official, with one's library, one's garden, one's modest patrimony, one's invitations, cannot be "enough." Such a "stupid world" can be lived in only if one has that secret self staring out from behind the mask. ("It wouldn't have been failure to be bankrupt, dishonoured, pilloried, hanged; it was failure *not to be anything*" (*Be*, 296, my emphasis.) But such a secret self, precisely because hidden to save it from ordinariness, can be real, counted on, relied on only if that gaze is met and recognized, and not just by a fellow secret sharer confronting one with her own secret self. That is Marcher's paradox. His secret, if known, would become (would be seen as, could only then mean) an ordinary, even fatuous fantasy. But if kept secret, it can't bear up, stay "real," under the suspicion of wish-fulfillment, or even wishful thinking. (That is likely what happened to it before he met May again.) He is saved by May's "art."

> It was only May Bartram who had, and she achieved, by an art indescribable, the feat of at once – or perhaps it was only alternatively – meeting the eyes from in front and mingling her own vision, as from over his shoulder, with their peep through the apertures (*Be*, 288).

This is, though, not an "indescribable art"; it is a fine evocation of the possibility of love, and the moral question in the story turns on Marcher's refusal of that love, or rather his refusal to face what he owes May by accepting her love, since he refuses only that open acknowledgment, not the (nearly lifelong) love itself. This is not a crudity of mutual resistance, but one-sided resistance, and Marcher senses this often; that he takes, but does not give. His "realizations," though, are pathetically inadequate. "I sometimes ask myself if it's quite fair" (*Be*, 290). "It was one of his proofs to himself, the present he made her on her birthday, that he had not sunk into real selfishness. It was mostly nothing more than a small trinket, but it was always fine of its kind, and he was regularly careful to pay for it more than he thought he could afford" (*Be,* 289). "How kind, how beautiful you are. How shall I ever repay you?" (*Be,* 293). "Marcher had been visited by one of his occasional warnings against egotism. He had kept up, he felt, and very decently on the whole, his consciousness of the importance of not being selfish" (*Be,* 292). (As usual, the small turns of phrase give away the irony. It is indeed a mere "trinket" that he brings her; that he pays more than he "thinks" he can afford, not more than he can; that he keeps up his "consciousness" of not being selfish, rather than not *being* selfish, and so on.)

It might seem too strong a way of putting things to frame the problem as what Marcher "owes" May. And it might seem, anyway, that many of the pictures of attempts at human love in James suggest a kind of "vampire" theory of affection, as if love must be a zero-sum game (a theme comically stretched to its limits in *The Sacred Fount*).[6] But *The Sacred Fount* is deeply ironic, and there is no general claim intimated here. Marcher does owe May a kind of mutuality in their regard, and there is no suggestion he could not give what he owes. May Bartram can. And he does not owe May acknowledgment simply as a duty, as something, without further ado, she is entitled to. Without such an acknowledgment and engagement, he loses *his* life, the chance to lead a life at all. Without her, he has realized from the beginning of the renewal of their contact, he "isn't anything," even his secret hope to be something eventually depends on her reflection, response, regard.

The great tragedy of Marcher's life is that he seems to believe that any acceptance of what seems May's view of things – that the Beast is the great good fortune of having found each other and made a life – would be too ordinary, would not make his life distinctive or worthy enough. But, as it turned out, it was, in all its ordinariness, enough. It was the life he led with her, even as he refused to live it, and even as he accepted its quiet satisfactions, intimacies, and pleasures. He refuses to acknowledge any of this because he holds on to the destructive hope that something must undergird or redeem or "give" a meaning, a teleological structure, to his life. But there not being any such Beast is just the Beast itself, an absence James is willing enough in other contexts to call "modernity." That absence is what makes his life with May the only kind of event that could now make a life, though he foolishly keeps "waiting for" it and cannot acknowledge and enjoy it.

The turning point of the narrative – the beginning of Marcher's great, final panic about all this – is, appropriately, a slip in the use of verb tenses by May.

> "Yes," Miss Bartram replied, "of course one's fate is coming, or course it has come, in its own form and in its own way, all the while. Only you know the form and the way in your case were to have been, – well, something so exceptional, and, as one may say, so particularly your own" (*Be*, 290).

Marcher senses immediately the "has come" and "were to have been" and begins an unrelenting, almost hysterical, somewhat merciless interrogation of May, even through her illness and up to her death, hounding her for "news" even as she collapses onto her maid's arm, and he has to be shooed away.

But May, as at the first meeting, cannot simply tell him what she knows, largely because, she keeps intimating (again as from the first), that "what it was" is "what it would have been" – their (possible but now lost) life and love together – and that now it is too late; Marcher will "never find out" (*Be*, 292), and that all that is what was to have happened. As he keeps trying to find a way to pin down what she seems to know, he remarks,

> "Well, I thought it the point you were just making – that we had looked most things in the face.
> "Including each other?" She still smiled (*Be*, 298).

She returns to that theme in their final talk before her death, again insisting that it has all happened and that his not knowing was the "strangeness in the strangeness." She goes so far as to say,

> "What I said long ago is true. You'll never know now, and I think you ought to be content. You've *had* it" (*Be*, 303).

This compressed formulation says a great deal, however ambiguously. The temporal reference ("long ago") is not clear, but it could easily refer to very long ago, when May mentioned that love, now clearly her love, might have been the Real Truth. And she says, with a hint of impatience, almost of rebuke, that he ought to be content, saying it that way even though she knows how important some dramatic revelation of a great event had been to Marcher. It is almost the only expression of her own side of things, a small crack in the facade she has created for Marcher's sake. As usual, though, May lets him off by not pursuing these questions ("each other"?) or formulations ("you ought to be content"?), but he certainly never gets the "answer" he wants from her, not even in the dramatic final scene, as he once more reverts to the myth that has formed his life, rather than, finally, giving it up.

Marcher, visiting May's grave after a year, sees in the eyes of another mourner real grief for a woman "when she had been loved for herself." This affects him horribly; it presents him with "the sounded void of his life," and he realizes that "she was what he had missed." But even this realization does not yet seem to escape the "chill of his egotism"; it remains framed in the terms of the Myth, the idea of a Real Truth.

> The fate he had been marked for he had met with a vengeance – he had emptied the cup to the lees; he had been the man of his time, *the* man, to whom nothing on earth was to have happened. That was the rare stroke – that was his visitation (*Be,* 311).)

Because this revelation seems so painful to Marcher and thereby so much a just punishment for his egoism, we tend to accept such a revelation. But it is still one more turn of the same screw, of his refusal and egotism. He still gets to be that "one man" with that special fate, to have missed his chance with May and so a chance for anything, any kind of life, but all as a fate that happens to him. He is right, in a sense, that "the escape would have been to love her," but he would not thereby have escaped his unique fate. That would have been (actually was) his fate, his life. There is now, still, for Marcher, a sense only of what he missed, not of what he made May miss, that his "missing" and "hers" were linked. (He thinks of her and regrets using her, but still, in a last ironic twist, only to envy poor May: "She had lived – who could say now with what passion – since she had loved him for himself" (*Be,* 311).)

In the story's magnificent closing sentences, the Beast (or Marcher's insistence that there be a Beast) returns, and Marcher enacts again, rather than frees himself from, what it means to see one's existence in the shadow of such a Beast.

He saw the Jungle of his life and saw the lurking Beast; then, while he looked, perceived, as by a stir of the air, rise, huge and hideous, for the leap that was to settle him. His eyes darkened – it was close; and instinctively turning, in his hallucination, to avoid it, he flung himself, on his face, on the tomb (*Be*, 312).

"In his hallucination," indeed, a phrase that could have and would have changed everything, had James simply left it out. Here and throughout the story, Marcher enacts his fantasy one final time, now as a catastrophic fate that still pursues, especially, him. He still cannot let his Beast go, still does not realize that it was his anxiety and narcissism that created the Beast and doomed his life with May. It all ensures that with eyes darkened, face down, unseeing, his final embrace of May can only be of her corpse.

III

There is a kind of companion story to "The Beast in the Jungle," written some five years later, perhaps even a "mirror" story, the very name of which suggests a different and far more positive "place": "The Jolly Corner." It helps clarify how James might see the link between a kind of moral acknowledgment of another, especially in relations of deepest trust and fidelity, or in love, and the problems of understanding and meaning, again figured as a problem of secrets, beasts, or, here, ghosts.

Spencer Brydon is back in New York after an absence of thirty-three years. He is fifty-six, and has been living what seems some sort of vaguely bohemian or artistic life "in Europe." He has now inherited the family house – the house where he was born and raised – and has returned to oversee renovations in preparation for its sale. In the course of this, he has taken up again with an old friend, Alice Staverton. She becomes his May Bartram-like confidante ("watching with him," in effect) as his connection with the house takes an unexpected, bizarre turn.

The setting again plays a determining role, as in "The Beast in the Jungle," though, as with many such parallels in the two stories, a kind of mirror role. Now the scene is hardly stalled, like Weatherend, and is more like a wholly unstoppable, breathless time, endless weather, the tumult and building and money-making of what is referred to as "the awful modern crush" of modern New York (*JC*, 315). He likes what he sees now – the "'swagger' of things, the modern, the monstrous," even less now than when he had "waked up to a sense of the ugly" and fled. "They were as so many set traps for displeasure, above all for reaction, of which his restless tread was constantly pressing the spring" (*JC*, 314). A house begins things again, but not as a museum; just the opposite. All these fine old homes are being redone. In the neighborhood now,

> . . . the old people had mostly gone, the old names were unknown, and here and there an old association seemed to stray, all vaguely, like some very aged person, out too late, whom you might meet and feel the impulse to watch or follow, in kindness, for safe restoration to shelter (*JC*, 317).

Brydon has been doubly out of such changes and accelerating pace, away from America and away from its modern spirit; he's escaped to Europe as if to hide out somewhere where the "crush" will someday finally appear but that has still escaped it, and into a life where money, power, and perhaps even the forward push of history can at least be ignored. Marcher had his secret life; Brydon has his exile. He seems a bit like Merton Densher in *The Wings of the Dove*, unsuited, perhaps because of his "ideas," for the roles history has now made available to young men, aware that he thereby isn't "fit" ever to make money. One imagines him, too, looking "vague without looking weak" and "idle without looking empty" (*WD*, 34). (Like Densher, like Strether too for that matter, without such a role or social function, the question of who he really is, what he stands for, what he owes others and so on all assume more interesting dimensions.)

But as he begins to supervise the construction, Brydon comes to realize that he has a talent for business, that he had "for too many years neglected a real gift" (*JC*, 316). He can stand up to contractors, negotiate effectively, has ideas for how things might be done. This sets him to wondering what he would have been like if he had stayed, how successful in business – simply as an American, a modern man – he would have been. (He begins to act out, that is, what might be called a common academic fantasy, the usual response to the usual question: "If you're so smart, why ain't you rich?" That is: "Of course I could have been. I chose not to try.") But as he begins to think through these counterfactual speculations with Miss Staverton, it all takes an odd, dramatic turn.

> He found all things come back to the question of what he person-ally might have been, how he might have led his life and turned out,

if he had not so, at the outset, given it up. ". . . I keep forever wondering, all idiotically, as if I could possibly know" (*JC,* 320).

Remarkably, however, Brydon gets his chance. His sense that there is an "alter ego" within him is, first, wholly accepted by Alice Staverton. Like May, she believes; in the context of the story she claims to have seen this alter ego in a dream, twice. And like May, when asked, "What was the wretch like?" demurs, says only "I'll tell you some other time" (*JC,* 322). Like May, she seems to know what Brydon wants to know, but, like May, knows in some other way that there is really nothing to be known, no simple fact of the matter that will settle who Spencer Brydon is.

Brydon doesn't have to wait long though for his revelation. He visits his empty, rebuilt house, his possible past, every night, wandering through the vacant rooms aimlessly, in effect looking for himself, until finally, frighteningly, he becomes convinced that the house is haunted, and that the ghost is none other than his alter ego. He becomes obsessed with catching actual sight of "who he would have been" had he not "given up," as he sees it.

And finally he gets his wish. After some grand scene-setting by James, there is a great confrontation scene. Courage is again the issue, and Brydon has it; he faces the apparition. But his "other self" is finally more pathetic than frightening. He (the alter ego) is almost cowering, hands (damaged hands, missing two fingers) covering his face. But most importantly, in one of James's most complex ironies, Brydon does not recognize himself as himself.

> . . . for the bared identity was too hideous as *his,* and his glare was the passion of his protest. The face, that face, Spencer Brydon's? – he searched it still, but looking away from it in dismay and denial, falling straight from his height of sublimity. It was unknown, inconceivable, awful, disconnected from any possibility – ! (*JC,* 335).

So, like Marcher, we have a man obsessed with a possible "self," someone who wants to hold himself apart from the "crush" and ordinariness of the emerging "American" world, and just by having held himself apart, has a life that turns now on the question of his real self. But now the character doesn't, like Marcher, expect some redemption in the future, but looks for it, or some resolution of the question of who he is, in the past, and is more than willing to think through the idea that he made a mistake with his distaste for the ordinary modern, money-dominated world, or that he made his decision badly, without knowing himself well enough. The self he has become is only one of many possibles, and it is quite possible that he "really" is or should have been a self he did not become, the tycoon "with a million a year." A beast will not leap this time, but a ghost will appear. Brydon will know, he thinks, who he really is, not by knowing who he will become, but who he might have been, who his better self might have been, the one with all the unappreciated talent. In both cases, both characters have some sense that "who they are" has somehow been taken out of their hands, that they are one of only many possible selves who could be or could have been, that there is no real way they could determine or could have determined their "fate." And so they are "haunted" by the question of such possibilities, because they seem to think (in a typically modern, romantic fantasy) that if they do not have a special fate (or an unrealized special self), they have none, are nothing at all.

And in both cases, the question of love is at stake and determined largely by their reaction to these issues (to the question of how one settles the issue of "who one is").[7] Staverton does not believe in a beast to come, but she believes in something like Brydon's view of the matter: that Brydon is not essentially or necessarily who he is; she thinks she too can see who he might have been. She believes, remarkably, in him and in his various possible selves. And their whole relationship to each other begins also to turn on the question of the ghost/beast, of who Brydon is, and how one could determine that. Alice, like May, seems to know from the beginning that that question is not to be settled by a revelation, a fact, or a ghost, even as she senses that Brydon cannot yet believe that, and so cannot accept what she is offering him (a life, let us say, and not a resolution or revelation).

Brydon wants to know from her, for example, such things as if he "is as good as he might have been. "She tells him "No, far from it," but also "I don't care" (*JC*, 322), an answer he cannot yet appreciate. She reminds him that really he doesn't care either "but very differently: You don't care for anything but yourself."[8]

This changes, however, and the result is something relatively rare in James's fiction: successful love, or in the moral terms we have been using, some way is found around the "crudities of mutual resistance," and something like the reciprocity or right sort of acknowledgment of dependence necessary for love is finally possible. The usual Jamesean ending, with its renunciations and failures, does not occur. It is avoided largely because Brydon can now give up his obsession with himself, his haunted notion of some determinate real self, his hunt for who he really is or might have been, and his hope that there might be some fact or revelation that could finally settle all that. The world Brydon has returned to, the ever more indeterminate, mobile, chaotic world of New York, has created such contingency in lives and possible lives that it is understandable that one might become "haunted" by the question he raises for himself. (The so-typical modern question of authenticity is best seen as a reaction to a specific kind of threat created by a specific form of social life.) And this is understandable in all sorts of senses. Not taking for granted that one's self-representation is reliable, or having some sort of distance from such a representation, is to have avoided the dangerous pomposity and morbidly rigid self-satisfaction of characters like Osmond. And insisting on one's own way through life is to have insisted on an integrity without which a free engagement with others is not possible, and which is particularly threatened in the new world of inheritable, powerful wealth. It is what makes us admire Isabel, what Strether comes to appreciate about the conventionally immoral Madame De Vionnet. But the "Real Self" issue can also be a spectral and useless issue when it emerges as it does for Marcher and Brydon, when, that is, it evinces a hope for finality, determinate revelations, revealed secrets, a fixed anchor in the unsettled waters through which the characters must somehow chart a course.

Although the line between the appeal of the integrity ideal in a society like this (Isabel's appeal, say) and a narcissistic fantasy of self-importance (Marcher's, say) is often very thin in James, we get some sense of how he thinks it all works, what is crucial from keeping the former from slipping into the latter, by noting how the "exorcism" of the ghost issue is connected to the themes of reciprocity and trust. What is finally so interesting about Brydon's "non-recognition" of his alter ego, that is, is that his "giving up his ghost" is the issue around which his relationship with Alice turns, finally in her direction. He has fainted away after his confrontation; Alice was concerned when she didn't hear from him, and has had the housemaid open the house. They find Spencer sprawled on the stairs, and he revives, in one of the most unabashed and direct of the romantic scenes James ever wrote. After reviving, Spencer says,

. . . "You brought me literally to life." "Only," he wondered, his
eyes rising to her, "only in the name of all benedictions, how?" It took
her but an instant to bend her face and kiss him, and something in
the manner of it, and in the way her hands clasped and locked his
head while he felt the cool charity and virtue of her lips, something in
all this beatitude somehow answered everything. "And now I keep
you," she said (*JC*, 337).

This startlingly positive, affirmative moment (which comes as something of a shock to anyone who might have made his way through so many
of James's failed-love, frustrating endings for so many years) then occasions
a vaguely metaphysical debriefing of each other about the ghost and Alice's
dream. (Alice claims to have seen the same "black stranger" in her dream,
at the same time, and, contrary to Brydon, to have known that it was and
was not "him.") Brydon can't at first get over the fact that the apparition of
his alter ego was actually not him, the "him" he now is anyway. He clearly
expected some reassuring redemption, the same "him," but rich and prosperous and happy. That would have meant that he could count his actual
life and missed possible life as his own, not all a mistake or an accident; he
could take comfort in the fact that he could have still been "him," and rich
and powerful. It would then have been his having walked away from that
possibility that determined his life, not a mistake or matter of luck or fear
or just inability. He would be master of his past as well as his present and
future. He is puzzled, though, and disturbed by not being able to recognize
himself in the figure he saw. Alice keeps trying to help him understand that
that is basically the whole point about "who one might have been," and
that believing otherwise (or thinking that somehow the contingency of
one's actual life cheapens or degrades it, makes it accidental and arbitrary,
that there might be some other, truer self one has "missed" being) is all a
destructive fantasy, a way of not living, or of living only in resentment.
There is no question that the "awful modern crush" of New York can
create anxieties like Brydon's, so many forks in the path of such a rushed
life, so quickly and often irretrievably taken, with so little awareness then
of why or what else might have been available. Any ego would have to seem
an alter ego in such a world, and it would be expected that the temptations
of the idea of a special determinate fate, or a real, perhaps better ego, would
be hard to resist.

But this fantasy of resolution, answers, secrets revealed, and so forth is better described as a kind of narcissism, or in the historical terms we have been using, a refusal to accept the risks and uncertainties Jamesean modernity requires. (A narcissism in the sense described by Freud in "Mourning and Melancholia" as a refusal to mourn a loss – the loss of traditional certainties in this case – a sense that one is so important, so central, that such a loss could not have happened to one, a sense that one's importance would be so diminished that no mourning-work is possible, no "libidinal re-cathexis thereby possible." In many of the stories, too, the loss in question, occasioning such obsession and melancholy, is simply the loss of the past, the irretrievability of the historical past or of one's own youth. In the face of this, so think some, there must be secrets, ghosts, papers, figures in the carpet. As Freud points out, one mourns melancholically in order to deny the loss, and to deny the loss of self-importance one thinks the loss would mean.⁹) It all especially counts as a resistance to what Marcher experiences but cannot fathom: that he needs May to be who he is, not a Beast that will finally make it all clear. So when Alice speaks of having "accepted" the stranger, she is making that point about her willingness to tolerate and accept such uncertainties and contingencies, even to the point of expressing her regard for whoever Brydon might have been. He would still have been in some way the person she has come to love, or at least she is expressing her willingness to keep faith with the ravaged and maimed capitalist, as with the unravaged and charmingly monocled Brydon. On hearing her out, Brydon can give up his fantasy of who he might have been, unlike Marcher, who cannot escape his fixation on who he might become (even if that means accepting that he is the only one who becomes nothing). And the story ends with perhaps the most successful social moment in James's work.¹⁰

> "Ah!" Brydon winced – whether for his proved identity or for his lost fingers. Then, "He has a million a year," he lucidly added. "But he hasn't you."
>
> "And he isn't – no, he isn't – *you!*" she murmured as he drew her to his breast (*JC*, 340).

## I V

Brydon's obsession is more typical of the Jamesean secret and ghost stories, though it has its odd counterfactual twist. Mostly the genre is not about what would have happened, but about what did happen, as if the "key," the one thing one must know, is something in the past, some determinate content, the revelation of which will put some dead author's life in its final perspective, illuminate the essence of somebody, settle a question of interpretation, or resolve a moral question of evil and guilt.

All of these stories typify the kind of resistance and anxiety we have seen before, and in almost all of them the fantasy about the final identity of ghosts or the final possession and revelation of secrets also typifies a resistance to someone else, a refusal to accept how much of what "it meant" or "who" someone was, is not a subject for some private revelation or not to be settled as some fact of the matter, but requires a kind of multiple reflection, negotiation, and engagement among genuinely reciprocal subjects, or requires the Jamesean moral ideal, let us say. So when the narrator in *The Aspern Papers* wants, no matter the costs or moral shortcuts, his great subject's private correspondence with Juliana Bordereau, he is not simply the crass journalist, the "publishing scoundrel" Miss Bordereau judges him to be. He believes in Aspern and believes in his poetry, and understandably thinks that the details of Aspern's love life might shed some light on the poems. But it is what he expects from such papers, how he expects them to be of use, that puts the story firmly in the genre we are considering and creates the many ironies in the first-person narration. (It is of course also a modern hope that the narrator evinces, despite his nostalgia: not papers about the work, drafts of poems, and so on, but letters about his life, again about what is private and secret and hidden. Only those sorts of letters can reveal. The poems themselves are presumed not to be enough.)[11]

The setting again tells us as much, as evocative of the past, of old Venice, of old people (Juliana like a "grinning skull"), of the old world as James could make it. (James himself stresses the "haunting presences" of the "visible past" in the story, "the poetry of the thing outlived and lost and gone . . . played out in the very theatre of our own modernity" (*APP*, 1176). For the narrator, though, this past is not just visible, but still somehow alive, although the images of that life used in the story call to mind a living death. The old palace with its two old spinsters evokes again the stalled time of Weatherend, the romantic illusion about the worth and beauty of such a past undercut by the bits and pieces we hear about Aspern's own life, and Miss Bordereau's willingness, up to a point, to barter those memories for cash. It is, I think, for James all "outlived and lost and gone," not to be forgotten, surely, but not to be reanimated or obsessively romanticized, as if planting all those flowers in the garden could re-create a life by force of will alone.

The triangle that this creates this time (the narrator and Miss Tina facing each over the papers) has considerably more pathos than the Marcher-Beast-May or Brydon-Ghost-Alice triangles. Neither one of them now has any real connection with the papers, or understand what's in them. (There is even enough self-deceit and wishful thinking in the Venetian air in this story that it would not be impossible to construct an interpretation of the story in which there were never any papers.) They are like fetishes that have acquired human powers in some mysterious way, perhaps by virtue of how much such resolutions are needed. They have drawn the narrator to Venice, and they have given Miss Tina her first link to the real, adult world. (Contrary to his reputation, James is perfectly able to treat exaggerated hopes for aesthetic values in general as a fetishization of such values; this is especially true of his treatment of collectors or nostalgists or high culture priests.) Thus, those readings of the story that have James himself evoking some nostalgia for the pre-modern scene of Aspern and Juliana have missed the pathos and futility of the narrator's hopes. His pathetic self-deceit about whether he was, with all those flowers, all that kindness and attention to a lonely woman, "really" making love to her or not is a mirror of his self-deceit about the past and about Aspern (on the question of why he wants the papers). The tone of dignity and humanity with which Miss Tina offers herself in marriage, even though, remarkably, she is bargaining with the papers, throws a strong light on where James's sympathies lie. Tina is willing to give them up for what is almost certainly her last chance to get out of that house and that past, even to have some sort of compromised, less than very romantic life on the outside, in the present. (She is willing thus to bargain away what she recognizes as her debt to her aunt, and to turn the papers over to a journalist.)

The narrator cannot at first accept, not because he just doesn't want to get married. He is in love with Aspern and the past and is ironically more a recluse and more a conniver than Juliana. And not just because he is a scholar or interested in the past. Again, it is the way he is interested, his hopeless sense that there is simply something decisive "in" those papers, that so distorts his relations with everyone else and sets up his abuse of Tina. It should be a great, liberating feeling to the reader when Tina burns those papers, as liberating as the end of Brydon's ghosts. It is not, of course, liberating for the narrator, who spends the rest of his life, we are led to believe, worshipping at a shrine, under the picture of the dead poet, feeling the loss of the letters interminably, mourning an absent and hidden meaning. There is an exchange in the story that however finally ambiguous, indicates how much is at stake for James in giving up Archer's hopes.

Juliana had cautioned, "The Truth is God's, it isn't man's: we had better leave it alone. Who can judge of it? – who can say?" To which Archer responds, in a familiar and understandable tone heard often in such debates: "We're terribly in the dark, I know, but if we give up trying, what becomes of all the fine things? What becomes of the work I just mentioned, that of the great philosophers and poets? It's all vain words if there's nothing to measure it by!" Julianna's answer seems to me to have the air of a Jamesean response:

"You talk as if you were a tailor" (*AP*, 158).[12]

V

A young, unworldly girl from a religious background, a vicarage, we are led to believe, so remote (so pre-modern perhaps) that it might be on another planet, a girl with no experience even of novels, plays, who has never even seen herself in a full-length mirror, with a father said to be eccentric, is engaged by a mysterious, wealthy man, very much of the world, to care for his dead brother's children, Miles and Flora, at a remote estate, Bly. The one condition is that however legally and morally responsible he is for the children, he wants never to be reminded of the fact. He is never to be bothered with any detail about their upbringing. Our would-be *deus absconditus* gives us no reason for this odd condition. The governess accepts, and takes up residence at the magnificent estate in Essex, finding there a confidante in the rather simple Mrs. Grose, chief servant and former maid to the owner's mother. The boy, Miles, is about to return home from school for summer vacation, and therein begins the tale. A letter arrives: Miles has been dismissed from school for some unnamed offense, and this either prompts or is simultaneous with (depending on one's reading) the appearance to the governess of two ghosts, presumably the former servants, Peter Quint and Miss Jessel. The governess fastens on the idea that they have returned to somehow reclaim the children who, she also supposes, were perversely corrupted earlier, probably sexually, by the servants. The governess is convinced that the children also see the ghosts but are engaged in a conspiracy to hide it and, eventually, to get rid of her. After several encounters (only with her; there is never a shred of independent evidence for the existence of the ghosts) and a deteriorating relation with Miles, she confronts first Flora, whom she absolutely terrifies with such claims, leading to Flora's illness, utter alienation from the governess, and rapid departure with Mrs. Grose, and then, in a truly horrifying scene, confronts Miles himself, who is also terrified and confused, so much so that he dies.

Especially since the publication of Edmund Wilson's essay "The Ambiguity of Henry James,"[13] which argued that the ghosts were complete fantasies, hallucinations, or projections of the governess, all to be explained in Freudian terms (the governess's repressed sexual desire for the unnamed "person in Harley Street"), a great deal of discussion of this story has turned on the question of the reality of the ghosts. Wilson's claim has often been countered by those who suspect James did want to write a straightforward (if eerie, modern) ghost story, and/or that his interest lay much more in the possibility of evil in the appearance of innocence (truly corrupted children who remain nonetheless children) and, correspondingly, in the evil that good intentions can do (the governess does after all destroy Miles in her attempt, as she puts it, to "save" him). Is the story "about" the governess, in other words, and her fantastical obsession with the ghosts, or is it, as say Dorothea Krook claims (and claims that James claimed), "about" the children and the spectral, real presence of evil in their lives?[14]

As the current of the discussion in the previous sections of this chapter will quickly indicate, I am somewhat on Wilson's side in this debate, but not for his psychological reasons. In the first place, there is indeed something "real" about the ghosts, but not simply as real demons or, certainly, as psychic phenomena. As noted, the basic structure of the story is not unconnected with a pattern in many other such stories. Here the question of love, or a certain openness to and regard for another, is not a matter between a man and a woman, with some cipher, mystery, ghost, or secret between them, presumably needing to be resolved before resistances between them or confusions and misunderstandings can be dropped or resolved. But the same kind of triangle is here, now between the governess and the children, still with ghosts in between, her affection for them and theirs for her, confusing the issue of who they "really" are and what she "really" knows.

And a similar issue arises, as with the other stories. Something has certainly happened at Bly; the former servants do appear to have been careless and somehow, oddly, too intimate with the children, especially Peter Quint with Miles. Miles and Flora do appear to know how to talk in ways grossly inappropriate for children, and Miles's rather adult perspective on things is what appears to have gotten him tossed out of school. This something is still not much, and it all could still be relatively innocent, but in the religious-allegorical context James is setting, or playing with, this original, corrupting event, even as such a vague possibility, assumes some significance. There is, in a way, an absent, now angry "God"; the authority and master of this domain has "left the building" and doesn't want to be bothered. It all does resemble a kind of garden of Eden after some Fall, some original sin (or, given the mystery, absence of innocence in the children, God's "departure," and so on, one supposes there must have been some Fall), and we have some poor human being, unequipped to deal with or fathom such mysteries, but sensitive enough to know that something has gone on that has not gone away, that still haunts the general meaning of life at Bly. But like so many other characters we have seen in this chapter, the governess conceives the view that this is a something that can be found, and not just found as a fact, but understood, and if found and understood, exorcised. It is this expectation and fierce insistence that constitutes the ground for the fantasy that there are demonic forces that must be named and destroyed "by confession." What is real in the situation is the maddening and nearly intolerably frustrating experience of this uncertainty, suspicion, mystery, and this intimation that their not being nothing to the question of the reality of evil means it must be a something. It is a temptation to resolution that, we can imagine, would be especially tempting for this poor parson's daughter, thrown into the thick of it.

But it is, as with so many other cases we have seen, a destructive expectation and insistence, extreme enough in this case to require, for a woman like the governess, spectral presences as real meanings, and it is enough of a dangerous, life-threatening insistence to end up destroying Miles. This may all seem a rather abstract or metaphysical way of putting the point, and there are still all the old questions about evidence for any fantasy view of the governess and her ghosts, especially one tied to the claim that the notions of resistance, anxiety about moral indeterminacy, and implications for any possible mutuality and love are all in play. But James himself, I would suggest, is rather careful in his remarks about the story and within the story itself, to stay pretty much out of the ghosts/no ghosts issue, and to concentrate both on the governess's and, interestingly enough, on our expectations.

Here is a good example of what I mean from James's New York Edition Preface.

> Otherwise expressed, the study is of a conceived "tone," the tone of suspected and felt trouble, of an inordinate and incalculable sore – the tone of tragic, yet of exquisite mystification. To knead the subject of my young friend's, the suppositious narrator's, mystifications thick, and yet strain the expression of it so clear and fine that beauty would result: no side of the matter so revives for me as that endeavour (*TSP,* 120).

There is something to be discovered; this very general, allegorical setting does suggest that life itself cannot begin without some implication in a moral stain of some sort – the great power adults wield over children seems in itself the inevitable, unavoidable culprit, if we read archetypally enough. The children do seem to have private, guarded, already damaged lives. And it is a sore (a kind of ego held secret, exempted from what must hold for all) that it is not safe simply to ignore; the presence of the content-to-look-the-other-way Mrs. Grose helps establish that premise, by contrast. Moreover, the beginning of the written tale insists in a grandly intricate fashion that the problem for anyone hearing the tale will be as complex as the governess's task within it, separating what anyone might need to believe from what might have happened.

The beginning is a great set of perspectival boxes, stacked within each other and set off in a distant time in ways that raise multiple reliability issues, and it raises immediately the question of what our attitude should be toward the stories' own mysteries and ghostly ambiguities, what we expect from it. We are hearing the memory of a recounted story; an unnamed narrator is telling us what he heard another person, Douglas, narrate at a country house on some winter night. Douglas, though, is not telling us what happened to him, and not remembering, though he says he is adding, at the beginning especially, his impressions and touches. He will read a transcript written by the main character, the governess. (We are also supposed to believe that the unnamed narrator has written down verbatim the preliminary remarks, and upon Douglas's death, inherited the "red, thin, old-fashioned gilt-edged album" itself.) The body of the story is this first-person account by the governess, given to Douglas, who sets the stage that evening in his own words (which words stress explicitly his view that her main motive in accepting the job was a romantic or sexual interest in the Master, his "seduction" of her) and who passes on the manuscript to our narrator.[15]

There are all sorts of nice little touches in the elaborate prologue. The waiting theme returns; the party has to wait for the manuscript, for the revelation of the tale (Douglas has to send to London for it; some large group of ladies could not wait, and in impatience hurry off before the revelation, too busy apparently with the social calendars to hang around). It is, ironically, Christmas Eve (as they celebrate the "advent" of another "ghost"?). The governess has been dead for twenty years; she had been the governess of Douglas's sister twenty years before that, when Douglas was a young man in college. So the story is forty years old and distant, and grew, in its telling, out of an unusually close relationship between this governess and another child in the family she was serving. Everyone in the present party assumes, because of the devoted way Douglas speaks of the governess, that he was in love with her, and given that she told only him, that once, the story, that she was in love with him. We thus begin, oddly, with a pre-vision of sorts of something like the great sin that occupies the center of the story itself, even if suitably cleaned up. (Douglas must have been about eighteen or nineteen; she was ten years older. Still, since it is Douglas who tells us that she was the "most agreeable woman" he has ever known, and further vouches for her sanity and stability, and since we immediately see how complicated his motives are, and since we are put in some complex, multi-mediated relation to the story itself, the question of anyone's being able to detach the account from the narrative points of view and biases within which it is embedded is probably as hopeless, and the attempt to do so is unavoidable – very much what James's characters so often face.) Not for nothing does the governess use a particular image when she first reports seeing Quint: "So I saw him as I see the letters in this page. . . ." (*TS*, 17), reminding us that we too are looking in these letters for Quint, or for what it meant that she saw Quint.

In the story itself, James is careful to create as much doubt as possible about the credibility of his suppositious narrator and the rather credulous, a bit too trusting source of household information, Mrs. Grose, even as he also makes it difficult to deny that there is something amiss at Bly. Even when supposedly directly in front of Mrs. Jessel, Mrs. Grose cannot see her (even the children, she finally has to admit, despite her conspiracy suspicions, see nothing); the governess is carefully introduced as painfully naive, presumably religiously devout, profoundly inexperienced (what can she, given her background, imagine Miles and Peter Quint did?), much too taken with the idea that she shall do some great thing, some "act of heroism," in protecting the children, and so win the admiration of the Master (*TS*, 28), and so forth. However, it is not so much what she claims to see that raises questions of credibility about the governess; it is what she so rapidly assumes it all means, and therein lies the theme we have seen before. She makes several, ultimately quite damaging inferences with breathtaking leaps of imagination, and I think we are to have some sympathy with poor Mrs. Grose's gasps at each of them, her obvious concern with whether the governess is being fair to the children. The governess immediately assumes, having just laid eyes on the ghost once, that Quint's has "come back" for Miles, come back to drag him further into the forever unnamed initiated evil. This is largely because, having once heard Mrs. Grose's story about Quint's spending so much time with Miles, which the humble woman clearly intended to be about inappropriate crossing of class boundaries, she assumes straightaway that something else must have gone on between them, some dark evil, and that Miles must have known about, or possibly been witness to, an affair between Quint and Jessel. (All this because Miles and Quint spent time together, and Miles, like so many billions of boys before him, prevaricated a bit to Mrs. Grose in order to continue adventures he enjoyed.) Then, because poor Flora doesn't see (or, in the governess's imagination, pretends not to notice) Mrs. Jessel at the lake, the governess leaps to the view that the children are involved in a conspiracy with the ghosts, working with them to conceal their (the children's) relationship with them. The governess has to explain at one point to a gasping Mrs Grose, as the fabulations about Miles and Quint are pouring out of her at a truly reckless rate, "You haven't my dreadful boldness of mind . . . but I shall get it out of you yet!" (*TS*, 36).

These suspicions make up the basic moral problem of the tale, raise the question of the governess's culpability for what happens, or her responsibility for demanding from this situation what cannot be demanded, all to the point of being the unmistakable agent for Miles's death. (I can't see how any interpretation of the story can ignore the near-comic ironies of the confrontation with Flora and then the dreadful intensity of her interrogation/persecution of Miles.) Whatever one thinks of the reliability of evidence about the ghosts, one has also to deal with the separate question of how the governess understands what some sort of lingering past ambiguity means, on what basis she forms the view that the children are in great danger of continued abuse, that they must be saved, and that they must be saved by confessing. (The governess is desperate enough to assign such a meaning that, James lets us see, she is willing simply to lie, straightforwardly and unambiguously, to Mrs. Grose in order to firm up the latter's allegiance. After supposedly seeing Mrs. Jessel again, who had merely been sitting at a table, the governess invents a non-existent conversation, gives the ghosts words that conveniently confirm all that the governess had been saying about the motives and plans of the visitors. She lets Mrs. Grose believe that it was the ghost who made clear that she "wants Flora," although nothing of the sort was ever said (*TS*, 60–1).)

Perhaps her guilt at her own sexual desire for the Master plays some role in the projected fantasy of abuse and redemption. I don't think we have much to go on there, however many towers and hats and lakes from the Freudian lexicon show up. But her rather obsessed resolve to assign a meaning to Miles's apparent (and likely inevitable) loss of innocence, the simplistic world she creates of abusers and victims, and her air of ferocity and anger at the children, as co-conspirators in their own supposed depravity, all begin to emerge from this to present us with a very clear sort of moral distortion in her relationship with everyone else. (The children are so accused mostly because they will not admit this depravity to her and, especially in Miles's case, want simply to live their lives, as he so charmingly puts it, simply to "get on," not to be trapped in this question of why they cannot remain innocent).

The importance for her of some morally determinate fact of the matter behind all this uncertainty is apparent at several points, never without a touch of some irony. After she has demanded from Mrs. Grose an explanation of an earlier remark that Miles was not uniformly good, and after having heard that he sometimes lied, she remarks,

> His having lied and been impudent are, I confess, less engaging specimens than I had hoped to have from you of the outbreak in him of the little natural man. Still, I mused, they must do, for they make me feel more than ever that I must watch (*TS*, 37).

That "little natural man" phrase speaks volumes about what lies behind the vast suppositions built by the governess on the little bits of narration supplied by Mrs. Grose and what James is so distancing himself from in this and other like stories. We also return to the governess's "nature theory" one more time in a way linked directly and so, one would assume, importantly, to the story's title. We had heard at the beginning that if a ghost story is all the more eerie when the human appeared to is a child, it would count as "one more turn of the screw" if it were two children. The following reference gives a much more general sense of the title.

> Here at present I felt afresh – for I had felt it again and again – how my equilibrium depended on the success of my rigid will, the will to shut my eyes as tight as possible to the truth that what I had to deal with was, revoltingly, against nature. I could only get on at all by taking 'nature' into my confidence and my account, by treating my monstrous ordeal as a push in a direction unusual, of course, and unpleasant, but demanding, after all, for a fair front, only another turn of the screw of human virtue. No attempt, none the less, could require more tact than just this attempt to supply, one's self, *all* the nature (*TS*, 80).

But of course, nature is not a thing that can be "supplied," and the "eyes shut tight" phrase just about gives completely away the question of the governess's reliability. It is her rigid will, and that alone, that is responsible for the moral framework within which she sets out to free the children from these evil things. She has some sense that there is no nature here, that she is beyond even her own notions of the original stain of sin in human nature (the "little natural man" in Miles), and that whatever has happened cannot be understood in these terms. But she resolves to do so anyway, and therewith the unmistakable cruelty suggested by the title. Another turn of the screw of human virtue indeed, and it is poor Miles who is on the rack.

The application of such a screw to Miles is painful to read. This is mostly because of the contrast between the content of Miles's "confession" – (the governess finally simply asks him about the school, breaking the bizarre silence about Mile's past and future that Miles himself had tried to end) – and the grand guignol dancing around in the governess's febrile fantasies. Yes, he stole the letter to the Master, read it and burned it. Yes, he was dismissed. For what? Saying things. To whom? I don't remember. All the while, as little Miles catalogues his childish sins, as if in some standard confession box for a boy his age, the ominous vision of Quint has appeared again to the governess, looming ever larger in the background, through the window. She finally yells at the ghost, "No more, no more, no more" (ironically echoing many readers' words as she keeps turning her screw). This alerts Miles to the fact that she thinks someone is there, and he immediately leaps to the supposition that she is repeating with him what went on with Flora. (We can easily suppose, as does the governess, that they have found a way to talk in the last day.) That is, even though his great sins were supposed to have been committed with Quint, he reacts instead to what he apparently knows is the governess's belief that Mrs. Jessel is wandering about, and not at all with any sense that his supposed conspiracy of silence about his dead friend has been discovered. The governess though, presses on, insisting, even in her own document, that she admits Miles could never see the supposed ghost.

> At this, after a second in which his head made the movement of a baffled dog's on a scent and then gave a frantic little shake for air and light, he was at me in a white rage, bewildered, glaring vainly over the place and missing wholly, though, it now to my sense, filled the room like a taste of poison, the wide overwhelming presence (*TS,* 88).

Too many turns of the screw with all this, apparently, for the "baffled dog." Miles keeps staring where she keeps pointing, but, seeing "but the quiet day," dies; his "little heart, dispossessed, had stopped." The governess has succeeded in making him dispossessed in her sense, and whole and innocent again in the only way one could fit such norms. That "dispossessed" functions here with the same telling irony as the "in his hallucination" in "The Beast in the Jungle," and we have again our principal clutching a corpse. (And speaking of irony, there is the famous ambiguity about whom Miles means to refer to in his last, "you devil!")

I don't mean to say that James would have us see the governess as a finally only silly, superstitious, and vaguely insane, destructive moralist. We can never forget that she has no recourse to anyone, no help. (She must rely instead for her bearings on the likes of Mrs. Grose, and we sense enough of Mrs. Grose's personality to suspect her own motives in her hostility to servants who put on airs, her strategy in dealing with an invading new governess, and so on.) And there is no doubt that she needs help, that the children have been neglected, and, very likely, have been as irresponsibly cared for as poor Masie. (James's Preface makes clear he wants us to believe that something evil had gone on, thanks to the former servants; they were indeed "false friends" to the children (*TSP*, 123).) She has been dropped into the undoubtedly corrupt consequences of upper-class English society and she needs some bearings, somehow, and her ability to fathom any of it requires all she has to work with: her lame categories of nature, the unnatural, and the supernatural. But we also see clearly that this insistence on the truth and a final resolution and confession is all not merely inadequate. It is literally deadly; it means the end of life itself.

VI

Finally, this all, throughout the major ghost and secret stories, amounts to a self-conscious inversion of the conventional Gothic narrative frame (so important to the romantic vision, or nightmare, of modernity), and this in a way of relevance to the major themes introduced here. More accurately, it allows us to see that James is in effect quoting the Gothic conventions rather than using or invoking them. There certainly are such Gothic conventions everywhere in his tales – hauntings, ghosts, mysterious, doomed sites, forces beyond or underneath consciousness that cannot be mastered, past secrets, or powerful challenges to the sufficiency of modern, middle-class self-understanding. (Leslie Fiedler notes that the purpose of eighteenth-century Gothic was "to shock the bourgeoisie into an awareness of what a chamber of horrors its own smugly regarded world really was."[16] And such Gothic suspicions about ourselves play ever more dominant roles in everything from Freudian views about internal hauntings to modern fiction (Morrison) to mass culture, as Mark Edmundson shows so well.)[17] Yet, as we have seen, James is treating such conventions and the fears that inspire them as reactive fantasies, not as the literary or mythic bearers of a deep truth. Such fantasies are defensive strategies in the face of the disorientation and apparently endless irresolution and uncertainty unavoidable in the modern social world James depicts. And this would mean that influential interpretations, like Eve Kosofsky Sedgwick's of "The Beast in the Jungle," where Marcher's anxiety is understood as prompted by homosexual panic (there is a beast "in the closet"),[18] or other (at least initial, earlier) Freudian readings, of *The Turn of the Screw* in particular, would have to count as equally defensive, reactive, Gothic readings. They assume precisely what James is trying to problematize or ironicize: that there must be a real, determinate "beast" or "ghost" lurking behind or underneath and that it must just be properly, finally named by our sharp-eyed, excavating critic (almost as if to name it is to kill it or tame it). (Marcher is at least willing to try, dialectically if also pathetically, to turn the fully acknowledged absence of a secret into his secret again; but critical readings, perhaps by nature, continue to hunt the beast.) Such critical responses seem motivated by the same anxieties, and continue and extend the same forms of resistance that we have been noting in this chapter and that James is citing and undermining rather than affirming.[19] (Again, James comes close to giving away his irony completely in *The Sacred Fount,* but, apparently, for many critics, not close enough.) Or, to paraphrase Nietzsche, in the world according to James, it would appear that we would at least rather will there to be a ghost than accept that there is nothing.

NOTES

1. Truffault (1967), p. 99.
2. *Frankfurter Allgemeine Zeitung,* 27 May: 35.
3. Cf. Tanner's remarks on the "avoidance of specification" in *The Wings of the Dove,* a theme he rightly links both to the moral faults of Kate and Merton, and to the problem itself, the unavoidability of the problem of specification. (1985), p. 14.
4. Compare this recent complaint in Philip Roth's novel *American Pastoral:* "You might as well have the brain of a tank. You get them wrong before you meet them, while you're anticipating meeting them; you get them wrong while you're with them; and then you go home to tell somebody else about the meeting and you get them all wrong again. . . . The fact remains that getting people right is not what living is all about anyway. It's getting them wrong that is living, getting them wrong and wrong and wrong and then, on careful reconsideration, getting them wrong again. That's how we know we're alive; we're wrong. Maybe the best thing would be to forget being right or wrong about people and just go along for the ride. But if you can do that – well, lucky you." Roth (1997), p.35.
5. *IH,* 155.
6. This is a theme in many of the earlier stories. See Tanner's summary (1985), pp. 9–15.
7. In fact, the question of the possibility or more often impossibility of love is never far from these "resolution" (or more often, "no resolution") stories. See not only the narrator's obsession with Hugh Verecker's "little point," the "figure" in his carpet, but also what the obsession does to Corvick and Gwendolen (*FC,* 357–400).
8. This echoes the beginning lines of the story, where Brydon's narcissism is first on view: The question of what one thinks of anything is "silly," because his thoughts "would still be almost altogether about something that concerns only myself" (*JC,* 313).
9. I develop this use of Freud's category in "Nietzsche und die Melancholie der Moderni-tät," forthcoming.
10. There are other exceptions to the "love is a zero sum game" reading. The friendship between Dencombe and Dr. Hugh in "The Middle Years" might be another example. Indeed, what could be taken as that story's summary sentiment could well serve as an

epigram for James's whole treatment of moral life: "We work in the dark – we do what we can – we give what we have. Our doubt is our passion and our passion is our task. The rest is the madness of art" (*MY*, 258).

11. The origin of the story concerned the half-sister of Mary Shelley, Claire Claremont, the mother of Byron's child, a story James heard about a researcher who was offered letters on condition that he marry the niece of Miss Claremont.

12. I don't think the issue here is epistemological, but more like the way the problem of truth is raised in Nietzsche, as a "condition" or putative measure of life, or what we expect the truth will do for us, as a matter of life, than whether there is any truth. See my discussion in Pippin (1997c).

13. Wilson (1934).

14. Krook (1962), pp. 115–6.

15. For more on the role of Douglas, and on the questions of authority and social power raised by the tale, see Rowe (1984), pp. 119–46. The most interesting account known to me of the story's prologue, and the erotic, transference and authority issues it raises, is Felman's extraordinary reading (1982), pp. 113–38.

16. Fiedler (1992), p. 135.

17. Edmonson (1997).

18. Sedgwick (1990), pp. 182–212. Sedgwick, of course, is wary of "essentializing" in the use of the category of homosexuality, and is quite sensitive to some of the historical issues that frame the narration, but her account still seems to me "Marcher-esque" in its hunt for the Beast, and it makes far too much of the one encounter with a male described in the story, the graveside epiphany. Cf. Bernstein's criticisms (forthcoming), p. 21. (And when James wants to come close to writing openly about homoerotic desire, he can. See, for the example, "The Pupil.")

19. The exception to such a temptation is Felman's brilliant Lacanean reading (1982), an interpretation rich and dense enough to require a sustained, independent response. In this context, I can only vote with her against the way the pro and con sides of the Edmund Wilson/Freudian debate were posed and for her much more sweeping treatment of the problem of ambiguity. There are, of course, a number of similarities between her treatment and Lacanean themes in Chapter 3 and elsewhere here, but that issue, not to mention the relevance of philosophical treatments, like Kant's and Hegel's, throughout and especially in Chapters 6 and 7, is also clearly unmanageable in this context.

# 5

# ISABEL ARCHER'S "BEASTLY PURE MIND"

It is not accidental that our greatest art is intimate and not monumental, nor is it accidental that today only within the smallest and most intimate circles, in personal human situations, in pianissimo, that something is pulsating that corresponds to the prophetic pneuma, which in former times swept through the great communities like a firebrand, welding them together.

Max Weber[1]

In the scenes he sets and the histories he assumes, James seems to have created a great many dangers and threats to any moral resolution of anything, even as he does not finally undermine the reality and unavoidability of such moral problems. So a natural question would finally be: How far does he think his best characters can go in the acknowledgment of any moral mutuality (especially in the possibility of love, understood as, among other things, an ethical relation of trust and fidelity)[2] or in the resolution of any interpretive question?

This question might be understood to have two specific foci. First, "reciprocity," in the way we have discussed, it might look more like a danger in Jamesean modernity than an ideal, the experience of dependence in the modern world more like a pathology than an acknowledgment of mutuality (as Rousseau first predicted in the *Second Discourse*).[3] The extraordinary complexity of social reality, or the link between the content of any self-perception and the experience of being-perceived, together with the range and complexities of material dependencies in modernity, might seem to threaten to dissolve the integrity of any self into its social constitution. Always to internalize the views of others, to think of oneself as nothing more than the accumulation of such views, or to be so materially dependent on others that one's deeds and passions (even love itself) can never be experienced as one's own, but just "theirs," "what they require," is not to have satisfied the first condition of my life's having worth: that it be, and be experienceable as, my life. Madame Merle's eloquent defense of social form and mutually reflecting dependencies might turn out not just to be a corrective to any exaggerated hope for "one's own private self," but to be the last word, a Rousseauean nightmare, "Osmondism," let us say.[4] And Isabel is introduced to us as someone ferociously pledged above all to escape such dependencies, and by a great stroke of luck she inherits enough money to attempt to do so. The fact that she nevertheless ends up as Mrs. Osmond is a sobering thought if the context for that event is not merely her individual psychological needs and weaknesses, but the general problem so often at issue in James: the possibility of independence at all.

On the other hand, the great adventures in endless indeterminacy, hesitation, even retrospective reconstitution of psychological and moral meaning, raise a parallel threat: that whatever heart is left to any notion of the moral importance of such autonomy seems, in the light of such adventures, too weak to do much pumping, too endlessly qualifiable, to serve any real moral, judgmental purpose. It might all just leave us with something like James's vague aesthetic expression of his moral ideal: see as much as you can, feel as much as can be felt, imagine intensely, appreciate and acknowledge the overwhelming complexity of your own and another's particularity, and so forth. One spectacular example of that problem: Strether's apparently endless and perhaps never resolved speculations about the proper judgment to make about Chad's affair with Madame de Vionnet, and the bearing of such an issue on his own decision about what to do, even on the issue of "who he is." Both such problems, let us say, Isabel's putative experience of the impossibility of the sort of heroic freedom or moral integrity she once thought possible, and so the impossibility of any true moral mutuality, or any reciprocity among free persons ("love as a zero sum game"), and Strether's turn back to America, his inability, apparently, to accept Maria Gostrey's offer of love, or resolve the question of his identity, suggest that the kind of life James would have us live, if it deserves to be called a worthy life, simply cannot be lived. Perhaps in the light of that supposedly tragic result – norms without which we cannot lead a "modern" life, but which cannot ever be realized, or realizations that must always come "too late" – the renunciations of life that seem to characterize so many of James's endings, especially in his first truly great novel and in his favorite novel, are all we are left with.[5]

I

As usual, we begin, in *The Portrait of a Lady*, with a setting as much historical as natural, the images as much temporal as geographic. It is late afternoon at a great old English estate now occupied by rich Americans. As the sun sets, we see, as if framed in one of the "portraits" that make up the imagistic structure of much of the novel, a dying old man, Mr. Touchett, his dying son, Ralph, and his pseudo-radical English friend, clearly a sort of dying breed (Lord Warburton, who professes to be for great changes, but seems about as politically conscious as his two dim-witted sisters[6]). There are too many jokes nowadays, complains the old man; no one seems to appreciate what serious changes are coming. The dying young man is said not to care, to be "a regular cynic. He doesn't seem to believe anything" (21). The full familial context, the broader picture for this part of the scene, we soon learn, is a cold, loveless, failed marriage between Mr. and Mrs. Touchett. He in his money making (he is a banker), she in her "independence," have produced nothing of any substance, moral or otherwise, to pass on to Ralph, who, like many modern characters, seems to be sick and dying because of nothing much to live for.[7]

We quickly get some sense too of the terms within which we are to understand the problem of "the future." They all three hope it will have something to do with the fresh, charming, eager "tall girl in a black dress" whom they soon meet, Mrs. Touchett's niece, the American, Isabel Archer. But they fear it will more likely look much more like her friend, Henrietta Stackpole: industrious, pragmatic, moralistic, tasteless, simplifying, and charmless. ("Henrietta, however, does smell of the future – it almost knocks one down" (88). This is a woman who sees in the death of Mr. Touchett, a man she barely knows, a chance for a story to sell, and she has no hesitation in inviting herself to the death watch.[8])

This familial context – the question of what is to be "passed on" now, in this awkward age, what renewal or future is possible in the state of exhaustion, sun setting, or dying so described – is announced frequently, if only negatively and bleakly, and it helps give the question of Isabel's future an ambitious historical dimension (since she is soon to be as suddenly as spectacularly rich and promising as America itself). The generational question is important, first, in the other central family in the story, Gilbert Osmond, Madame Merle, and their daughter Pansy. In some grotesque imitation of European manners, she has been made fit for nothing but pouring tea. Madame Merle thinks of herself as "born before the French Revolution," belonging to "the old, old world" (170), and seems later, to Isabel, to be "the product of a different moral or social clime" than hers, to have "a different morality" (275). This contrast and problem is already figured, as noted, in Ralph's illness and the diseased Touchett family, in the death of Isabel's baby, and in the death of the three children of the Countess Gemini (as if really to stress the point about her moral vacuity, her lack of any generative power)[9].

Enter, then, Isabel, and the picture comes to life, is set in motion, and the question of what she might help renew or inaugurate is posed. As is already clear, James from the start will give her the great burden of his American theme with all its social and historical implications, and his presentation of her fate will reveal a good deal about the moral dimension of his international theme. She will make a bad marriage, face that fact, and make a decision about what to do about it. It will be the most complex of the international marriages James arranges, between an American who believes her great luck and money and energy will make possible a new open-minded and free exploration of taste and appreciation (a form of greatness that will serve as a kind of redemption of the money and power itself), with some specter of traditional, pre-modern European culture (a Europeanized American perhaps because there can't really be much of Europe left, just these stylized imitations, this idea of it). Her mature sense of the meaning of what she did and what it requires is the moral and dramatic pivot of the novel, and a very great deal hangs on what we think she learns. But the historical framework that James creates, the question raised about the possibility of the future, inheritance, generational transition, and the weight already placed on the "American vs. European" moral conventions in so much of his fiction, lifts that issue out of melodrama and romance (where it is wonderfully complex in its own right) and gives it that dimension we have seen in so many other contexts. The question of what it is finally right for Isabel to do (or, alternatively, why she went wrong) will return us again to the question of how or in what sense anything could be said to be right at all, given what now seems unavailable as a guide or norm for such a question (and so to the possibility, suspected by so many readers, that there really is no such question left by the end of the novel, that it is all "really" a matter of sexual fear, repression, or simple despair).

These issues are all in play because Isabel has so many "ideas," ideas that scare Lord Warburton and faintly amuse, irritate, and finally infuriate Osmond. In this regard, Isabel has by chance escaped the fate of most American girls, has not been socialized to be like a Ludlow in Albany, and so, unusually, does not regard the insistent, ever erect and manly Caspar Goodwood (as fine a name as there is in James) as all that great a catch. (Goodwood appears to Osmond "the most modern man" he knows (420), although Osmond is surprised, apparently, that Goodwood is not hopelessly crude.) Isabel had had the odd good fortune to have been carted back and forth across the Atlantic three times before she was fourteen, and so European tastes were as much a part of her as American aspirations. And, especially, her bohemian background has broken the hold of the conventional expectations of bourgeois girls. An unsatisfiable and infinite desire has been created in Isabel, a longing not just for what has been offered her, or what she must settle for, but for what might be; for, especially, what simply is not a part of the narrow world of Albany, but part instead of the world of "the music of Gounod, the poetry of Browning, the prose of George Eliot." ("Her reputation of reading a great deal hung about her like the cloudy envelope of a goddess in an epic"; young men feared "that some special preparation was required for talking with her" (41). All this even though she reads "in translation.")

This all means two things for the role Isabel plays in the larger moral drama of the novel. First, since she has had no guidance, no interlocutors, has been formed in the unformed culture of America, has had no help weighing and distinguishing what is important to know from what isn't, since she is so self-educated, she steps into the first scenes with a jumble of ideas, many of them clearly half-baked, none of them really attached, connected, thought through, or deep. "Forgotten things came back to her; many others, which she had lately thought of great moment, dropped out of sight. The result was kaleidoscopic. . . ." (42). Whatever chance circumstances allowed her father to escape the hold of the only authoritative culture there was in young America, the utilitarian and Puritan conventions that would so crush characters like Waymarsh and would produce Goodwood and Henrietta, also managed to free his brightest daughter from the same fate and to create enough suspicion and dissatisfaction and strength of will to make possible all this longing, reflection, reading and theorizing, but all in a haphazard, context-less way.

Since the question of how Isabel changes is so important, and since James is introducing her and that theme with such an emphasis on her radical rather than conventional American background (self-taught, self-reliant, brave, longing for some cultural redemption, some dimension higher than the Albany aspirations of her sisters), it is important to emphasize how much attention James draws to the consequences of her catch-as-catch-can program of self-education. James has created such a likeable character, that we might not notice that she is at first, a brash, know-it-all, somewhat self-important twenty-three-year-old, pronouncing on this or that with great confidence and authority, but who knows, finally, very little and, more dangerously, does not know what she does not know. Even our narrator, in an odd twist, "likes" her so much he hesitates to point this out!

> Meanwhile her errors and delusions were frequently such as a biographer interested in preserving the dignity of his subject must shrink from specifying. Her thoughts were a tangle of vague outlines which had never been corrected by the judgment of people speaking from authority. In matters of opinion, she had had her own way, and it had led her into a thousand ridiculous zigzags. At moments, she discovered she was grotesquely wrong, and then she treated herself to a week of passionate humility. After this she held her head higher than ever again; for it was of no use, she had an unquenchable desire to think well of herself (53).

Her opinions can have a "slender value"; she often only "seems to feel and think" (57); she wants mostly not to "appear narrow-minded" (62), she is capable of such fatuous remarks as "Oh, I do hope they'll make a revolution!" . . . "I should delight in seeing a revolution" (71); and we are told that "the love of knowledge coexisted in her mind with the finest capacity for ignorance" (173). Clearly something of both her desire for someone like Osmond, her need for such aesthetic, high-minded appearances (or even for someone who does finally seem to "speak from authority,") as well as her inability to understand what he really stands for, will have had something to do with the culture-less context within which such American "ideas" were formed.

Even more important, though, and even more American is the general shape of her most important idea, the idea that makes her at once so admirable to modern readers and that will lead her straight to her doom. What is most important to her and what others notice first about her is "independence" and her great views about independence. For that is how she understands that paradigmatic modern ideal, freedom. (The importance of this issue is signaled by the telegram the Touchetts first receive, where Mrs. Touchett describes Isabel and her sister as "quite independent," a comment that raises the question (for them and for us) of what that means: "'In a moral or financial sense?..that they wish to be under no obligations? Or does it simply mean that they are fond of their own way?'" (24).) This ideal is often presented with an air of paradox by James, and that is certainly appropriate since somehow the consequence of Isabel's aspiration for a "free exploration of life" (101) will be her stepping freely into the gilded cage of Gilbert Osmond's villa and life.[10] It is the paradox or problem at the heart of the moral issues of independence and dependence, or freedom and convention, on which so much in the novel hangs.

The paradox has first to do with Isabel's view of her fate. She has "no choice," she says, but to refuse Warburton, because she "must" be free; she "can't escape [her] fate" (118) even though her fate largely consists in, and is expressed in, moments of negation: not being Mrs. Warburton or Mrs. Goodwood. (She tells him, too, that her reason for refusal was "I like my liberty too much.") And aside from "wanting to see Europe first," the negative sense is about all the content there is to this aspiration about her fate. At one point, she finally seizes the paradox (of being fated not to have a fate; even to be something like "condemned to be free") when she insists "I don't wish to be a mere sheep in the flock. I wish to choose my fate and know something of human affairs beyond what other people think it compatible with propriety to tell me" (143). (This claim, of something so paradoxical as choosing a fate, brings to mind James's puzzling formulation in his Preface, that Isabel "affronts her destiny.") She is particularly eager to flaunt the idea of not making a great match, or proving her independence, when she is confronted by Goodwood: "I'm marrying a perfect non-entity. Don't try to take an interest in him. You can't" (279).

So among the jumble of her shifting and half-formed ideas, there is one general ideal that has taken hold, deeply enough to come to her mind first, before anything as simple as lack of desire or love in the explanation of her two refusals: she must be free, and freedom means first of all independence, not being attached or committed anywhere, not being identified with a role or function, not, indeed, "being" anything (at least, she seems to think, not yet, not for a while). There is, she suspects, little freedom in anything now conventional, especially in being Mrs. Goodwood or Mrs. Warburton, and yet there can be no value or merit in any sort of life that is not deeply one's own. So there seems only one option in being free, and that is simply not being conventional, or in choosing some course of action manifestly risky, dangerous and unpredictable. (Like her father, she is a gambler; playing it safe is selling out.) These are the views that will lead her to Osmond, both because his life itself is "nothing" ("No career, no name, no position, no fortune, no future, no anything.) "Oh yes, he paints. . . ." (172),[11] and because his relationship to everything is so much the embodiment of a certain form of freedom she would have to find attractive – that is, irony – and, because there is nothing conventional in marrying him. It may not be clear what marrying him amounts to, but for Isabel's purposes, it is especially clear and important what the marriage is not: "what is expected of her" (as in, a catch like Warburton or an American captain of industry). Because Osmond is an aesthete, a connoisseur, because he manufactures nothing and rules no great estate, she assumes he must be free from conventional dependencies and that he can embody an older form of moral and aesthetic purity – disinterestedness. As we shall see, she is misled, but her failure to see is not merely a mistake or something that happens to her. It results from what her views, all too typical and paradigmatically modern, American aspirations, won't let her see. Likewise, that Osmond's aestheticism is a disguised egotism, a demand to be appreciated and worshipped, is also a characteristic, not merely a personal pathology. It reflects how little life there is in the social forms he manipulates, how much they simply now cover over the Countess Gemini's meaningless love affairs, Madame Merle's machinations, Pansy's vacuity, and Osmond's monumental vanity.

There is a final twist to this paradoxical formulation (that her fate is to have to choose her fate, that freedom for her will be largely a negative stance toward the world, more declining to act than acting). It is an extreme vision of her future, one where the insistence on her freedom, on not planning out her life conventionally or even prudentially, seems to lead her to an acceptance of an anarchy or passivity, even a fantasy of violation and abduction. When asked by Henrietta, "Do you know where you are drifting?" she responds,

"No, I haven't the least idea, and I find it very pleasant not to know. A swift carriage, of a dark night, rattling with four horses over roads that one can't see – that's my idea of happiness" (146).

In the light of earlier discussions here, Isabel's ideal, or her fantasy, is quite understandable. The new American conventions of work, thrift, respectability, a public world kept strictly distinct from the private consolations of romance, all as offered by Goodwood, and the museum-like, and even rather silly, lord of the manor existence proposed by Warburton, look eminently rejectable. She wants something more bohemian, something that could look unpredictable, and because unpredictable or even imprudent, more likely "her own," less determined by venal self-interest or the security of reputation. Understanding a free life, a life really of one's own, as successful avoidance of such options (and nothing but), is quite attractive for a mind and spirit like Isabel's. But the paradoxical (and hubristic) tone of being powerful enough to "choose one's fate" (or "affront one's destiny" or determine by her action and will alone what such deeds will "mean"), her romantic images, and the specter of Osmond and his supreme irony,[12] all suggest that something is going very wrong with this sort of moral ideal, this putative "duty" to live independently, not to live conventionally.

It is all well enough to want not to be Madame Merle, whose whole life is a kind of fine social form, but there looks to be some deadly inadequacy in this modern alternative of Isabel's. A free life so understood looks either to be some still unattached "nothing," or an attempt to avoid the conventional in a way that is as inauthentic or as much trapped by convention as what one is trying to escape. (Osmond's life is a version of this. His apparent contempt for the conventional only reflects a narcissism that can find no real appreciation for his genius there. He cannot "be" anything; that would be unfree and vulgar and compromised, and this is the Osmond that Isabel first sees. But if he is not seen and appreciated to be above all such attachments, he is literally nothing. This means he must keep searching for the special few who can truly appreciate him and his special, cynical, aesthetic embodiment of convention. He is hardly free from the search for such affirmation. He wants, most of all, to be the Pope, to be the object of worship for nothing at all, for being the Pope.)

If this is how James would have us understand the course of events that now unfold, then, to return to the question asked earlier, the question of

Isabel's failure, what it means, and what she ought to do about it, cannot at all be read as a general comment on either the possibility of modern freedom or some sort of genuine mutuality or love. Whatever comment there might be on the general issue of the realization of a free life will have to be an implication or inference from what goes wrong with Isabel's particular aspiration. That will again have a great deal to do with what one thinks she learns, what kind of "Bildung" has gone on.

### II

Isabel moves toward her "destiny" by chance, the unexpected inheritance of seventy thousand pounds or so. Ralph has persuaded his father to "put some wind" in Isabel's sails by settling such money on her rather than him. (Ralph, thus, as Madame Merle points out, does as much to create Isabel's fate as anyone; he "makes her marriage" as much as anyone, since there is very little chance Isabel would have been led to or attracted to Osmond, and none, vice versa, had she not the fortune that Ralph arranges. She will, it turns out, choose very little of her fate.) Given Isabel's unformed state, that is, as Mr. Touchett knows immediately, very dangerous (as dangerous as America's rapidly growing power and wealth), a little like pouring a lot of gasoline on an uncontained fire. In this instance, it can even be "immoral" to alter someone's life so unilaterally. And there is little question that Ralph has not, at the outset, understood Isabel well enough, that he has moved too fast, both out of impulsive generosity and out of a love that is too idealized (as if of a portrait), all this as a consequence of his "sidelines" status in life. He must admire her non-conformity and boldness, but he expects somehow that all that potential and dangerous wildness will stop at his expectations, that she will do what he expects ("make a great marriage"), and that turns to be a fatal miscalculation (perhaps she wants most of all to upset his expectations).

He does understand some of the risks though, and at one point utters what appears to be a paradigmatic Jamesean speech, a prefiguration of the famous "live all you can," little Billham speech in *The Ambassadors*.

> Take things more easily. Don't ask yourself so much whether this or that is good for you. Don't question your conscience so much – it will get out of tune like a strummed piano. Keep it for great occasions. Don't try so much to form your character – it's like trying to pull

open a tight, tender young rose. Live as you like best, and your character will take care of itself. . . . Spread your wings; rise above the ground. It's never wrong to do that (192).

This is quite a complex, difficult piece of advice, as if of a piece with the dialectical problem of freedom just noted. In the first place, as Ralph quickly realizes, he is preaching to the converted; when it comes to any conventional view of the right, or of what ought to form a character, no one could be already more on Ralph's side than Isabel, more sure of her capacity to avoid the expected, to "spread her wings," and even to be able to stop "thinking" and jump in that carriage. (As Ralph realizes after Isabel's enthusiastic response: "You're a capital person to advise," said Ralph; "you take the wind out of my sails" (192).[13]) On the other hand, in the obvious ironic twist, however Isabel conceives of her fortune and what to do with it, it will be a conception, a piece of her "conscience," her sense of what she ought to do, and why. There could be no other way to act than for "what she thinks best," even if, as with her marriage, it is in defiance of what everyone thinks the worst. The trick will be not in having a conception, or having none at all, but in how one has it, with what sort of expectations, confidence, and so on. Moreover, one's action are too intertwined with others, with their reactions and their own desires and wills, to make it possible ever to take this advice about spontaneity or to enact Isabel's fantasy. There may be such a carriage and a dark night, and one may not know where one is going, but someone does, someone is driving, and it is a superficial and dangerously romantic view to pretend not to care. Ralph, that is, to some extent already shares Isabel's illusion that by not acting conventionally, by being bold and trusting herself, as special or a distinct individual (one of the "great," not the "weak"), she will have acted freely, as herself (will have risen above the ground, in the conventional image of freedom as flight). The irony in such advice is already evident in the images: She will not thereby have escaped her conscience and made her fate; she will have acted out a naive ideal of conscience, and made her fate over to those eager to manipulate such types.

Isabel is aware that "a large fortune means freedom," and she is afraid, for all her bravado. She intuits that despite her agreement with Ralph about not overusing her conscience, "one must keep thinking; it's a constant effort" (193), but she has no sense yet of how long it might take to form such thoughts, how fragile, defeasable, and tentative all such thinking must be, and so how dependent such thoughts are on a social world of mutuality and reciprocal independence, on the reassurances, interchanges, corrections, and challenges of others who can react freely, not in response to one's money or their own greed. For all of their obvious affection for each other, the great pathos of this culminating scene between them is that she can't yet find that in Ralph. He has become somehow infatuated with her view of the world (perhaps it seems such a breath of fresh air, so bold to have turned down a rich, virile American and an English lord) and is only encouraging her to act on it, not helping her think about it. The deepest irony of all here is that acting also on her own intuitions, Isabel's calamity results primarily from her following Ralph's advice, and her mythical carriage turns out to be the gilded cage of a marriage to Osmond. She "takes flight" and flies right into the cage.

The latter half of the novel turns on her realization of this fate, or rather on her slow realization (i) that Osmond is an egotist, vain and pompous, and that since she will not bend completely to his will, he had ceased even to like her, that he will be cold, petulant, and angry the rest of their lives together (his crude attempts to marry off Pansy to Isabel's ex- and still ardent lover, Warburton, make all this clear to her); (ii) that Madame Merle had indeed, as Mrs. Touchett charged, acted deceptively and manipulatively, in order to arrange the marriage of her old friend to Isabel; and (iii) that the intimacy that Isabel has begun to suspect between Madame Merle and Osmond is of long standing, that they had had an affair that began during Osmond's first marriage and that Pansy is Madame Merle's daughter. The moral question of judgment and reaction is played out in a series of electric scenes in the last third of the novel – a long night alone in which Isabel realizes her marriage has failed and tries to make sense of that, a brief, very tense scene with Madame Merle in the convent where Pansy has returned, a decision to defy her husband and visit the dying Ralph, and a notoriously ambiguous final scene at Gardencourt with Caspar Goodwood, complete with "white lightning" kisses, impulsive rejection, and flight back to Rome.

And Isabel's is indeed a "moral" reaction to all of this. That is the language she comes to about the "serpent" Osmond and Madame Merle's "wickedness." What Isabel must assess concerns the various possible interpretations one might give of Osmond's aesthetic aspirations, what it meant for him to have stood so apart from the world around him, to have judged it all so vulgar, profane, ugly, and wanting, and she begins to apply moral and not psychological or personal terms. His stance and his actions, toward the world and toward himself, have been "false" and thereby simply wrong. Since, as we have noted throughout, it is not hard for some readers to think of James himself as having adopted Osmond's aesthetic stance, it is quite important to appreciate what Isabel comes to see. For she decides that:

> Under his culture, his cleverness, his amenity, under his good-nature, his facility, his knowledge of life, his egotism lay hidden like a serpent in a bank of flowers (360).

Isabel had thought him "the first gentleman of Europe" and she finds she was wrong, but what she has discovered is something like the implications of self-importance, Osmond's role in the world itself, what else he did and did not do, would or would not do, how he valued and understood his relationship to others. She had conceived of Osmond as many conceived of her, as a "portrait," and had thought one could understand him in a pictorial way, as having that sort of determinate, fixed meaning or identity.[14] Her own view of liberty was like that; it is one of the things we mean when we call such views romantic. But what is important about the meaning of a great picture is what we don't see, but must try to construct in order to make sense of what we do, an uncertain and indeterminate, possible construction that requires a community of appreciators, a culture of mutually educating taste. Isabel's imagination wasn't up to that when she first met Osmond, and she has had little real help, certainly no such appreciators, even if a lot of criticism. But she has now seen him in motion, and she can even begin a bit to fill out the possibilities implied by the picture of Madame Merle standing while he sat. The moving picture as a whole is now clearer to her because she can see what else would be, must be, if this is.

> But when she began to see what it *implied* [his gentlemanly self-importance] she drew back; there was *more in the bond* than she meant to put her name to. It *implied* a sovereign contempt for everyone but some three or four very exalted people whom he envied, and for everything in the world but half a dozen ideas of his own. That was very well, she would have gone with him even there a long distance; for he pointed out to her so much of the baseness and shabbiness of life, opened her eyes so wide to the stupidity, the

depravity, the ignorance of mankind, that she had been properly impressed with the infinite vulgarity of things and of the virtue of keeping oneself unspotted by it. But this base, ignoble world, it appeared, was after all what one was to live for; one was to keep it forever in one's eye, in order not to enlighten or convert or redeem it but to extract from it some recognition of one's own superiority (360, my emphasis).

To her horror, Isabel has discovered not only that Osmond's aestheticism is just a display of narcissism, but that her husband has found a final way to express his views about the unsuitability of the modern world, its not being a proper arena for his beauty. He can spend the rest of his life demonstrating his superiority by expressing daily contempt and hatred for his inferior, all too modern wife, with her "sentiments worth of a radical newspaper or a Unitarian preacher" (362). Given her youth, background, experience, there was perhaps little chance that Isabel could have anticipated what her own view of independence might mean, how close it was to Osmond's irony and willful negation. But her stubborn confidence that she did know has been her undoing, and so there is an element of tragedy in these reflections, a necessary tension between innocence and experience.

And there is also a note of great guilt throughout, since Isabel had so eagerly, despite warnings, signed on to this project of high-minded anti-modern aestheticism, without appreciating that what it meant could not be contained in a satisfying single portrait, that it could mean a wide variety of possible things the understanding of which required a more dedicated and intense imagination than she had brought to the issues or, at the time, was even willing to undertake.[15] So she can finally "see" Osmond in his treatment of Pansy, his inability to appreciate anything of Pansy's own life and his complete inability even to begin to question the old norms and expectations according to which a marriage to Warburton would of itself, simply and unequivocally, be a great thing. Osmond, it said very often, "takes himself too seriously." In an attitude all too typical of conservatism and traditionalism, his irony and negativity do not extend to himself; he can conceive no suspicion of himself and his ancient forms.[16] Ralph, on the other hand, may be "cynical," but he doubts himself as well (perhaps too much) and so can forgive. "It was simply that Ralph was generous and her husband was not" (363). Ralph yields nothing to Osmond's distaste for aspects of the world developing around him; it is bad enough that when dying, he can pronounce, "death is good," but can also add, with unusual Jamesean simplicity, "life is better, for in life there's love" (477).

As we have seen in other contexts, Osmond's "evil" is of a piece with this willed resistance to the instability, ambiguity, and uncertainty of the world he inhabits and the kind of mutuality and dependence that that world requires. He prefers the world of ritual, rigid traditionalism, and form, so he pretends he lives in this "papal" world, that his daughter can be hidden away in a convent, that his American wife can be crushed and remade. The same is true of Madame Merle, with her modern "wickedness," not perhaps of "Biblical" proportions – manipulating matters to arrange a dowry for your daughter is hardly murdering your brother – but "wicked" nonetheless in being "deeply false . . . deeply, deeply, deeply" (431). Isabel had been used as an "applied handled hung-up tool, as senseless and convenient as mere shaped wood and iron" (459) because Osmond and Merle simply cannot conceive that what they think they are doing could have any dimension other than the conventional meaning that would be assigned to arranging a marriage for a convent-educated daughter, or to securing a good match as a stepmother. It is, and is only, what it would be seen to be. There is never the slightest hint that they ever would allow themselves to think otherwise. What all such actions mean are, for them, as fixed and obvious and visible as one of Osmond's coins. But the world now has Isabel Archers in it, shooing off Lord Warburton, defying her husband's wishes, trying to figure out what she thinks right, refusing to abandon a dying friend. They are flabbergasted and horrified, but that is the extent of their capacity to respond. It is Isabel who can appreciate the multiplicity of meanings, how and why things looked to whomever they did, had to look then, how they must look and mean now, why.

But she is also lost at the end; such a humbling experience has occurred, as it often does in James, too late; as if no one's imagination is powerful enough to anticipate what a course of action might imply, what else it might require, and so what finally "would have been" one's motives, as if only retrospection, "after" a life is lived, can help establish that. (One could not say that she has "discovered" that she intended at the earlier time of courtship to present herself falsely, to dissimulate and pretend to be the type Osmond obviously expected. But that is how "that Isabel" must look to herself "now.") A kind of collective imagination, especially an engagement at a level of deep trust, intimacy, and love, would help a great deal to anticipate and reflect, and that might have been so in Isabel's case, had she had Ralph. But she then had her ideal of independence, and Ralph could see himself only as a burden, an interruption in a life that had a future longer than his tubercular existence would allow. He held back, and she doesn't "ask for help" until much later.

But finally, after all the recriminations, Isabel does appear to take something from all this, to conclude something. She makes a promise to Pansy – "I won't desert you" (462) – and she has to act, apparently, on that promise very soon.[17] For Goodwood presses his case, and literally himself, on Isabel one last time, in one of the most famous of James's scenes.

### III

Goodwood has heard from Ralph of Isabel's misery and has heard Ralph's supposition that Osmond will never forgive Isabel for going to Ralph, that he will make her pay the rest of her life. So Goodwood makes a long and impassioned case: that Isabel must leave Osmond, that there is no reason for her to stay. "You must save what you can of your life; you mustn't lose it all simply because you've lost a part" (488). And "We can do absolutely as we please; to whom under the sun do we owe anything" (489). Isabel feels herself sinking, as in "fathomless waters" as she hears all this, a possibility that with all its images of darkness and possession, returns us and this fatherless girl, intimidating to boys and scary to lords, back to her own fantasy of wild carriage rides and decisive male action.

> . . . this was different; this was the hot wind of the desert, at the approach of which the others dropped dead, like mere sweet airs of the garden. It wrapped her about; it lifted her off her feet, while the very taste of it, as of something potent, acrid and strange, forced open her set teeth (488).

And,

> His kiss was like white lightning, a flash that spread, and spread again, and stayed; and it was extraordinarily as if, while she took it, she felt each thing in his hard manhood that had least pleased her, each aggressive fact of his face, his figure, his presence, justified of its intense identity and made one with this act of possession (489).

But still, neither the case nor the passion moves her. When she returns to her senses, she was, it is said, in another ambiguous use of the word: "free." She races toward the house, and we hear, "She had not known where to turn; but she knew now. There was a very straight path" (490).

After reading such scenes, one might be tempted to conclude that Isabel just "cannot handle" this sudden appearance of unmediated, powerful sexual passion, either in Goodwood or herself, and she is simply running away in fear; that her renunciation is, as in many other such cases in James where one has to make this choice, better explained in psychological than moral terms.[18] But this would assume that a life with Goodwood now makes some sense for her, that it makes more sense to rush back to Albany and risk turning into a Ludlow, or at least a Goodwood. She did not and does not now love Goodwood, and the sexual excitement she feels at being so passionately, finally loved need reflect no such love on her part. He is still the same earnest boy he always was (almost the same; he is now much more decisive) and while she now, in this situation, can appreciate all the elements of his "hard manhood" she liked least before (because so insistent, one-sided, aggressive), that means only that he can and will help her, that someone will finally act on her behalf, forcefully. Of course she wants help, and even at this point in her desperation wants most of all to die; running away with him would be a wonderful leg up on that option, she notes, but that is not what one might call high praise. Most of all, this would all enact again her (and Ralph's) earlier fantasy of "soaring away," of choosing her fate, or willing her destiny. This, this dark night escape, is precisely the romantic fantasy that led her into this trap. After all she has gone through, and all the shadows that the past, and what she will be consigning Pansy to, will forever cast on her future, there is something pathetic and paradigmatically American in Goodwood's claim: "Why shouldn't we be happy – when it's here before us. When it's so easy?" (490).

Isabel's "straight path" is not something one can simply applaud as if it were a great, straightforward moral triumph. It is all too sad and complicated for that. Her "awakening" by Goodwood has only brought out how much of intimacy, passion, and love she is giving up, not necessarily just with him, but forever. But she has, after all, saved Pansy once, and has promised to try to do it again, and that is not an unworthy or self-deceived goal. Moreover, as we have seen in other contexts, what it means for her to have achieved a self-determined life is to "recover" her past as her own, and the way to do that depends on what she will do now. Her marriage to

Osmond becomes at least hers, depending on how she acts now.[19] And in the novel's final ironic twist, her rejection of Goodwood's proposal turns out not to be a "renunciation of a life that cannot be or is too frightening to be lived" but the rejection of the fantasy of independence and will that sealed her fate in the first place. Her future is not a rosy one, but it will be hers in the only sense now available, tied inextricably to others (a helpless child who is liable to become another "hung up tool" without whatever protection she can afford) and a life "led" in a much more tentative, interrogative, and humbled way.

Well, perhaps not the final irony. The novel ends with Caspar's hearing from Henrietta some of his own optimistic, American, can-do advice about infinite future possibilities, ". . . just you wait." Hearing that he is young, that he can always meet someone else, adds "on the spot thirty years to his life," and the two Americans walk away in misunderstanding, Henrietta convinced that "she had now given him the key to patience" (490).

NOTES

1. Weber (1946), p. 155.

2. This is, of course, only a limited perspective on the possibility of love; there are surely many others. But its being limited does not make it any less real or pressing, and it is surely an element that James often concentrates on.

3. There are small allusions to the Rousseau problem – the possibility of a moral sense, being free and acknowledging each other as free, within civilized dependence – scattered throughout James's fiction. In *The Ambassadors*, for example, where the main question for Strether is the role of a moral sense in a civilized life (or what a civilized life amounts to, even whether it is inherently decadent), Madame de Vionnet, not insignificantly, was educated at Rousseau's Geneva. The narrator remarks: "She was another person however – that had been promptly marked – from the small child of nature at the Geneva school; a little person quite made over (as foreign women were, compared with American) by marriage" (139). I assume these allusions are not accidental, since much later, when all of the "secrets" of Madame de Vionnet's civilized life are known, she is referred to as "Madame Roland" on the scaffold (317). Madame Jean Marie Roland (nee Jeanne Philipon) thus lends her names to the two main French characters (see Holland (1982), p. 273) and suggests a certain "post-revolutionary" stance, the moderate Gironde, victims of the Jacobin (in this case, American, puritanical) terror. That Madame de Vionnet is thereby thought of as "post-revolutionary," not pre-, and even though a sacrificial victim to the more extreme forces, the true heir of the Genevan's demand for freedom, is unquestionably on James's mind in these associations.

4. Isabel intuits this problem in Madame Merle right away. She "was not natural . . . her nature had been too much overlaid by custom and her angles too much rubbed away. She had become too flexible, too useful, was too ripe and too final. She was in a word

143

too perfectly the social animal that man and woman are supposed to have been intended to be; and she had rid herself of every remnant of that tonic wildness which we may assume to have belonged even to the most amiable persons in the ages before country-house life was the fashion. . . . One might wonder what commerce she could possibly hold with her own spirit" (*PL*, 167). As usual, there are several ironies in this observation. First, like Isabel literally, Osmond and Merle are also American "orphans," without the traditional resources and inheritance, as Americans, to form a life "out of the past." So they "adopt" an older, different parent, or formal European culture, and so the priority of old social form. But Isabel is such an orphan, too, without a father who could pass on a moral form. (He was an American par excellence: a gambler.) So she also craves and finally embraces precisely the kind of formality and ritual that she here hesitates before. That is, of course, the central problem around which the novel turns: the meaning of her decision to marry Osmond, and James's treatment is played out exactly in the terms of these dialectical ironies about dependence and independence. Second, she gets right that Merle is nothing but the web of her social relations, but sadly she does not know how right she is, that this means Merle is interested in nothing but her former lover and a dowry for her daughter, all much to Isabel's eventual disadvantage. (As if to drive home the point about Americans and heritage, James also makes Henrietta "without parents" (*PL*, 55).)

5. Or one reads in a similar vein that James has produced some bitter eulogy for the dying culture of a beloved aristocratic, conventionally stable, high culture Europe, inclining his reader towards a kind of "tragic pessimism," admiring only those characters who somehow find a way to "love and suffer" nobly, in Stephen Spender's words, "so as to some extent atone for the evil which is simply the evil of the modern world. Spender (1938), p. 67. In Crews (1971), moral issues in James are treated in a similar way. Crews emphasizes both the great difficulties of individual moral integrity (something, he thinks, that would require far too much separation, even alienation, from society) or any clear moral judgment about others, even though called for (given the great difficulty in assigning personal responsibility and the obvious complexity of meaning and motives). Hyacinth's suicide in *The Princess Cassimassima*, or Strether's sacrifice and loneliness in *The Ambassadors*, are presented by Crews as "tragic" expressions of such unresolveable Jamesean dilemmas. See p. 83 on "the two parts" of James's "moral awareness" and their irreconcileability, "intuitive inclusiveness," and "social conscience." There is unmistakably a tragic dimension to the later novels, but we also need to investigate first and in some detail what sorts of moral and ethical issues come to gain some purchase on the lives of individual characters and why, especially given James's awareness of the historical uniqueness of this context. When we do, I think we can begin to see that not every tragic situation implies a claim about fundamentally tragic human alternatives. Said in a simpler way: "Tragedy" is not the right ultimate category for the later novels. The invocations of melodrama, comedy, fairy tale, and the general tone taken suggest something at once lighter, more tranquil, and deliberately undefined.

6. I suggest later that this theme is connected with a view of meaning, a view false even of pictorial meaning in art, but more at home there: an idea of stable, determinate, "frozen," out of time typologies, categories, and styles. It is a view most associated with Osmond, though Ralph tends to think this way, and Isabel is subject to the temptation. The image of seeing or thinking in painting is scattered throughout the novel: pp. 195, 197, 222, 224, 230, 235, 237, 258, 271, just to take one brief stretch.

7. There is a great deal of tenderness between Ralph and his father, but their intimacy is always qualified, perhaps even intensified, by the awareness of the absence of any future for Ralph.

8. One things she is not, of course, is stupid, and she is as admirably independent as Isabel. (She also, of course, genuinely loves Isabel and will later cross "the stormy ocean in midwinter because she had guessed that Isabel was sad" (406).) She knows, for example, that Isabel lives "too much in the world of [her] own dreams" (*PL*, 188). She has also settled for far less in life than Isabel will, and this makes her much less vulnerable than Isabel, less susceptible to people like Madame Merle and Osmond, however much that also means that she is considerably more prosaic. She has no trouble, therefore, seeing right away that Osmond is a creep. But then, again, all she seems to want out of life is hard work and a pair of sensible shoes.

9. Cf. Holland's discussion (1982), pp. 17–27.

10. It is Ralph who reminds her that she is entering a "cage," something she tries to defend by saying it is "her" cage, that she has chosen it, can accept her fate because she has chosen it (*PL*, 288). And, of course, she hasn't chosen much of anything. Ralph has engineered her inheritance – it was the result of an idea, not chance – and Madame Merle has "made" her marriage. One might say that no more subtle "dialectic of Isabel's enlightenment" could be imagined.

11. According to Isabel, he also has a "genius for upholstery" (*PL*, 324).

12. Osmond's version: "Not to worry – not to strive nor struggle. To resign myself. To be content with little. . . ." "Do you call that simple?" she asked with mild irony. "Yes, because it's negative." "Has your life been negative?" "Call it affirmative if you like. Only it has affirmed my indifference. Mind you, not my natural indifference – I *had* none. But my studied, my willful renunciation" (*PL*, 227).

13. This is, of course, a reference to the main image Ralph had used in trying to persuade his father to settle such a fortune on Isabel: that he wanted to "put a little wind in her sails." This explicit reinvocation of the image suggests that by doing so, he has taken the wind out of his sails, or that he is not, cannot be, as much a spectator on the sidelines as he would like to think. He will not know what he has done, or even, cannot yet understand what he meant to do, until much later when he and Isabel try to figure it out, but it is already clear, at least imagistically, that they "share" the same wind.

14. When finally Isabel has been turned into a "portrait of a lady," made to correspond to Osmond's view of the world, of meaning, of taste, the results are painful. Ralph's reactions: "Poor human-hearted Isabel, what perversity had bitten her? Her light step drew a mass of drapery behind it; her intelligent head sustained a majesty of ornament. The free, keen girl had become quite another person; what he saw was the fine lady who was supposed to represent something. What did Isabel represent? Ralph asked himself; and he could only answer by saying that she represented Gilbert Osmond. 'Good heavens, what a function,' he then woefully exclaimed. He was lost in wonder at the mystery of things" (*PL*, 331).

15. There is, in other words, also the question of what Isabel did not want to see or even refused to see, and so her own moral culpability. See Dorothea Krook (1962), p. 59.

16. Osmond has perfected what the Bellegardes aspire to in *The American*: "the art of taking oneself seriously" (*A*, 111), and is thereby just as morally suspect.

17. There is this too: "You'll come back?" she [Pansy] called out in a voice that Isabel remembered afterward. "Yes, I'll come back." Perhaps that "afterward" refers to the

moment when Isabel "listens a little" at the door of Gardencourt in the novel's closing scene (*PL,* 490).

18. For example, Mazzella (1975), pp. 610–11.

19. There is a fine discussion of how Isabel's decision defeats Osmond's "freedom-killing" powers and reclaims her life as her own in Weisbuch (1998), p. 116. See his final summation: "The world is now completely before Isabel, and all before us, we who have been shorn of the comforting simplifications, and who must live now by our wits and by our love" (p. 119).

# 6

# THE "STRANGE LOGIC" OF LAMBERT STRETHER'S "DOUBLE CONSCIOUSNESS"

"The real hero, in any of James' stories, is a social entity of which men and women are constituents."

T.S. Eliot, "Henry James"

I

James situates his characters in a social world where various uncertainties in any common form of life, and the profound and unstable dependencies now characteristic of modern societies, have made much more difficult such basic elements of mutual understanding as the assignment of motives, reliance on a stable self-understanding or identity, comprehending the implications of one act description rather than another, assessing the salience and relevance of characteristics and act properties, and so forth. The collapse of the authority of traditional and religious conventions, the prevalence and different sort of power made possible by newly accumulated and vast wealth, the partial breakdown of social class structure (and even to some extent new uncertainties about gender roles, family roles, the nature of marriage, and the meaning and value of work) and the social mobility of the newly powerful, have all thrown our characters on each other for recognition and reassurance without many fixed navigation points, and appear to have suggested to James a historicist thesis about social meaning, together with an equally radical claim about the intersubjective and unstable nature of subjectivity itself. There are now no "social facts," to paraphrase Nietzsche, only socially negotiated and perhaps ultimately unresolvable, contesting interpretations.

Characters must still of course somehow finally be able to depend or to count on each other, both for the security and stability of social life itself, and for the very possibility of shared meaning in their interactions (or for a deeply and unavoidably shared consciousness itself), but they must do so within the suspicions and uncertainties created by these unequal and rapidly shifting dependencies, power relations, limited imaginations, and unmanageable complexities and possibilities. It is now a cliche, after, say Baudelaire's reflections pointed it out, that too much happens too fast and too complexly in modern societies for experience even to be "taken in" somehow, much less understood or assessed, but the details of such an experience turn out not at all to be cliches in James's treatment. He is quite aware, I have argued, of how profoundly this situation can affect the possibility of any mutuality and therewith any reliable moral acknowledgment and trust, any relationship based on some mutual regard for or expectation of the right thing. "Managing" this situation appropriately, not falsely or resistantly (not acting as if all this were not now the case or as if it were avoidable) is partly what emerges as the moral dimension in James's novels and tales.

As noted in Chapter 3, one prominent figure assumed and manipulated by James to suggest this issue of dependency and the moral complications that issue from it is the triangle, especially the most frequent Jamesean triangle: the heiress, the deceiving friend, and the fortune hunter.[1] *The Portrait of a Lady, The Wings of the Dove,* and *The Golden Bowl* (or, depending on what one thinks of Basil, *The Bostonians)* make direct use of this structure, and it is introduced in a somewhat different form in *Washington Square* (where we also see the important supplement to the triangle, the tyrannical father).[2]

Such a repetition of narrative structure, wherein desire is manipulated and even intimate engagements do not mean what they seem to mean, also works to suggest a quite general dependence in attachments on reflections of such attachments in the consciousness of others.[3] The very fact that this structure is so common (and shows up in so many similar forms in *The Bostonians, The American, The Spoils of Poynton, The Awkward Age,* and many others)[4] at least suggests that the friend or reflector, the other, turns out to be necessary, indispensable in the origins and sustenance of desire itself. The narrative structure suggests a profound need for the "confirmation" of desires in the like desires of others, and therewith suggests the susceptibility of uncertain and unstable desire to external manipulation.[5]

Without fixed or natural or divine standards of worth or firm, authoritative traditions, or even the possibility now of the self-intimacy and authenticity on which the romantics counted so heavily,[6] we know so little of what we really want, so little of what is worthy of inspiring and sustaining any wanting, that we can self-consciously desire and sustain desire only if the desire is mediated by, or manipulated by, a third. We want, inevitably, weakly and dependently, what others want or can get us to want. We want this way in the simplest sense, because otherwise we would not know what is wantable; do not now (and given the intensity of these dependencies, cannot) simply feel what we want personally and immediately. It is this dependence and the uncertainties and vagaries that it creates that make at least any straightforward reliance on a moral virtue like integrity or the moral acknowledgment of others' freedom at worst very questionable or at best simply very difficult and risky, given how much of "who one is" or what one tries to acknowledge in others is already a reflection of that dependence.[7] James complicates things enormously by suppressing, keeping hidden the role of the mediator (the attraction is arranged and so the desire is mediated, but the heiress thinks she simply wants what she wants) and by introducing deception, thereby pointing to the sort of power this gives the mediator in such an environment. Maggie, that is, may still want the Prince as she has always wanted him, simply as reflected in, as desirable to, other women (most of all now because of what she has found out about his affair with Charlotte), and the coldness of her "amputation" of Charlotte may still both raise moral doubts about her status. But this dependence on this reflection and recognition and the complications (and envy and competition) it creates is not simply a singular moral fault in her character. It reflects a threat to free and therefore worthwhile lives that James paints on a much broader canvas.[8]

*The Ambassadors* presents again such a triangular sketch, but, as if to confirm how self-consciously and seriously James takes such a structure, deliberately, almost painstakingly, inverts most of our expectations (expectations that his own fiction teaches us to have) about the heiress, fortune hunter, and deceiving friend. Now the young American heiress is an heir, Chad Newsome, and not at all a passive object. The friend is not a female but older and male, Lambert Strether. The presumed European fortune hunter is now a woman, Madame de Vionnet. The tyrannical father is now a tyrannical mother, Mrs. Newsome, and not onstage, but offstage. The complex, deliberate gender reversals are only the beginning. There are reversals and inversions everywhere. The presumed fortune hunter is not taking advantage of the heir; the heir, in effect, is deceiving the "fortune hunter," who genuinely and selflessly loves the heir (but not vice versa). The friend – the man occupying the Charlotte Stant, Kate Croy, Madame Merle position – is not a deceiver but an enlightener, and as fine and admirable a character as James ever created, his best hero by far. He does not try to gain by manipulating the relationship; he loses everything (his own future marriage and presumably his very livelihood) by trying to sustain and encourage it.

The central romantic relationship is not a preparation for marriage, but adulterous. And finally, and most remarkably, two further moral inversions. First, as with so many other plots, there is a lie at the center of this triangle, too, though now the character in the position of the friend is the one deceived, and is not the deceiver. Strether is led to believe by little Billham that the relationship between Chad and Madame de Vionnet is "virtuous," or Platonic, mentor and student, not sexual. When, in one of James's greatest scenes, Strether comes upon the two of them enjoying a weekend together, and learns the truth, neither he nor we are outraged or morally discomfited. He had been lied to, but, on the other hand, there was indeed a genuine, unavoidable ambiguity in the characterization "virtuous," and even in more senses than the sexual/Platonic ambiguity they are all first concerned with. (It was virtuous in the sense that Chad had not simply been seduced, manipulated by an adventuress, as Strether believed when Billham told his "technical lie"; it was a relationship that had helped and nurtured them both. And the sense in which it wasn't virtuous actually had nothing to do with Billham's meaning, but with Chad's "lack of imagination," his own moral limitations, as we shall see only later.) Second, until we have a sense of those limitations in Chad, our moral intuitions are all, like Strether's, on the side of the adultery. The return of everything to its ordained social order (Chad back home to marry a good American girl, to create his "monopoly") is hardly affirmed in the tone James creates.

These inversions create a complex setting, to say the least, in which James raises both the questions of dependence, power, and freedom in modernity on the one hand and, as noted at the beginning of the last chapter, the question of the resolution (if any) within such a world of moral ambiguity and moral meaning in Stretcher's initial and ultimate relation to Chad on the other. As always, the two themes are linked, the possibility of some sort of independence and mutuality of independent subjects having a great deal to do with the quality of the determinations settled on by the participants.[9]

II

At the outset, though, we are shown a man not at all very independent, a mere ambassador, the representative of someone else, his friend and bene-factress back home in Woollett, Mrs. Newsome. He is to represent her interests in convincing her son, Chad, to return home to Woollett and take over control of the family business. If successful (and the condition is clear from the start to Strether (*AM,* 56)), he will then marry the rich widow. The twenty-eight-year old Chad has been in Europe for five years now, far longer than the originally planned six months, and all of Woollett society has come to believe that an evil European seductress has him in her clutches. It is from those clutches that Strether is to free him.

But the only freedom that the fifty-five-year-old Strether begins to care about is his own. From the moment he gets off the boat, he begins to enjoy a "consciousness of personal freedom" (*AM,* 17), "an extraordinary sense of escape" (*AM,* 59), begins to experience "the strange logic of finding himself so free" (*AM,* 60). (Strether had not been to Europe since a honeymoon trip with his wife many years before. These memories now called up are quite painful. They remind him that he has failed to be the great figure he had hoped to be, failed even to keep faith with his love of Europe, with his hopes for high culture and art, and they remind him of his unlucky life. His wife died very young, and he grieved so for her that he could not care for his son, who was sent to boarding school, and died there of diptheria. Strether blames himself for neglecting him.) But Strether does not just experience and remember such failure and dashed hopes. He also begins to relive the Europe he once experienced, the chance, then and perhaps now, to escape the fate that crushed Waymarsh and linked Strether so tightly to a widow's money. This new sense of freedom has a "strange logic" because, among other thing, he begins to experience this sense of possibility and freedom, even though still strictly "contracted," to carry out the will of someone else, a contract whose meaning will be more and more being simply subjected to that will, not having one of his own, not being free. The possibility of independence, in some form, according to this "strange logic," will also introduce us to all the aspects of his various dependencies, the senses in which his life is not his own, but wholly ambassadorial. (These latter restrictions, we will see, make possible, even easy, a certain kind of judgment about Chad, the judgments so comfortable for Waymarsh and the Pococks. But the more independent Strether becomes or feels himself to be, the more difficult any such judgment becomes, and paradoxically the more his judgements they seem to be guided by another sort of dependence-in-his-new-independence, first on Maria Gostrey, then on Madame de Vionnet.)

He has, then, more properly described by James, a "*double consciousness*," first described psychologically: "There was detachment in his zeal and curiosity in his indifference" (*AM*, 18). His heart is not really in the ambassadorial mission that he is supposed to be zealous about; his real curiosity, under the guise of indifference, is for a continent not yet thoroughly modernized in the American sense, and thereby a place where the paradigmatic virtues of the new America have not yet taken root.

But, we find, this duality is polysemous, and already so visible, as always, in the names of the characters. Strether's doubleness is clear: He yearns to "stray," yet he must remain tied to his "tether." The advice given him by his guide is clear from her name, Maria Gostrey, or "Go stray!" and his traveling companion reminds us of the moral and cultural bogs and fens he has left behind: Waymarsh.[10] This is the dominant form of that doubleness, a paradigmatic modern position for James (or, as it could be said: "Money! Can't live with it; can't live without it"). He is, almost wholly, dependent, inextricably linked to Mrs. Newsome, her money, Woollett, and so on, the ever-more influential American way of making and thinking about money. But he is also self-consciousness, ironic, incapable of being simply a representative of such a world. The Woollett point of view is from the start more borrowed than wholly genuine in Strether, a coat that doesn't quite fit.

However, in many other senses, too, the "strange logic" of that double consciousness creates manifold and eventually unbearable tensions for Strether, in an almost classic now familiar sense, in which alienation counts as *the* modern form of unfreedom.[11] He really is not what he nevertheless is (an ambassador), and he somehow is what he most of all is not (not being of Woollett, anything but Woollett). The tension created thereby is evinced in manifold ways. There is, of course, the International Theme again, and here both in a simple, and again in its own double, sense. That is, he comes over to Europe bristling (genuinely, at the start, we are to believe) with "Woollett categories," or the kind of simplistic and naive moralism that is the darker side of American innocence. The woman must be bad, the liaison must be a moral disaster, Chad is simply irresponsible, he owes it to his mother, family, and Woollett to return, and so on. Yet Strether is already, even before his adventure and transformation, an outsider as an American (he is, but just as much is not, such an American); he shares none of the dominant sensibilities about work and rectitude that go together with this moralism. He tells himself and Maria that he is a "failure" because he hasn't made money (*AM*, 40), but we sense he only half believes it (just "look at the successes!" Maria points out ironically and appropriately), and it would seem he never bothered to try all that hard to be a "good American" in that sense.[12] He is a critic, an analyzer, not a doer or a maker, and that aligns him already with the observers in "Europe" who now must watch the game rather than play it, or with Europe in its mythic Jamesean function. Or at least one of the functions; as noted, this sort of doubleness in Strether has it own dualities. For Strether is also "American" enough to believe not merely in "life" itself, but in a life of one's own, and so to be disapproving when confronted with that standard Jamesean figure of the other side of European aestheticism and ambiguity and even cynicism about "innocence: the arranged marriage." (The announcement by Madame de Vionnet that "we are marrying Jeanne," her daughter, as if she had just sold a pet, jars both Strether and the reader and reminds us at an opportune time that the European dimension is itself double, that Strether cannot "be" a European in that sense.)[13]

And, finally, Strether's consciousness is temporally double, divided. For one thing, not being "who he is" means being always in between his duty to the past and his aspiration about his future; it means that he can never, as he says, "take things as they come" (*AM*, 61). So, as Maria first puts it, he suffers from a "failure to enjoy" (*AM*, 25). In his case, he sees so much in the light of his future, of the forever postponed gratification so familiar in critical treatments of capitalism (that is, in terms of what he needs from Mrs. Newsome and so what he must always postpone), that much of the present is lost on him (or would be without her initial help) and, especially sees so much in terms of the past (and his own guilt and regrets) that he has a difficult time making his way to life itself before him, in getting out from under the shadows of his own past in a way that might let him lead a life, rather than just remember one (all so that his "long ache" for a life "might at last drop to rest" (*AM*, 61).) The "yellow covers" of the French fiction he sees in shop windows can only remind him of his own optimism and "promises to himself," when he collected his own supply during that first trip with his young wife, convinced he could keep some private faith with art and high culture, could arrange his own private redemption in the world of commerce he returned to. Now such memories only remind him of the present state of those volumes, "somewhere at home, the dozen – stale and soiled and never sent to the binder . . . the mere sallow paint on the door of the temple of taste that he had dreamed of raising up. . . ." (*AM*, 63). Chad, the central "problem" in the story (what to make of his dalliance, how to understand it), is the perfect figure for this temporal duality; at once an evocation of another and perhaps last chance for Strether to care for his lost son, as well as the beginning of a relationship with his future step-son.[14]

### III

Narratively, all such divisions suggests a great tension that must be re-solved, and that is certainly the surface structure of the story, and would appear to suggest a certain kind of answer to the questions we have been raising about determinacy of meaning and moral resolution. So it would appear that this is a narrative of liberation, not deception and tragedy (hence, one might suggest, all the inversions in Jame's own carefully cre-ated archetypes). The tension is resolved by a break with Mrs. Newsome, American Puritanical moralism, a prescribed future, and a break with Strether's feeling that he is somehow imprisoned in his past, that every-thing is now, for him, too late. The newly found independence makes it finally possible to appreciate the Chad-Madame de Vionnet liaison "as it is," in its specificity, and to judge its worth and any moral questions of harm, duty, and promises, not as an ambassador, but for itself, in a possible engagement with others who also want to escape from the play of self-interest, domination, and merely imitative desire. This all costs Strether a great deal, essentially costs him the possibility of a life in a world where such ambiguity and freedom is not tolerated, but he bravely pays the price, and is willing to live with the costs (isolation, marginality, powerlessness).

Yet the bulk of the evidence already presented about James's sense of the possibility of any kind of modernist morality makes that conventional summary seem a bit too pat. The first question to be raised is one of the central ones we have been pursuing: How does Strether resolve the various possible interpretations of what Chad had been doing, resolve them with others whom we come to admire for not simply maneuvering to get out of Strether what would be useful to them, but who do want to help him "see": Maria, little Billham, and Madame de Vionnet. And any exploration of that issue must take some account of the depth, unavoidability, and persistence of Strether's "double consciousness" and so all the implications of such a position. That is, the deepest and most important irony (or, again, doubleness) in the story concerns the supposed resolution itself, the liberation and insight summarized earlier. For Strether's coming to see that Chad's relation with Madame de Vionnet is "virtuous" remains double in many senses, in itself and for him; it is not "resolved." It is not what he took it to be: a more experienced and more powerful woman manipulating a younger man selfishly, either for her own amusement or gain. And that realization looks like an initial resolution of his American prejudices and his European-inspired doubts. (Early on, Strether could go so far as to say confidently: "She's base, venal, out of the streets" (*AM,* 45).) But it turns out that it is also not what he next takes it to be, a kind of tutorial in taste and culture. (He waxes poetic when he is in this "Platonic pair" phase of his evaluation, when he wants so badly to see it in its best "European" light: "It's a friendship, of a beautiful sort, and that's what makes them so strong. They're straight, they feel; and they keep each other up" (*AM,* 168).) But, it turns out, they were far freer than Strether supposed. The relationship is sexual, Madame de Vionnet is still married, and everyone on her side has deceived Strether. He then seems to make his peace both with the adultery and with this deceit, and finds a way still to hold onto the former (second) or virtuous reading as well, and some sort of more stable duality seems possible. (He takes full in the face the lie they had told him, but tells himself that it was "such an inevitable tribute to good taste as he couldn't have wished them not to render"; and even, in a remarkable turn of phrase, that he could "trust" Madame de Vionnet "to make deception right" (*AM,* 318). But then he finds that that is too simple as well. Chad is, in some sense, much better than he was or would have been (although Madame de Vionnet's being responsible for some "immense moral lift" may exaggerate a bit (*AM,* 168)), but Chad is certainly not "good."[15] He gives her up too easily; he is even callow and thoughtless. He wholly "lacks imagination" (*AM,* 290), and because of that, does not seem to see what his leaving would mean for Madame de Vionnet, does not even seem to think about it. ("He spoke of being 'tired' of her almost as he might have spoken of being tired of roast mutton for dinner" (*AM*, 337).)[16] It is the basic irony of the novel that, fundamentally, Waymarsh was in some fact-of-the-matter sense right all along: Chad is not seriously involved and will come home when he's finished.[17]

But to return to Strether's own duality, it is not surprising that Strether would want to see everything as virtuously as he can, even as the evidence mounts against it, just as it was not surprising that initially seeing it all in the former way would have been attractive. That meant then keeping faith with Mrs. Newsome and going home to marry a fortune. But now, seeing it as virtuous means he can be free; he has a way of forcing the break by insisting on "the truth," on letting that do its work effecting his liberation from Mrs. Newsome, even if he is greatly exaggerating the virtue of the relationship and has some good reasons to know full well that he is. (At one point, little Bilham, the author of the "technical lie" about virtuous friendship, simply lets slip that Chad can't marry Jeanne de Vionnet because he had been in love with the mother. A confused Strether asks," But isn't it exactly your idea that he isn't in love with her mother?" Billham can only reply, "Well, he isn't at any rate in love with Jeanne," and Strether marches on, without attempting to resolve what he has heard (*AM*, 169).) So Strether encourages Chad to stay, not go; his bridges are thereby burned, and out come Mamie and the Pococks. As noted, he continues to hold to this view of what the relationship means, even as he can clearly and unambiguously see that Chad would not only go then, but go easily, that the decision doesn't seem to cost him much; no agony, no tears, no regrets. He takes the "European" side because Chad's staying no longer can mean for him "disloyalty and irresponsibility to Woollett," but his leaving would now mean "disloyalty and irresponsibility to Madame de Vionnet" (as well as a betrayal of all that has come to be "better" in himself). His leaving/ staying now seems better illuminated, more what it would actually mean, when reflected in the consciousness of someone for whom the possibility is not tied up with Woollett or money or power, even though someone not "independent" in the "disinterested" sense, Madame de Vionnet. Why this should be so is one of the central questions raised by the events in the novel, and is obviously connected with the themes we have been following throughout these works.

So the first view (in the clutches of an adventuress) is not the truth, neither is the second (virtuous tutorial), and neither, it would appear, is the third (adulterous and deceptive, but still true love and morally transformative for Chad). And each of these positions adopted by Strether still reflects his own complex double consciousness, his dependence and yet his dissatisfaction with such dependence, and his (genuine) willingness to understand and appreciate in some way that is free even if not wholly independent. Each such stage of liberation appears to reflect also a new stage of, and a different sort of, superior dependence, the last one, especially, to anticipate a bit, as he appears to have fallen in love with Madame de Vionnet. (The doubleness, in other words, knowing and not-knowing himself at the same time, is not self-deceit or wishful thinking, or simple alienation. A better word might simply be finitude, the unsatisfactoriness of many modern forms of dependence, which make having one's own life impossible, but the impossibility of any final independence, and the acknowledgment of forms of dependence that realize rather than qualify one's freedom. Strether is not resolving all such dualities, in other words, but learning to live with the impossibility of such a notion of resolution.)[18]

IV

All of which would appear to push us closer to either a moral skepticism and/or a wholly psychologized understanding of the characters' moral aspirations (simply what he needs to see in Chad, morally). I do not think so, and argue that there is nothing especially surprising or deflating (or skeptical) in the fact (i) that the moral ideal at stake in the novels (freedom, understood in both its negative sense as freedom from subjection to the will of another or positively as a kind of self-understanding and therewith authenticity) has no unambiguous realization (as we discovered in Isabel's case), or (ii) that the moral dimensions of mutual understanding and appreciation should remain so unresolved and unresolveable. Appreciating such ambiguities about a free life and coming to terms with interpretive problems all already amount to an appropriate moral stance. But this conclusion anticipates here elements of Strether's development, to which we need to return.

There are three turning points in this development, each of which contributes something to the position sketched here: Strether's "live all you can" speech in Gloriani's garden (really the beginning of his decisive turn away from the American position, and his eventually encouraging Chad to stay, not go); the discovery scene in the country when Strether learns the truth about the affair and his subsequent "coming to terms" with it with

Madame de Vionnet in her apartment; and his final decision to return to America and not stay with Maria, who "would do anything" for him.

Virtually everything in Strether's famous speech to little Billham is qualified by the same dualities we have been noticing, and those qualifications make it difficult to take in what is supposed to be the content of Strether's moral advice. It is here, in the midst of this beautiful scene, a garden party for a famous sculptor (in the middle of one of the "temples of taste" Strether had had such hope for much earlier), where Strether first realizes, much to his shock, that Madame de Vionnet is not "bad" at all; on the contrary. (All this even though he also learns for the first time that she is still married, and even though Madame de Vionnet seems to "cut" Strether by not introducing him when appropriate.) Greatly moved by the spectacle and the reversal of so many of his expectations, and the confirmations of so many of his doubts and suspicions about the World of Woollett, he unburdens himself to Chad's friend. What seems to be a torrent of regret, sad self-recrimination, and a very broad, somewhat vague ethic pour out of him and, from the point of view of the reader, seem to state the principle on the basis of which Strether's turn away from Woollett and regret about his own past are based.

The theme concerns yet another doubleness, a life that is lived "too late" to be appreciated as lived (as if one might live for what will have been one's life). The opening premise encourages Billham to resist this way of living:

> There were some things that had to come in time if they were to come at all. If they didn't come in time they were lost for ever. It was the general sense of them that had overwhelmed him with its long slow rush (*AM*, 130).

Such a premise also begins the paradoxes. Strether will now regret that so much had passed him by, and that it was now too late. But the statement ends with it's being clear that something is happening to him now, precisely this experience, this new sense of what had happened to him. Nothing has really rushed by him; the general "sense" of everything is now "overwhelming" him. In a perfect example of the doubleness we have been discussing, it is Strether who can appreciate how much of life must be actively lived, led, risked, not merely endured, and not (or not fully, yet) Bilham. One has to be old to appreciate the possibilities of youth (in the usual tragic sense of "youth is wasted on the young"), and he is appreciating them; they are "overwhelming" him. The novel is, after all, about how exquisitely and fully Strether has begun to live, finally.[19] (The speech contains within it this point of view. As Strether begins to talk about the "right time" for life, the time he has supposedly missed, he says: "But that doesn't affect the point that the right time is now yours." And then some consciousness of his own position seems to return suddenly; actually "the right time is *any* time that one is still so lucky to have" (*AM,* 132).)

"Live all you can; it's a mistake not to" (*AM,* 132), is the most quoted piece of advice in the speech, something one highlights especially because James wrote in his New York Edition Preface that the whole novel grew from imagining such a scene and such an outburst. It is clear that the way one might, by existing, still not "live" would be not to have "one's own life." ("It doesn't so much matter what you do in particular, so long as you have your life. If you haven't had that what *have* you had?" (*AM,* 132).) And so the question raised concerns the conditions for achieving such a distinction. Just what must one do in order to achieve "having *one's* life," or presumably not having it be someone else's? Strether, our ambassador, himself raises mostly, and oddly in this context, a doubt about any such possible freedom, noting instead that,

> The affair – I mean the affair of life – couldn't no doubt have been different for me; for it's at best a tin mould, either fluted and embossed, with ornamental excrescences, or else smooth and dreadfully plain, into which, a helpless jelly, one's consciousness is poured – so that one 'takes' the form, as the great cook says, and is more or less compactly held by it: one lives in fine as one can. Still, one has the illusion of freedom; therefore, don't be, like me, without the memory of that illusion (*AM,* 132).[20]

Herewith yet another duality, this time between the consciousness of one social determinations, one's all too tightly fitting mold, and one's freedom, at least as an experience, subjectively, as the presumably necessary "illusion of freedom." We are not given much to go on in understanding what James calls Strether's "philosophy" at this point, how to take the status of such an "illusion." The image is extreme and somewhat ugly: consciousness poured like jelly into a mold that contains it and gives it a shape. Given this, all this passionate advice about "live all you can" would make little sense if it only amounted to: Be the mould you must be! Yet for all the philosophical unclarity, the phenomenological point is clear enough: Consciousness is yet again dual, at once formed by social and economic and historical conditions, and in some way, perhaps by being aware of them, understanding their meaning and implications, not merely determined by them, not simply what these conditions decree. Life itself, the practical requirement to lead a life, choose, maneuver, react, and so on would seem to require such an assumption. Or else, given the logic of the image, we would simply be fated to sit like poured jelly, and advice of any kind would be useless.

Finally, there is a neat duality in the "logic" of life itself as promoted here by Strether. In the Preface, James draws our attention to the crucial condition that makes it possible for Strether to become aware of life, not merely to exist, or to carry out his role as ambassador, but to begin to lead his own life. ". . . (I)t would take a felt predicament or a false position to give him so ironic an accent. One hadn't been noting 'tones' all one's life without recognizing when one heard it the voice of the false position" (*AM*, 5). It is this very falseness of his Woollett role, the impossibility of continuing that life, that James counts for Strether as "no small point gained," which in effect begins to give him back his life. Again, in some sense, the Woollett view of Chad is factually true, but it will not allow, if held to as the whole, many other things to be noted and pursued. If it is the whole truth, then so much else of what is now seen and appreciated could not be so, so many of the conversations he has had, and senses as possible, could not be, and they all are. It is just not possible to confront all that he sees in the garden and hold fast to the Woollett categories and judgments: vanity, laziness, treachery, egoism, and so on. James even evokes Strether's own vessel image to make his point about what has changed in Strether.

> He had come with a view that might have been figured by a clear green liquid, say, in a neat glass phial; and the liquid, once poured into the open cup of application, once exposed to the action of another air, had begun to turn from green to red, and whatever, and might, for all he knew, be on its way to purple, to black, to yellow (*AM*, 6).

Strether, of course, must be already somehow receptive to such reactions, but however tightly held by the vessel of his past and circumstances, he can so react, appreciate, evaluate, discuss, and in that sense is also free.

This means that it is the very break down he can suffer ("people's moral scheme *does* break down in Paris" (*AM,* 7)), which now makes it possible for him to regain or now lead a life. That is, the advice is not at all the call for romantic immediacy it might seem to be, as if simply to dive into experience, risk, gamble, avoid constancy or familiarity or whatever. Just the opposite. One would not be leading a life in such cases of immediacy, but, as we saw with Isabel's ideal, either blindly existing or living, openly or furtively, in subjection to someone else. Live by *not* simply living out a role seems the full practical import of the advice, or even "live doubly," even if not yet well recognized by Strether, who himself seems for a time simply to have leapt into the European garden as if it just were life, and Woollett death.[21] As we have already indicated, this too will be reversed and qualified, and we shall have to ask what we and Strether are left with when that happens.[22]

The passage winds up with a flurry of dense dialectical ironies. Strether, of course, had been encouraging Billham to live his own life, but thought of himself as thereby encouraging "innocent gaiety." Billham had turned instead "quite solemn." And Strether had also wanted Bilham to be free of surveillance, subjection, the expectations of others, yet he remarks, "And now for the eye I shall keep on you!"

This prompts Billham to say that in effect, he would be happy not to have his own life, but Strether's life, to be like Strether is now. In a way, this would confirm what Strether has been encouraging: to have some point of view on one's life, not just to be oneself; but Strether, evoking again the doubling of gaiety and seriousness, retorts: "Ah prepare while you are about it to be more amusing." Billham says that Strether is plenty amusing enough for him, and Strether, in effect, ends the scene with the question of the book:

"*Impayable,* as you say, no doubt. But what am I to myself?" (*AM,* 133).

He speaks French, adopts the perspective of an other ("as you say", and thereby begins to work out (thereby is able to work out) how much his new sense of independence paradoxically relies on his reflection in the consciousness of these foreigners, and he then expresses the fear this perspective evokes, that he might again lose himself. He, at the very least, has now had his breakdown, the question of who he is to himself can be raised, and so by having his life interrupted and confused, can actually begin to live.

v

This picture of sociality not as slavish or material dependence, and so not as some simple contrast to romantic authenticity, but as endlessly struggling, mutually reflecting, refined, interrogative, imaginative consciousnesses, is given its clearest figure in the relationship between Strether and Madame de Vionnet.

This aspect of their relationship – her need for Strether's reaction, her need that he reflect to her some view of her affair close to her own and thereby help make it mean that – establishes for the reader much of the genuineness of their relation. That is, this need couldn't be fulfilled if Strether were manipulated or tricked; he must see who she is, and he must be free to do so. (This is a theme already established with respect to Chad – that he cannot really be "squared" without Strether, that the affair can't mean anything except in the consciousnesses of the various involved parties, the quality and freedom of the mind reflecting being the crucial issue.[23]) When Strether runs into Madame de Vionnet in Notre Dame (evoking already what will be the implied themes of their discussion, mystery, and faith, at least in the social world that comprises the sacred for James), their conversation begins to reveal to Strether that she needs him not just to keep Chad around; she needs him to believe in her in order for her to have the relation with Chad she wants. She needs his faith in her, not just his permission, and she needs that for herself, not just strategically.[24] The tone in her voice, its "deference to the solemnity around them" (*AM*, 175) (as if at some founding act of the trust necessary for sociality itself), she spoke in a way that "seemed to make her words mean something that they didn't mean openly." And further,

> Help, strength, peace, a sublime support – she hadn't found so much of these things as that the amount wouldn't be sensibly greater for any scrap his appearance of faith in her might enable her to feel in her hand (*AM*, 175).

She needs a "firm object" to "clutch" at, and Strether resolves to be one, not just to hold to his emerging views that the affair was not venal or insignificant, but, much more important, to let her see that he so thought. (She had herself already let him see how much she needs such approval; she does not bluff it all out, pretend the issue is settled and obvious.) He spontaneously invites her to what turns out to be an intimate breakfast, to establish this new dependence "over their intensely white table-linen, their *omelette aux tomates,* their bottle of straw-coloured Chablis. . . ." (*AM,* 176). It is basically at this late breakfast that her relationship with Chad simply becomes in Strether's mind a moral issue in its own right, an issue of what they owe each other because of what good they have done for each other, and not a question of adultery, betrayal of his mother, or irresponsibility. If it were the latter, what Strether and Marie can now see in each other would not be possible, could not be a practical implication of such a truth. This experience is not something that can be reformulated as an argument or in any sort of brief, and all James can do is let us see something of what Strether sees. It is because of what they do see and feel that Strether can later answer Mrs. Pocock directly, when she is flabbergasted that Strether can even hesitate about Chad's "real duty." He answers, well aware of the "sore abysses it revealed," "Of course they're totally different kinds of *duty*" (*AM,* 276, my emphasis), and he gently defends everything about Madame de Vionnet in the face of Mrs. Pocock's violent and final attack.

Yet the relationship between Chad and Madame de Vionnet is not what it still seems, either to Strether or to Madame de Vionnet; Strether's own sense of the "duties" involved in their relationship begins to contrast with Chad's conduct, and so a final tension must be confronted.

VI

After the real affair had been discovered, Madame de Vionnet asks Strether to come see her, and he willingly goes. This is the scene where her profound vulnerability with respect to Chad is on full view; she is terrified of losing him, breaks down in great sobs before Strether, and helps us realize how risky and anxious that relationship had always been for her. We again hear from Madame de Vionnet of her dependence on Strether and on Strether's views, "How can I be indifferent to how I appear to you?" (*AM,* 320), and a final element in what she is and what the affair might mean is added.

That final element is Strether himself. For Strether has now become, intimately, a part of the affair, however much he (and many readers) want to see him as ("tragically") a mere observer, a vicarious agent. He has become a part of the actual love affair, not just a part of the business of managing it. Strether feels a bit of this himself, when, for all his protestations about what is "too late," he makes his way to the telegraph office to set up his rendezvous, and notes with a kind of pride and a noticeable thrill, that "he was mixed up with the typical tale of Paris, and so were they, poor things – how could they all together help being?" (*AM,* 315). And even more directly later (evoking yet again all his many "dualities"),

> He had absolutely become, himself, with his perceptions and his mistakes, his concessions and his reserves, the droll mixture, as it must seem to them, of his braveries and his fears, the general spectacle of his art and his innocence, almost an added link and certainly a common, priceless ground for them to meet upon (*AM,* 319).

Their triangle is now as tightly bound together as ever; and so is the depth of their dependence on each other, dependencies that do not now qualify or restrict as much as make possible "one's own life," a life one can only comprehend as one's own in the freely given recognition by others. As we have seen before, the moral question they face is the appropriate acknowledgment of such dependencies, the right comprehension and enactment, so as not to be "false" and so as to end up "squared." In this case, this means that they both now have also come to love Chad through his reflections in each other's conciousnesses, and both now clearly love each other, though unequally and obscurely, "through" or on the basis of, these reflections of Chad. (Madame de Vionnet keeps remarking on how much now Strether is part of it all; he has climbed into their boat,[25] even though he keeps trying to tell himself that he is "well in port, the outer sea behind him, and it was only a matter of getting ashore" (*AM,* 327).) Unmistakably, keeping Chad between them, keeping him in Paris, also means something for them, keeps them together, preserves their intimacy. (He is "between" them in the reverse of the way Milly and the money is between Merton and Kate, uniting them even as he separates them.) The somewhat bizarre, familiar, even intimate tone of their reflections on Chad, as if he were the talented, unpredictable son of these worried parents, is only occasionally undercut by the evidence of the intensity of Marie's physical passion, and by the adult intimacy that their common bond has created between them. (Chad had himself evoked this when he first introduced them, as if arranging a date for a divorced parent, declaring they were "made for each other.")

However, the great accomplishment of this scene, especially its human and deeply sympathetic tone, is that the presentation of the density of these mutual dependencies (virtually the opposite of the "crudities of mutual resistance" discussed earlier with respect to *The Golden Bowl*), also presents persuasively the tangle of moral implications or acknowledgments that follow from such dependencies. Madame de Vionnet wants Chad to stay, but not simply on any terms. He must stay freely, on his own terms as well, and her desperation is already a measure of the realization she has come to that he cannot stay. There is no recrimination, no condemnation of Chad, no "jilted lover" scene. Instead, she is full of worry about her "wretched self," "always there" to "take" happiness. But that is in this case only an unrealized worry; she is ready to act on her maxim that the only real happiness is not to take but "to give" (*AM*, 321), and I take that maxim not to mean a simple self-sacrifice, an offering up of herself in selfless love. What she says about it sounds the moral tone that underlies that moral element in all James' fiction: "It's what plays you least false" (*ibid.*). Chad's lack of imagination notwithstanding, he cannot stay, and it would be "false" for her to pretend he could. (She herself remarks to Strether that she had "felt him to have the makings of an immense man of business" (*AM*, 341) and cannot really pretend that their present life can stretch out indefinitely for Chad.)

The whole thing's coming to an end robs Strether of his chance to stay too, but he realizes as well that whatever happens must not simply and exclusively happen for him. He will go and try to persuade Chad one more time to stay, but not in any unqualified call to obligation. It is first (and already weakly, recognizing its limits) an appeal to Chad simply not to go "before," before the benefit of staying had ceased, but this is an appeal also open to "who Chad has already become" and who he nevertheless still is, where he fits (that is, with a concession that he is, after all, an American, not an ersatz French count, with Strether even conceding, acknowledging Chad's actual talents: "Advertising is clearly at this time of day the secret of trade. It's quite possible it will be open to you – giving the whole of your mind to it – to make the whole place hum with you" (*AM*, 339).) Chad, as we learned earlier, is, after all, "only Chad."

Finally, it yet again appears that the ultimate moral category used to describe the implications of these dependencies at the end of a James' novel – what must happen for anyone to end up "right" – is sacrifice, even a tragic self-renunciation. It would appear that to put Chad in the right, Strether has to sacrifice himself, where that means not staying in Europe and marrying Maria. Of course, Strether has already sacrificed Mrs. Newsome and Woollett simply by hesitating. To some extent, he willingly takes on himself the Woollett wrath at Chad's sins (his five-year delay), and does so as if to exorcise his own guilt at his earlier neglect of his "first" son. However, as noted before, such a straightforward logic (Chad's gain, Strether's loss) does no justice to what has happened to Strether or the double logic pursued throughout. He doesn't give up going back or give up Mrs. Newsome. His loss is also his gain. She has remained the same, "But, he says, "I do what I didn't before – I *see* her" (*AM*, 343). Once he had acknowledged the inappropriateness of the moral logic of "adultery" or "irresponsibility," another moral logic of integrity, and new loyalties, were inescapable.

Yet Strether also enacts what appears to be another sacrifice, and that one is more puzzling. James goes to great lengths to set a certain scene in Strether's last interview with Maria. It is in her "little Dutch-looking dining room" (Dutch perhaps to suggest the great felicities and comforts of middle-class life so clear in Dutch painting), a setting especially said to be "saved from modern ravage" (*AM*, 340). There Maria does everything but propose to Strether, telling him that she wants her place to be for him a "haven of rest," and, twice, that there is nothing she wouldn't do for him. But Strether declines, in effect declines this haven saved from modern ravage, and prepares to return to Woollettean modernity. (To make it clear to us just what he is going back to, and so to increase the appearance of sacrifice, he offers to tell Maria what sort of vulgar product constitutes the secret of Woollett's wealth, and she, like Marie, declines the honor.)

He says that he wants it to be clear that his view of the rightness of Chad's delay, of the superiority of "Europe," all had to do with the thing itself, not with his own attachments, interests or commitments. It is not enough to make such a claim; it must *look* that way (for Chad's sake), and for that he must act accordingly and come back with "nothing" for himself. That, he seems to sense, will help Chad's history actually be what it should be taken to be, will help constitute the meaning of Chad's delay in Europe. No part of the fate of that meaning, bound as it now is with Strether's fate, will then be shadowed by any of Strether's "wretched self." Strether says that his "only" logic must be now "to be right" (*AM*, 344) and Maria would make him "wrong."

This has become a familiar question by now, whether the explicit invocation of moral categories is trustworthy, whether Merton Densher's return of the money, our moral assessment of Maggie Verver, Isabel's return to Rome have any sort of ultimacy or independence in the psychological world created by James. Here again, with Strether, many critics find only an abandonment of Maria and the "limitations" of Strether's "capacity for love."[26]

But, in the first place, it would alter the implications of his support for Chad if it were to look as if his rejection of Mrs. Newsome and Woollett were a part of his own self-justification, as if he too had simply fallen into the decadent European maelstrom and polished up Chad so as to look right himself. This claim for going back with a kind of integrity is not a mere rationalization of Strether's cold heart. The measure that it is not such a rationalization may be taken in the line spoken after Strether says Maria would make him wrong – "Honest and fine, she couldn't greatly pretend she didn't see it" (*AM*, 345) – a line with no irony that I can detect about her honesty and fineness.

But the "wrong" he speaks of is again ambiguous, what his staying with Maria would "do" to Chad's status back home's being only one side of it. For it has been clear for some time that Strether's great infatuation with Maria had cooled, almost in proportion as his imagination caught up with his surroundings and he didn't need her as much, or see her as so mysterious and indispensable. Her own acknowledgment that nothing of what Strether needed to see could be "seen" if she showed it all to him was clear in her generous departure from the scene for a long stretch. She must have known that that was also a risk. When she returns, it is clear to her, if not fully to Strether, that something has happened between them, and it is also clear that it is Madame de Vionnet. Were he to stay now, he would, honestly, now be staying not for Maria but for Madame de Vionnet, and that would in the first place be futile, in the second, grossly unfair to Maria, and third, would indeed have to cast that backward Jamesean shadow over past motives, inevitably altering their possible sense, not to mention any future relation with Chad. By leaving without "anything" for himself, he ends up both with nothing (loved by someone whom he does not love; in love with someone who cannot return his love) and yet with everything, the logic of being right and therewith having "his own life" ("and without your life what have you got?") The former situation amounts to the final duality in Lambert Strether's situation, the stuff of both comedy with Maria and tragedy with Madame de Vionnet. That it could be both at the same time ("She sighed it at last all comically, all tragically away") amounts to the "strange" and, I think, "modern" logic of Strether's double consciousness.

Maria alludes a final time to this duality, to the kind of alienation that has made possible and greatly complicated Strether's independence. She notes that "it" (James's mysteriously indefinite pronoun, signifying simply everything) "isn't so much you're *being* 'right' – it's your horrible sharp eye for what makes you so" (*AM*, 345). That "eye" is what makes it impossible for Strether ever to be, simply, comfortably, in some final, settled sense, right, but it is that duality and uncertainty that also most of all makes him, in the only appropriate sense left in the world he inhabits, right.

NOTES

1. As Bette Howland has noted in the *Raritan* piece (1996) cited in Chapter 2. The triangular nature of modern desire is explored brilliantly by Girard (1965). Cf. my discussion of this and the modernity theme in general in Pippin (1991).

2. The three shattered pieces of the golden bowl suggest one common reading of the results of such "triangularity, or of the always borrowed, or reflected, or observed or manipulated nature of desire: the impossibility of love in James's world." But while such triangularity, and its social conditions, surely represents a threat to mutuality and even intimacy, it also reflects a moral fault, I have been suggesting, not simply "the modern fate." If that is so, then the aspiration not only to a possible love, but to a general form of genuinely mutual recognition is not hopeless, if we understand the nature of and occasions of such faults.

3. In his Preface to *The Wings of the Dove,* James names his mediators explicitly: "My registers or 'reflectors', as I so conveniently name them (burnished indeed as they generally are by the intelligence, the curiosity, the passion, the force of the moment, whatever it may be, directing them. . . .)" p. xliii).

4. Basil, Olive, and Serena; Christopher, Valentin, and Madame de Cintré; Fleda, Owen, and Mrs. Gareth; Nanda, Van, and Mrs. Brook, *inter alia.* The triangularity assumes a macabre or even perverse dimension when one member is dead, as in "The Aspern Papers." See Bell (1991), p. 192.

5. This is a phenomenon clearly linked to the transition from folk, or indigenous or local culture, to mass culture, and so to the kind of commonality that makes mass culture possible, conformism, as well as to the power and status of advertising as the mediation of consumer desire in a mass culture. And this – the role of advertising in modern culture and its connections to reflected or manipulated desire – is not lost on James. Not for nothing, in the final conversation between Chad and Strether, does Chad appeal to his talent for and the new importance of advertising, as a reason to go back. "Advertising, scientifically worked, represented itself as the great new force. 'It really

does the thing, you know,'" concludes Chad (*AM,* 339). Chad knows a great deal about reflected, mediated desire, and has thereby stage managed (as in the frequent references to drama and play-acting) the reflection of his romance. Cf. the discussion in Girard (1965) of such "Vance Packard" issues.

6.  Since, if these assumptions are right, there is no temporal or psychological space ever free from such reflected or borrowed desire; no experience intense or bizarre enough not to be "always already" a reflection or imitation, even those experiences favored by modern romantics, like the anxious anticipation of one's "ownmost" death.

7.  This is a theme again in Girard (1965) and Pippin (1991).

8.  The simple name for all of this is, of course, "modern money." James has few equals in the sophistication of his comprehension of the meaning and implications of such a social currency, how much of the human condition that modern form of making and distributing money has changed, at how intimate a psychological level.

9.  The significance of the inversions comes out only later, and will be discussed then. (There are obviously psychological and even psychoanalytical dimensions to the triangularity issue as well.) The inversions help to suggest that this is a tale of liberation, rather than betrayal or tragedy. But there is, predictably, one final reversal or play on that expectation, too.

10. I borrow these suggestions about the significance of these two names from Bette Howland.

11. Like everything else in this novel, this also has a double meaning, since it is by virtue of his crisis, his coming to realize that he is not who he thinks he is, or even that he is not "anything," that Strether attains a kind of freedom he would not otherwise have, begins to be able to be himself.

12. He has failed "in half a dozen trades, *as he liked luxuriously to put it*" (*AM,* 61) (my emphasis). (It's almost as if he is proud of being a failure. Maria certainly is.)

13. The dualities go on: Strether is both the putative authority, the experienced voice of Woollett and an infant, he is forever approaching and withdrawing, committing and sacrificing, he begins to live here, but only vicariously, he is "in" it all, but "out" of it. I think he is thereby James's quintessentially modern character, unsatisfiable but not tragic or comic, finally "right" but not moralistic. Dawidoff (1992) points, in original ways, to a number of Strether's "American" traits: Strether is like a private detective in a detective novel; like the Western hero who cannot get the girl in the end, and above all, represents an intense challenge to bourgeois normalcy, to the world of work and regularity.

14. When this doubleness begins to lose its tension, and things don't seem as much for the past or for the future, then the following is possible: "They walked, wandered, wondered, and a little, lost themselves: Strether hadn't had for years so rich a consciousness of time -; a bag of gold into which he constantly dipped for a handful" (*AM,* 76).

15. "She had made him better, she had made him best, she had made him anything one would: but . . . he was none the less only Chad" (*AM,* 322).

16. Little Bilham had alreay sounded a warning about Chad: that he was about to tire of being so good, that "he isn't used, you see, . . . to being so good" (*AM,* 112).

17. Nothing can go unqualified here; any judgment about Chad must have its own double. A case can be made for him; his future really is not here in Europe. He does belong to the New World. By being made like Madame de Vionnet, he has been made old and young at once (his grey hair is often mentioned as a sign of this) and so able to take the longer view of his own life as well as his immediate obligations to Marie. But it is

nonetheless a qualified case, and Chad's lack of imagination, his inability to appreciate his own dualities and ambiguities, does not allow his case to rise to the level of tragedy.

18. On the issue of "virtuous attachments," see the fine discussion in Holland (1982), pp. 249–69, and the interesting links drawn by Holland between this theme and the "civilization" and "destiny of the middle class" themes in *The Ambassadors*. As will be clear later, I do not agree with the standard view of Strether that Holland, in his otherwise very illuminating treatment, advances about the "limitations" of Strether's "capacity for love" (p. 279).

19. Predictably, there is also one final turn of this screw, too. The extent to which Strether is able to appreciate life also constrains what he is able to do, or what he would be able to do if he were less self-conscious, less aware. He can fall in love with Madame de Vionnet, but acknowledging that means he can have no common future in Europe either with Maria or Marie.

20. In a way typical of such formulations, Strether does not say "Be free now," but something like "Be such that you will later have the memory of freedom."

21. This "living negatively" has of, course, the ring of Adorno. Both Posnock (1991) and Dawidoff (1992) are especially good at drawing our attention to the politically radical implications of the way James presents and treats Strether.

22. That is, this speech is only Strether's opening turn, and there will be enough more to have a dizzying effect. This first declaration also has the air of comedy (Billham has clearly no need of such advice, is in no danger of heading off to Boston to bury himself in a bank) even while, through Billham's "solemn" response, James creates an enormous air of sympathy and affection for Strether, despite the inappropriateness of the "advice."

23. Obviously, in another sense, Chad simply needs Strether's "cover," the authority of someone like Strether with his mother so as to give him a reason for staying so long, to mitigate the charge that he neglected his duty. But that self-interest does not mean that the right description of his affair does not require this social struggle and eventual reflection; it just means that that reflection may serve other purposes.

24. This is a theme so frequent in James that a list of similarities would soon grow unmanageable. See, among many other examples, the way in which Verena, in trying to persuade herself that she has "renounced" the prospects of a bourgeois marriage, cannot do so by searching her soul, but only by persuading Olive (*B*, p. 298).

25. Cf. Holland (1982), p. 260.

26. Holland (1982), p. 279.

# 7

## MEANING AND MORALITY

". . . without your life what have you got?"

There might be several reasons for the great interest taken by so many Jamesean characters in their freedom, reasons for the supposition that what makes a life most worth living is my genuinely being able to lead it. Surely reasons are needed, for it is a controversial interest and supposition. One might imagine other answers at other times in other forms of society, or one might simply imagine alternative philosophical claims. One might not have an interest in "one's own life" perhaps because there can be no such thing; perhaps one might seek, instead, at best, a virtuous life, the best life one could have, even if not so self-determined or in any other sense individually mine. One might seek a just life; one might even seek pleasure or power, even, if not in the fullest sense, freedom. (There are certainly plenty of characters in James who still remember such answers and still believe them.) It is controversial also because, as characters like Isabel discover, what makes for a free life is not obvious, and the risks are enormous when one ranks such a value so high and bets so much on some interpretation of its meaning.

These reasons might involve ambitious philosophical theories – a metaphysics of the person, a required presupposition of all practical life, a value theory. Such a theory might be constructed or inferred from the way James narrates his plots, because his treatment of value and evaluation seems to link these issues with something quite philosophically theoretical: the problem of meaning. What one "doesn't have" if one doesn't have "one's own life" is a life with any meaning, or with only apparent meaning or a kind of deliberately staged enactment of prior, no longer living, conditions of sense, or a manipulated life that is not one's own. Inside the social world James creates, one has no other choice but to try to make sense of what one is doing. A life plan cannot (or, I have argued, cannot for James any longer) have the point, implications, and claims on one that it does, just by being the kind of life it is, by playing a role within a fixed social order. (If the advent of modernity saw the collapse of any possible view of a natural order and hierarchy of the cosmos, the late modern world could be said to represent the collapse of any credible claim to a natural or fixed social order, and the advent of the intelligibility and meaning problems that follow from such a collapse.) And this making and negotiating cannot be done without some degree of freedom from the subjection of the will of others and an individual freedom from self-deceit in attempting to do so. If a life doesn't mean what one has taken it to mean, what others have led one to think it can mean, one's life hasn't that point and so, for one, then, suddenly, no point. (One can imagine a memory of a time with someone in the past, a memory for a long time sweet and completely uncomplicated, ruined forever by a later revelation that the assumptions made by one party then were false, that someone was untrue or unfaithful in some way. Nothing about what it was then, for one of the parties, how it felt then has changed, but it can no longer really be remembered that way, even as a memory of "then," the falseness in what one took it all to mean changes everything, irrevocably and forever, and "how it was" is no longer one's own.)

However much, to speak with the philosophers, I may have from a first-person perspective "identified with,"[1] freely "chosen," enthusiastically embraced, "second-order, strongly evaluated,"[2] my life, if it turns out that ultimately or at bottom, the whole show was stage managed by others, or almost wholly foreordained by institutional restrictions, my life could not have had the meaning I took myself to be settling on, could not be said to have had the significance I found in it, and so is thereby, with such a discovery, robbed of meaning for me.[3] This is also so when the sense-making practices and assumptions simply belong to "another (past) world," and these can't be integrated, despite the self-interested, self-deceived pretense that they can, with a "new world," as in all those potentially explosive marriages between Europeans and Americans. All of which considerations begin to suggest the full account that is implied by James's treatment: that freedom cannot be achieved alone, that the achievement of free subjectivity requires a certain sort of social relation among subjects, and that this relation of mutuality and reciprocity is highly sensitive to social arrangements of work and power and gender relations.[4]

This suggestion about what is required for a life to have a certain kind of sense, and so to be one's own, is so often what is at issue in James's basic plot. The deceived heiress is robbed of her freedom not just because she has been, as a matter of fact, deceived, but because the very conditions for any life's having a sense for her as hers – a kind of genuine mutuality in engagements with others – are absent. James has, as one modern moral philosopher has suggested we should do, put "meaning" in the place so occupied by "happiness" or rectitude in modern moral reflection,[5] and one might put all that in a theoretical form linking freedom with any such possible meaning.

But the instigations and motivations for this kind of yearning or striving for freedom might also be understood, as we have seen James suggest, historically and socially, not as if deduced from a large moral or philosophical theory. It might simply have happened that forms of agreement about a common or religious or supra-individual good (or point or meaning), or tradition-based hierarchy and convention, had broken down, and broken down so fundamentally and irreparably as to make it idle play to wonder if it was all a philosophical mistake, something we ought to argue against and try, by arguing, to restore. Their so breaking down means that moral life itself has changed, must be different. (As noted throughout, it certainly might be that there are other explanations for the phenomena James is interested in. It could be that our normal cognitive grasp of true moral value might have broken down somehow, become distorted under the temptations of all this money and the new mobility that the access to power makes possible. From a certain high altitude, it is not unreasonable to suggest that we have always known who the bastards are, and not that much has changed. But we have seen enough to be confident that this is not James's view, that that view sounds true only by being announced from too high an altitude, too high to tell us anything informative about what is happening on the ground.)[6]

As in the tone of Strether's remark, in the altered circumstances described by James, one's own life might be all one has left, and any presumption to take it from one and live it for one (in the name of some objective good or moral requirement) would have now to be immediately suspicious, an exercise necessarily in power, not beneficence or justice. Moreover, such a powerful *eros* for one's own life, in such a society, might be best understood as much a protest as an affirmation. A profoundly new sort of society might now have created forms of dependencies (not to mention outright oppressions and stultifying forms of labor) so intimate and pervasive and unavoidable as to make daily life a constant experience of some lack, a lack of subjectivity itself or an anxiety that one's own desires were mere reflections of what others desire.[7] Freedom becomes such a value at such a time when intrusions and constraints no longer seem justifiable (when such constraints can no longer seem self-constraints or no longer seem objective but contingent and arbitrary) and when those intrusions and constraints are everywhere and go deep and when the very point or meaning of one's existence comes to depend on such a contrasting freedom. (I don't mean that it has become such a value just because we "start valuing it," as if we just create it and impose it on the world. I mean, and I think James means, that the achievement of such freedom really has become what makes it possible to affirm, approve of, identify with, one's life, that without which there could not be any direction or real purposiveness in a life. The characters who aspire to such achievement have come to understand this, or appreciate it in some way, and they have understood something true.)[8] If, as we have also seen, a further component of the very possibility of some psychological stability and coherence, or the establishment of any shared meaning itself, now requires some free exchange and recognition between independent subjects, then what is now most needed turns out to be now the least likely, the most threatened.

But a yearning for, a protest in the name of, exactly what? A free life in what sense? The first condition or necessary component of any answer is clear enough. James is no bohemian or romantic; it is material independence, money. If the minimal or negative condition of liberty is the power to avoid (relatively) subjection to the will of others, then what makes that possible in this society is capital. But that answer is also rather drastically hedged, since James realizes that the conditions for achieving such a necessary starting point distort and shadow what it makes possible. Chad may have a lot of faith in advertising, but he is beginning the life that did what it did to Waymarsh and created the almost supernaturally self-satisfied Adam Verver. Money, yes, but if at all possible, never earned, better, much better, inherited, achieved very quickly, "found" or married. (Better, but hardly unproblematic. The distorting effects of money and the power and dependence it creates hardly vanish completely with such more fortunate acquisitions.[9]) This acknowledgment of the necessary role of material independence and the acceptance of the benefits of chance does not amount to a profound answer on James's part to this aspect of the question. It accepts the injustices of luck quickly, almost indifferently, and moves on, and it constitutes no great political thought.

But this is also only the beginning of what he presents. It is true that money makes possible what James is really interested in, and that James often rushes quickly to that topic: the cultivation of a kind of understanding, imagination, taste, awareness, felt life, that amounts to the fullest achievement of freedom and so the achievement of what amounts to the modern highest good, in the sense alluded to earlier. That freedom at issue does not involve the exercise of will, the absence of constraints, or the satisfactions of interests and desires. Strether's liberation involves an expanse of understanding, and so, finally in his life, a greater capacity both to take account of others better, and just thereby, to be himself. This is an expanse so subtle and delicate that it has no real content, no real new thing he learned, no straightforward moral truth. (In the book's most intricate and gentle irony, most of the expanse of his imagination and the development of his taste occurs about a content that is actually false, a lie. That that doesn't matter reflects the immense moral complexities for James in the question of whether Madame de Vionnet's treatment of Strether enhanced or constrained his new-found freedom, and in what various, multiple senses.) And it is in exploring the possibilities of this sort of awareness and so an expanded and more powerful subjectivity that the Jamesean question of morality – the nature of our affirmative, meaning-constituting dependence on others, and what we owe them in the light of that link – arises. Money is certainly one condition for such a possibility, but is not treated as exclusively so. The good fortune of a certain sort of intelligence, or the luck of an unusual upbringing can also exempt one sufficiently from the powerful capitalist machine and the slavish dependencies and malformations of character it requires. (Isabel Archer, pre-fortune, for all her early limitations, is a good example.)[10]

Of course, James raises this issue in many other ways too. That art and the life of the artist can also represent the achievement of freedom (sometimes almost in a Kantian sense, as the achievement of a kind of purity, disinterestedness, or even transcendence, at least as a kind of trans-bourgeois independence) is undeniable but complex enough to be the subject of another book. I have concentrated here on the implications for James of the simple fact that such freedom as is possible in modernity cannot be achieved alone, an implication that forms the basis of his understanding of moral life. If you have nothing without "your life," and that possibility requires some confidence that your life has the sense, the point, that you take it to have, and the very formulation of such a sense involves anticipations, expectations, and interpretations of others (even inside the deepest elements of a self-relation, in the formulation of my own motives), then a certain mutuality and reciprocity with others, a genuine reciprocity, could be said to be what we all must owe each other. In this situation, without that possibility, nothing can be settled, relied on, even, literally, understood, and I don't "have my life."

Naturally enough, once one begins to focus attention on such claims as elements of a position, as philosophical assertions, various other questions emerge immediately, and it is difficult to take them up and respond by citing passages in the fiction or elements of plot and character that could count as "answers." For example, this link insisted on between morality and a mutually realized freedom also has it that this link is a function of an engagement that appears in James's treatment to be conducted at a very high level of sophistication and interpretive sensibility. This would seem to imply that without the capacity to appreciate the complex implications of one's treatment of others, or to be sensitive to the various possibilities that must be counted as dimensions of meaning, a morally appropriate life with others would be impoverished, perhaps not possible. This would seem to reserve not only a fully free life (which James unquestionably links with a certain sort of intelligence and taste) to a small few, but also a morally justifiable life, and that seems quite counterintuitive. Whatever constitutes a morally righteous life, it would seem equally available to the good-hearted and innocent and well-meaning, even if such genuinely good souls might not be capable of handling the mental gymnastics of Jamesean plots.

On this issue, though, it would be a mistake to take James's treatment of extremely complicated cases as if a norm in moral life. When the participants are the likes of Kate Croy and Merton Densher, it is true that a proper appreciation of what is going wrong in their treatment of Milly requires, if it is to be just, an appreciation of their take on the events, and a sense of the possibilities realized and not realized in the actual events. Given the quality of minds involved and the complications of the events, all of this is dense, elusive and not easily accessible, even for all the participants. But cases like a swindle undertaken for self-interest, a callous disregard for familial duties for the sake of pleasure, a willingness to inflict pain and humiliation on the other for ego gratification need not be complicated at all, and our usual intuitions about moral mutuality and reciprocity need not at all be challenged by interpretive difficulties. There may be no such difficulties. But it would be wrong to invoke those sorts of categories unproblematically for the cases we have discussed, for respectively, Kate, or for Chad, or even for Osmond. (As Isabel notes, he did not really pretend to be other than he was, however much deceit about his relationship with Madame Merle was involved). When moral life becomes complicated, James has an account of the nature of those complications and their historical conditions. And in its complications, many more of its implications, dimensions, and underlying foundations can be seen and assessed. When the cases are relatively uncomplicated, his treatment helps us see (within certain kinds of societies and at certain historical times) what is going so clearly wrong when it does, and why we have become attached to what we want to go right.

But this is hardly the end of the questions that can be raised. If the issue remains the first one raised here, in effect Kate's "Golden Bowl" question to Merton about Milly – what is wrong, she wants to know, if we are happy and she can't find the flaw, or dies before she can? – then what amounts to James's treatment of an answer is compelling, but in philosophical terms, admittedly, still unfinished. I don't think there is any question that James is treating Kate's attitude as wrong, and the interesting issue has been all along why he thinks that, what else he must be committed to in order to believe it. It has, I have been suggesting, something to do with the loss we suffer when others are so treated, the way the absence of such free, opposing other subjects (an absence we often engineer) turns our own aspirations and projects into self-contained fantasies that cannot be satisfying because they cannot finally be "ours." This sounds immediately problematic for all sorts of reasons: Isn't immorality an evil done to another, a violation of what is just simply theirs, and not primarily something bad for me? Who cares if what seems to satisfy is a deluded fantasy of satisfaction, as long as I am subjectively satisfied? Who cares even if that means it is unfree? Even if the general principle is accepted, what is so wrong with one such unfreely treated person in a world otherwise populated by the appropriate, necessary others? To all of these could also be added the relativism, reductionist, and nihilism worries noted earlier.

James's fictional engagement with these issues has, I believe, shown why the assumptions on which many such questions are based, and the alternatives suggested by others, are either confused, or incomplete, or inappropriate as issues for the times and peoples he is treating. This does not amount to a systematic response because such a fictional engagement is not properly considered a systematic theory. It has its own compelling qualities and richness and gives us as just a picture of the modern moral situation as any other modern author, whether artist or philosopher, even though showing us that such a situation is not the same as philosophically interrogating it.

It is at this point enough to note what an uncomfortable, anxious situation it is, one wherein the primary Jamesean modern experience, dependence, can be thus both redemptive and destructive, often at the same time; when the times are in effect bad enough that no choice is ever fully right. This can lead to an anxiety intense enough to make understandable the hope for ambiguity-ending "revelations," secrets, disclosures, and so forth. In *The Wings of the Dove*, Densher even insists on such a resolution in a "modern" way often hinted at but rarely as explicitly treated by James. Unsure of what they (he and Kate) are doing, unsure especially of what he is doing and what is being done to or for him, desperate to be able to believe that the right category or explanation and excuse is love and devotion, he insists on what must seem to him an unqualified experience both of ambiguity-ending resolution and subjective power: physical sexuality. He will carry on with the plan only if Kate comes to him, alone, in his rooms, if she agrees to have sex with him, on his terms. That will, he seems to think, finally settle something between them, make finally clear where they stand, who is finally willing to do what for whom. (This is all already an echo of sorts for what Kate expects to be another unqualified, final, unambiguous resolution, beyond interpretation, and once over, locked away in past time: Milly's death.) But, of course, sex and death change matters only by complicating them, not resolving them; the shadows that Kate's agreement and Milly's death create for the future are intense and unavoidable. Nothing is settled – nothing is ever settled – and the hope that something could be so settled begins to look like a resistance or avoidance that has its own distinct, morally suspect tone.[11]

Densher, of course, also tries another tack; he will "stay still," do no harm, avoid active entanglements in anything, not create unbearably ambiguous meanings by, he hopes, creating none. But the tangles are already there, as they are everywhere in the world James thinks we have entered, and what he does or doesn't do in those last scenes in Venice will mean what it must to all those with whom his life is now so deeply tied, regardless of his pathetic attempt at passivity. Those scenes in Venice, parallel to those "crudities of mutual resistance" in other novels – here instead a studied, deceitful avoidance – with Densher wandering purposelessly back and forth to Milly's palazzo for dinner, waiting, expecting something will alter this stalled time, call to mind what is lost with Milly excluded and so much managed by Kate. For the meaning of what Densher has done or could do or would do or would have done is, it turns out, not something that can be stage-managed, controlled, relied on by force of will. Whatever the purposes that include Milly must actually include Milly, Densher finds, or they just cannot be such purposes for him, even however vaguely, passively he tries to characterize what he is doing. Those images in Venice – a city that seems itself an image of a stalled, dead, pre-modern time – lets us see what Densher or anyone loses by so grievously and fatally ignoring the new claims of freedom: one loses "one's own life."

NOTES

1. Frankfurt (1988).
2. Taylor (1985).
3. This recalls the way James treats the problem of consciousness itself as retrospective, as if no understanding of one's desires, intentions, and beliefs could be anything other than provisional until such dependencies could be clarified and thought through. One is always, in other words, living one's life "too late," not just because of some psychological weakness or fear.
4. One needs to take the point of Isaiah Berlin and others that some work is needed to show that whatever the desideratum James wishes to direct us to, it can rightly be called a state of freedom. That is far too involved an issue for a marginal remark, but it is an important worry. See Pippin (forthcoming).
5. Wiggins, in his fine essay (1991), p. 88.
6. For reasons at least suggested throughout, it is also not a very attractive position in itself. But that is another subject fit for a separate book or two. Cf. Williams's maxim (1985): "I must deliberate from what I am. Truthfulness requires trust in that as well, and not the obsessional and doomed drive to eliminate it," p. 200.
7. Cf. Anderson's (1992) treatment again. I have suggested that it is not individualism or social withdrawal that James encourages as a reaction to such a society, but a different form of freedom, one, ironically, very much inspired by sentiments like Anderson's, at the close of his remarks on James: "We shall not crack the money firmament or attain to the freedom we want until we see that such liberty always comes from the quality of our relations with other people, and in no other way" (p. 149). Precisely, and so James would insist.
8. It would be anachronistic in the extreme at this point to attribute to James some grand philosophy of history – within which the dependencies and acknowledgments of

modern society, and so the moral claims unavoidable in such societies, could be located – or to see him struggling against the conventionalist and relativist implications of the position I have attributed to him. These are problems that should be raised in other contexts, but they are problems and should be raised (and I am indebted to remarks by Richard Eldridge for pressing this point). I think one can defend a claim for the originally implicit and gradually realized claims of freedom in history, but that is obviously a much larger and different topic in any assessment of modernity.

9. In this sense, the problem of meaning in James is never resolveable, has no answer. But I have tried to show, especially in the last chapter, that this does not make everything so much a matter of reflections and iterated reflections on reflections, that everything substantial in such negotiations evaporates, or that James is a skeptic.

10. James himself, and the James family, would be another good example. See Freedman's discussion (1998a).

11. See the discussion, at the conclusion of Pippin (1991), of modernity as "unending."

# TEXTS BY HENRY JAMES

*A* = *The American,* in *Four Selected Novels of Henry James.* New York: Grosset & Dunlap, 1946.

*AA* = *The Awkward Age.* Edited with an Introduction and Notes by Ronald Blythe. Additional Notes by Patricia Crick. New York: Penguin, 1987.

*AB* = "The Author of Beltraffio," in *FC.*

*AC* = *The Art of Criticism. Henry James on the Theory and the Practice of Fiction.* Ed. by William Veeder and Susan M. Griffin. Chicago: University of Chicago Press, 1986.

*AF* = "The Art of Fiction," in *Selected Literary Criticism.* Edited by Morris Shapira. London: Heinemann, 1963.

*AM* = *The Ambassadors.* Edited by S.P. Rosenbaum. New York: Norton, 1964.

*AP* = "The Aspern Papers," in *T.*

*APP* = New York Preface to "The Aspern Papers," in *Literary Criticism, Volume Two: French Writers, Other European Writers, The Prefaces to the New York Edition.* Edited by Leon Edel, with the assistance of Mark Wilson. New York: Library of America, 1984.

*AS* = *The American Scene.* Edited with an Introduction and Notes by John F. Sears. New York: Penguin, 1994.

*B* = *The Bostonians.* Edited with an Introduction and Notes by Charles R. Anderson. New York: Penguin, 1984.

*Be* = "Beast in the Jungle," in *T.*

*CSI* = *Complete Stories 1892–1898.* New York: Library of America, 1996.

*CSII* = *Complete Stories 1898–1910.* New York: Library of America, 1996.

*DM* = *Daisy Miller: A Study* in *T.*

*FC* = *The Figure in the Carpet and Other Stories.* Edited with an Introduction and Notes by Frank Kermode. London: Penguin, 1986.

*GB* = *The Golden Bowl.* Edited with an Introduction by Virginia Llewellyn Smith. Oxford: Oxford University Press, 1983.

*H* = "Hawthorne," in *Essays on Literature, American Writers, English Writers.* New York: Library of America, 1984.

*IH* = *Italian Hours.* Boston, Ecco Press, 1909 (reprint).

*JC* = "The Jolly Corner," in *T.*

*Le* = *Letters.* Edited by Percy Lubbock, Scribner's, 1920, vol. I.

*MY* = "The Middle Years," in *FC.*

*PL* = *Portrait of a Lady.* Edited by Robert D. Bamberg. New York: Norton, 1975.

# Texts by James

*RHP* = "Preface to Roderick Hudson," in *Literary Criticism: French Writers, Other European Writers, Prefaces to the New York Edition*. New York: Library of America, 1984.

*T* = *Tales of Henry James*. Selected and Edited by Christof Wegelin. New York: Norton, 1984.

*TNT* = "The Next Time," in *CSI*, 486–524.

*TS* = *The Turn of the Screw*. Edited by Robert Kimbrough. New York: Norton, 1966.

*WD* = *The Wings of the Dove*. Edited with an Introduction and Notes by Peter Brooks. Oxford: Oxford University Press, 1984.

*WMK* = *What Maisie Knew*. New York: Penguin, 1975.

*WS* = *Washington Square*. New York: Crowell, 1970.

# BIBLIOGRAPHY

Anderson, Quentin. (1992) *Making Americans. An Essay on Individualism and Money.* New York, Harcourt Brace Jovanovich.

Armstrong, Paul. (1983) *The Phenomenology of Henry James.* Chapel Hill, University of North Carolina Press.

Auchard, John. (1986) *Silence in Henry James.* University Park, Penn State University Press.

Beidler, Peter. (1989). *Ghosts, Demons and Henry James. The Turn of the Screw at the Turn of the Century,* Columbia, University of Missouri Press.

Bell, Millicent. (1991) *Meaning in Henry James.* Cambridge, Harvard University Press.

Bernstein, Jay. (forthcoming). "Modernity as Trauma: Disenchanted Time in Benjamin and James."

Bersani, Leo. (1969). *A Future for Astyanax: Character and Desire in Literature.* Boston, Little, Brown.

Blackmur, R.P. (1934). "Introduction" to *The Art of the Novel.* London, Scribner's.

Blackmur, R.P. (1983). *Studies in Henry James.* Edited with an Introduction by Veronica A. Makowsky. New York, New Directions.

Booth, Wayne. (1962). *The Rhetoric of Fiction.* Chicago, University of Chicago Press.

Booth, Wayne. (1988). *The Company We Keep: An Ethics of Fiction.* Berkeley, University of California Press.

Brooks, Van Wyck. (1925). *The Pilgrimage of Henry James.* New York, Dutton.

Brudney, Daniel. (1990). "Knowledge and Silence: *The Golden Bowl* and Moral Philosophy," in *Critical Inquiry,* vol. 16.

Cameron, Sharon (1989). *Thinking in Henry James.* Chicago, University of Chicago Press.

Cranfill, Thomas, and Clark, R.C., Jr. (1965) *An Anatomy of Turn of the Screw.* Austin, University of Texas Press.

Crews, Frederick. (1971). *The Tragedy of Manners: Moral Drama in the Later Novels of Henry James.* Hamden, Archon.

Dawidoff, Robert. (1992). *The Genteel Tradition and the Sacred Rage. High Culture vs. Democracy in Adams, James, & Santayana.* Chapel Hill, University of North Carolina Press.

Diamond, Cora. (1995a). "Missing the Adventure: Reply to Martha Nussbaum," in Diamond (1995c).

Diamond, Cora. (1995b). "Having a Rough Story about What Moral Philosophy Is," in Diamond (1995c).

Diamond, Cora. (1995c). *The Realistic Spirit. Wittgenstein, Philosophy, and the Mind.* Cambridge, MIT Press.

Dupee, F.W. (1965). *Henry James.* New York, Delta.

Edel, Leon and Gordon N. Ray, eds. *Henry James and H.G. Wells.* London, Hart-Davis.

Edmundson, Mark (1997). *Nightmare on Main Street. Angels, Sadomasochism and the Culture of Gothic.* Cambridge, Harvard University Press.

Eldridge, Richard. (1989). *On Moral Personhood. Philosophy, Literature, Criticism and Self-Understanding.* Chicago, University of Chicago Press.

Eldridge, Richard. (1997). *Leading a Human Life: Wittgenstein, Intentionality, and Romanticism.* Chicago, University of Chicago Press.

Felman, Shoshona. (1982). "Turning the Screw of Interpretation," in *Literature and Psychoanalysis. The Question of Reading: Otherwise.* Baltimore, Johns Hopkins University Press.

Fiedler, Leslie. (1992). *Love and Death in the American Novel.* 3rd ed. (1960). New York, Anchor Books.

Frankfurt, Harry. (1988). "Freedom of the will and the concept of a person," in *The Importance of What We Care About.* Cambridge, Cambridge University Press.

Freedman, Jonathan, ed. (1998). *The Cambridge Companion to Henry James.* Cambridge, Cambridge University Press.

Freedman, Jonathan. (1998a). "Introduction: The Moment of Henry James," in Freedman (1998).

Furet, François. (1995). *Le passé d'une illusion. Essai sur l'ideé communiste au Xxe siècle.* Paris, Robert Laffont/Calmann-Lévy.

Furth, David L. (1979). *The Visionary Betrayed. Aesthetic Discontinuity in Henry James's The American Scene.* Cambridge, Harvard University Press.

Girard, René. (1965). *Deceit, Desire, and the Novel. Self and Other in Literary Structure.* Translated by Yvonne Freccero. Baltimore, The Johns Hopkins University Press.

Habegger, Alfred. (1989). *Henry James and the "Woman Business."* Cambridge, Cambridge University Press.

Hagberg, G.L. (1994). *Meaning and Interpretation: Wittgenstein, Henry James and Literary Knowledge.* Ithaca, Cornell University Press.

Haviland, Beverly. (1997). *Henry James's Last Romance. Making Sense of the Past and the American Scene.* New York, Cambridge University Press.

Holland, Laurence B. (1982). *The Expense of Vision. Essays on the Craft of Henry James.* Baltimore, The Johns Hopkins University Press.

Howland, Bette. (1996). "*Washington Square,* the Family Plot," in *Raritan,* vol. XV. No.4, pp. 88–110.

Hutchinson, Stuart (1983). *Henry James: The American as Modernist.* London, Vision Press.

James, Williams. (1983) *The Principles of Psychology.* Cambridge, Harvard University Press.

Krook, Dorothea. (1962). *The Ordeal of Consciousness in Henry James.* Cambridge, Cambridge University Press.

Larmore, Charles. (1996). *The Morals of Modernity.* Cambridge, Cambridge University Press.

Leavis, F.R. (1964). *The Great Tradition. George Eliot, Henry James, Joseph Conrad.* New York, New York University Press.

Liljegren, S. (1920). *American and European in the Works of Henry James.* Lund, C.W.K. Gleerup.

Lustig, T.J. (1994). *Henry James and the Ghostly.* Cambridge, Cambridge University Press.

Mackenzie, Manfred. (1976) *Communities of Shame and Honor in Henry James*. Cambridge, Harvard University Press.

Matthiessen, F.O. (1946). *Henry James. The Major Phase*. Oxford, Oxford University Press.

Mazella, Anthony J. (1975). "The New Isabel," in the essays included in the Norton *PL*.

McGinn, Colin. (1997). *Ethics, Evil, and Fiction*. Oxford, Clarendon Press.

Miller, J. Hillis. (1987). *The Ethics of Reading*. New York, Columbia University Press.

*New Literary History*. (1983). Vol. 15, no. 1. Special issue on "Literature and/as Moral Philosophy."

Nussbaum, Martha. (1990a), "'Finely Aware and Richly Responsible': Literature and the Moral Imagination," in Nussbaum (1990c).

Nussbaum, Martha. (1990b). "Flawed Crystals: James *The Golden Bowl* and Literature as Moral Philosophy," in Nussbaum (1990c).

Nussbaum, Martha. (1990c). *Love's Knowledge: Essays on Philosophy and Literature*. New York, Oxford University Press.

Nussbaum, Martha. (1995). "Objectification," in *Philosophy and Public Affairs*, vol. 24.

Olafson Frederick. (1988). "Moral Relationships in the Fiction of Henry James," in *Ethics*, vol. 98, no. 2, pp. 294–312

Ozick, Cynthia. (1993). *What Henry James Knew and Other Essays on Writers*. London, Jonathan Cape.

Ozouf, Mona (1998). *La Muse démocratique. Henry James ou les pouvoirs du roman*. Paris, Calmann-Lévy.

Pippin, Robert. (1991). *Modernism as a Philosophical Problem. On the Dissatisfactions of European High Culture*. Oxford, Blackwell.

Pippin, Robert. (1997a). *Idealism as Modernism: Hegelian Variations*. Cambridge, Cambridge University Press.

Pippin, Robert. (1997b). "Morality as Psychology; Psychology as Morality: Nietzsche, Eros and Clumsy Lovers," in (1997a).

Pippin, Robert. (1997c). "Truth and Lies in the Early Nietzsche," in Pippin (1997a).

Pippin, Robert. (1998). "Nietzsche und die Melancholie der Modernität," in *Konzepte der Moderne*. Edited by G. von Graevenitz and Axel Honneth. Forthcoming.

Pippin, Robert. "Naturalness and Mindedness: Hegel's Compatibilism." Forthcoming in the *European Journal of Philosophy*.

Porte, Joel, ed. (1990). *New Essays on The Portrait of a Lady*. Cambridge, Cambridge University Press.

Porter, Caroline. (1988). *Seeing and Being: The Plight of the Participant Observer in Emerson, James, Adams and Faulkner*. Middletown, Wesleyan University Press.

Posner, Richard A. (1998). *Law and Literature*. Revised and Enlarged Edition. Cambridge, Harvard University Press.

Posnock, Ross. (1991). *The Trial of Curiosity. Henry James, William James, and the Challenge of Modernity*. Oxford, Oxford University Press.

Posnock, Ross. (1998). "Affirming the Alien: The Pragmatist Pluralism of *The American Scene*" in Freedman (1998).

Rahv, Philip. (1978). *Essays on Literature and Politics, 1932–72*. Edited by Arabel J. Porter and Andrew J. Dvosi. Boston, Houghton Miflin.

Rimmon, Shlomith. (1977). *The Concept of Ambiguity – the Example of James*. Chicago, University of Chicago Press.

Roth, Philip. (1997). *American Pastoral*. New York, Vintage.

Rowe, John Carlos. (1984). *The Theoretical Dimension of Henry James.* Madison. University of Wisconsin Press.

Sabin, Margery. (1987). *The Dialectic of the Tribe. Speech and Community in Modern Fiction.* New York, Oxford University Press.

Sabin, Margery. (1998). "Henry James's American Dream in *The Golden Bowl,*" in Freedman (1998).

Sedgwick, Eve Kosofsky. (1990) *Epistemology of the Closet.* Berkeley, University of California Press.

Selzer, Mark. (1985). *Henry James and the Art of Power.* Ithaca, Cornell University Press.

Spears, Sally. (1968). *The Negative Imagination. Form and Perspective in the Novels of Henry James.* Ithaca: Cornell University Press.

Spender, Stephen. (1938). *The Destructive Element.* London, Jonathan Cape.

Tanner, Tony. (1985). *Henry James. The Writer and His Work.* Amherst, University of Massachusetts Press.

Tanner, Tony. (1995). *Henry James and the Art of Nonfiction.* Athens, University of Georgia Press.

Taylor, Charles. (1985). "What Is Human Agency?" in *Philosophical Papers, I.* Cambridge, Cambridge University Press.

van Fraassen, Bas C. (1988). "The Peculiar Effects of Love and Desire," in *Perspectives on Self-Deception.* Edited by Brian P. McLaughlin and Amelie Oksenberg Rorty. Berkeley and Los Angeles, University of California Press.

Veeder, William. (1975). *Henry James – the Lessons of the Master.* Chicago, University of Chicago Press.

Weber, Max. (1946). "Science as a Vocation," in *From Max Weber: Essays in Sociology.* Translated and edited by H.H. Gerth and C. Wright Mills. New York, Oxford University Press.

Weinstein, Philip. (1971). *Henry James and the Requirements of the Imagination.* Cambridge, Harvard University Press.

Weisbuch, Robert. (1998). "Henry James and the Idea of Evil," in Freedman (1998).

Wiggins, David. (1991). "Truth, Invention, and the Meaning of Life," Essay III of *Needs, Values, Truth: Essays in the Philosophy of Value.* Oxford, Blackwell.

Williams, Bernard. (1981a). "Moral Luck," in *Moral Luck.* Cambridge, Cambridge University Press.

Williams, Bernard. (1981b). "Persons, Character and Morality," in *Moral Luck.* Cambridge, Cambridge University Press.

Williams, Bernard. (1985). *Ethics and the Limits of Philosophy.* Cambridge, Harvard University Press.

Williams, Bernard. (1993). "Nietzsche's Minimalist Moral Psychology," in *European Journal of Philosophy,* vol. I, no.I.

Wilson, Edmund. (1934). "The Ambiguity of Henry James," in *Hound and Horn,* VII, 385–406.

Wollheim, Richard. (1984). *The Thread of Life.* Cambridge, Harvard University Press.

# INDEX

# Index